MASTER NARRATIVES

" Look in," said the old man, pointing downward with his finger. The child complied, and gazed down into the pit.

" It looks like a grave, itself," said the old man.
" It does," replied the child.

Master Narratives

Tellers and telling in the English novel

Edited by
Richard Gravil

Ashgate

Aldershot • Burlington USA • Singapore • Sydney

© Richard Gravil, 2001

All rights reserved. No part of this publication may be reproduced, stored in a retrieval system, or transmitted in any form or by any means, electronic, mechanical, photocopied, recorded, or otherwise without the prior permission of the publisher.

The editor has asserted his moral right under the Copyright, Designs and Patents Act, 1988, to be identified as the editor of this work.

Published by
Ashgate Publishing Limited
Gower House
Croft Road
Aldershot
Hants GU11 3HR
England

Ashgate Publishing Company
131 Main Street
Burlington, VT 05401-5600 USA

Ashgate website: http://www.ashgate.com

British Library Cataloguing-in-Publication Data

Master Narratives: tellers and telling in the English novel. – (The nineteenth century series)
1. English fiction – 19th century – History and criticism
2. Reality in literature
I. Gravil, Richard
823.8'09

Library of Congress Control Number: 2001787432

Printed on acid-free paper

Typeset in Times New Roman by the editor

ISBN 0 7546 0128 5

Printed and bound in Great Britain by MPG Books Ltd, Bodmin, Cornwall

For

Bill Ruddick

1939 – 1994

Contents

List of Illustrations		ix
Introduction		1
1	How pleasant to meet Mr Fielding: The Narrator as Hero in *Tom Jones* W. B. Hutchings	9
2	'Where then lies the difference?': The (Ante)Postmodernity of *Tristram Shandy* Jayne Lewis	21
3	*Old Mortality*: Editor and Narrator Mary Wedd	37
4	*Mathilda* – Who Knew Too Much Frederick Burwick	47
5	'Perswasion' in *Persuasion* Jane Stabler	55
6	*Wuthering Heights* as Bifurcated Novel Frederick Burwick	69
7	Negotiating *Mary Barton* Richard Gravil	87
8	Nell, Alice and Lizzie: Three Sisters amidst the Grotesque Alan Shelston	101
9	The Androgyny of *Bleak House* Richard Gravil	123

10	*Middlemarch* and 'the Home Epic' Nicola Trott	139
11	The Ghost of Doubt: Writing, Speech and Language in *Lord Jim* Gerard Barrett	159
12	Liking or Disliking: Woolf, Conrad, Lawrence Michael O'Neill	169

Endnotes 181

Notes on Contributors 199

Index 201

Illustrations

For *The Old Curiosity Shop* the titles are those allocated in Thomas Hatton's list of illustrations to the works of Charles Dickens in *Nonesuch Dickensiana* (1937).

1	Nell in bed. S. Williams	105
2	Nell among the tombs. George Cattermole	105
3	Nell dead. George Cattermole	106
4	The shop. George Cattermole	106
5	Mrs Quilp's tea-party. Hablot Knight Browne	107
6	Quilp's corpse. Hablot Knight Browne	107
7	Nell and the Sexton. Daniel Maclise	108
8	Alice with the creatures. John Tenniel	111
9	The Duchess with the baby. John Tenniel	111
10	Alice and the Queen of Hearts. John Tenniel	112
11	Alice and the White Knight. John Tenniel	113
12	Alice in the shop. John Tenniel	115
13	Little Dorrit's Party. Hablot Knight Browne (original title)	116
14	The Bird of Prey. Marcus Stone (original title)	117
15	Waiting for Father. Marcus Stone (original title)	118
16	Mr Venus surrounded by the trophies of his art. Marcus Stone (original title)	120
17	Alice in the drawing room. John Tenniel	120

The Nineteenth Century
General Editors' Preface

The aim of this series is to reflect, develop and extend the great burgeoning of interest in the nineteenth century that has been an inevitable feature of recent decades, as that former epoch has come more sharply into focus as a locus for our understanding not only of the past but of the contours of our modernity. Though it is dedicated principally to the publication of original monographs and symposia in literature, history, cultural analysis, and associated fields, there will be a salient role for reprints of significant text from, or about, the period. Our overarching policy is to address the spectrum of nineteenth-century studies without exception, achieving the widest scope in chronology, approach and range of concern. This, we believe, distinguishes our project from comparable ones, and means, for example, that in the relevant areas of scholarship we both recognize and cut innovatively across such parameters as those suggested by the designations 'Romantic' and 'Victorian'. We welcome new ideas, while valuing tradition. It is hoped that the world which predates yet so forcibly predicts and engages our own will emerge in parts, as a whole, and in the lively currents of debate and change that are so manifest an aspect of its intellectual, artistic and social landscape.

Vincent Newey
Joanne Shattock

University of Leicester

Introduction

Richard Gravil

The essays in this volume have been composed in memory of the late Bill Ruddick, a notable scholar and teacher, an inveterate reader and reviewer of nineteenth-century fiction, and, for most of the contributors, a close and beloved friend. The authors engage with a selection of literal 'master narratives', texts which in one way or another represent growth points in the development of the novel. All of the essays explore what Fredric Jameson called the 'objective' structures of particular texts: 'the historicity of its forms and of its content, the historical moment of emergence of its linguistic possibilities, the situation-specific function of its aesthetic'. Most of them reflect, also, on the function of such texts as what Jameson called 'symbolic move[s] in an essentially polemic and strategic ideological confrontation' with one or other of society's 'master narratives'.[1]

What makes some novels more indispensable than others, and what mysterious process determines their inclusion in a teaching canon? According to Terry Eagleton, 'Literature is a vital instrument for the insertion of individuals into the perceptual and symbolic forms of the dominant ideological formation'. In this somewhat monolithic view, 'Ideology adapts individuals to their social function by providing them with an imaginary model of the whole, suitably schematized and fictionalized for their purposes.'[2] This loosely Althusserian notion became so commonplace in the late 1970s and 1980s as to constitute a virtual critical hegemony today. Macdonald Daly, for example, tells readers of *Mary Barton* that the novel is canonized because it is crucial to 'the self-renewing programme of the bourgeois intelligentsia'.[3] Students are often taught, and may believe, that novels, especially canonical novels, simply reflect whatever cultural historians take to be the dominant cultural formations of the writer's epoch. Dickens wrote in an era of patriarchy: his novels, therefore, are interesting primarily as evidence of the pervasiveness of 'domestic ideology'; the use of his fiction, if any, is to provide examples of the pastness of the past. Yet, as Raymond Williams insisted, the making of art is 'always a formative process', involving a tension between what is thought and what is being lived: what is 'perceived' and 'dominant' is already past (to Blake and Nietzsche one's thoughts are already merely the bones of thought) but the novel belongs to the present. The novel exhibits tensions between what is felt and what is merely thought, between the objective and the personal, between what is 'believed' and what is 'experienced'; its proper realm, then, is the 'emergent'.[4] Mikhail Bakhtin's most characteristic proposition, the basis of his (debatable) claim for the primacy of the novel over other genres, is that the form includes dissenting voices and dramatizes fissures in what may appear a monolithic ideological formation: 'The novel comes into contact with the spontaneity of the inconclusive present.... The Novelist is drawn towards everything that is not yet completed'.[5]

So the premises, even of what might be considered an ideologically cohesive body of criticism, can generate fundamentally opposed views of what makes novels, and what drives canon-formation. A conservative model of canon-formation suspects the novel, especially the realist novel, of serving the dominant structures of value in the bourgeois state; a radical model might see the canon as constituted by those novels which have most successfully, if not always coherently, expressed an emergent consciousness, challenged most effectively the received social codes, created space for new structures of feeling. In the essays that follow, each writer has kept one eye, implicitly or explicitly, on this question, while focusing on the claims of the particular novel to have contributed something unique to our sense of what fiction can do; to have brought some new fictional element into being, mastered some facet of the art of telling.

Bill Hutchings, in 'How pleasant to meet Mr Fielding', takes up the vexatious business of the novel as history and the novelist as historian, a self-conscious model of writing that was playfully taken up by Sterne, Scott and George Eliot. For a Modernist such as Ford Madox Ford, as Hutchings points out, what is aesthetically desirable is to convey as immediately as possible (that is, without consciousness of any medium) the actuality of a scene or a character. 'All authorial intrusion should ideally be avoided, the scene being directly presented to readers as if they were themselves witnessing it'. Precisely this business of 'witnessing', however, is what Fielding as a professional lawyer is concerned with, and the illusions of realism, much contested in postmodern writing and by such a realist as George Eliot, are already suspect to Fielding. His narrator must, therefore, be overtly present and available for inspection. Fielding's age was occupied with the concept of objectivity. 'Objectivity is the result of a communal act of observation, a pooling of our perceptions towards a series of general truths.' Thus, *Tom Jones* foregrounds the inevitable subjectivity of any particular narrator, the problematics of objectivity. Fielding uses the judicial system 'as a running metaphor for how we judge human actions and motivation'.

Jayne Lewis's essay on 'The (Ante)Postmodernity of *Tristram Shandy*' explores what might be termed the wormhole theory of fiction, exemplified by *Tristram Shandy* even more than by *Roderick Random* or *Tom Jones*, whereby it and a work like Barth's *The Sotweed Factor* might appear to be contemporaries. Certainly, his novel seems to have much more in common with Proust, Woolf and Joyce than with Fielding, Richardson or Smollett. Its narrative technique, 'spun of interruption, digression, and all species of textual chasm', can make one feel that 'the English novel was postmodern even before it was modern'. Lewis's chapter acknowledges that *Tristram Shandy* gestures 'toward an atemporal dimension in the history of narrative', but its searching analysis of several aspects of Sterne's narrative technique shows that whatever *Tristram Shandy*'s lack of *intrinsic* difference from certain modern and postmodern novels, it exhibits profound *situational* differences from them. Ironically, Professor Lewis argues, some of the qualities that seem to make it timeless stem, when historically considered, from certain very eighteenth-century dispositions, for instance the period's neo-epicureanism and its 'sensibility'.

Historical fiction may have become academically marginalized, but the form Scott perfected has been the staple genre for a long tradition of cultural analysts, from James Fenimore Cooper to J. G. Farrell, concerned with the conflict of cultures and the birth of nations. The particular instance that Mary Wedd examines carries much scholarly baggage, of a kind that may at first appear remote from the matter at hand. Yet her '*Old Mortality*: editor and narrator' shows how Scott's editorial apparatus, with its presumption of scholarly and historical documentation, and antiquarian addenda, ironically undercuts the 'authority' of the narrative itself. Jedediah Cleishbotham, who introduces himself as editor of the 'tales of my Landlord' insists that he is 'not the writer, redacter or compiler', nor in any way 'answerable for the contents'. Peter Pattieson, the school teacher who has collected the accounts of 'Old Mortality', died before he could assemble them in publishable form. Not the landlord, nor the schoolteacher, nor Cleishbotham (whose initials mark many of the footnotes) is responsible for the narrative. Scott may not be much reputed as an ironist, but Mary Wedd's essay shows how this plurality of 'authorities' relates intimately to the ubiquitous ironies of *Old Mortality*. At the heart of the novel is a problem that has not become any less relevant in our times: that of the barbarous pursuit of rival 'goods', or as Mary Wedd puts it, 'idealism yoked to atrocity'.

As narrative device, Mary Shelley typically gives her central character an opportunity to study the literary tradition in which she has placed him or her. The creature in *Frankenstein* acquires an education in reading *Paradise Lost* and *Werther*. The action of *The Last Man* is suspended so that attention can be given to Defoe's *Journal of the Plague Year*. Frederick Burwick's first essay in this collection, on '*Mathilda* – Who Knew Too Much', shows how Mathilda, in telling the story of her relationship with her father, reveals expert knowledge of the literature of father-daughter incest, quoting from Alfieri's *Myrrha*, Boccaccio's tale of Tancred and Ghismunda, Fletcher's *The Captaine*. Written in 1819, but unpublished until 1959, the novel was sent to William Godwin, who blocked its publication 'by declining to return it to her'. Without imputing father-daughter incest to Mary Shelley's experience, Professor Burwick's essay recognizes (as Godwin presumably did) how the novel reflects the strained relationship between the author and her father, and makes use of a theme already prominent in the Byron-Shelley circle. As Nicola Trott has also suggested in a recent study of *Frankenstein*,[6] 'Mary', in Frederick Burwick's words, 'had good reason to reflect on a father's trespassing the boundaries of love'.

'Persuasion' is not only the title of Jane Austen's most engagé novel, but a key term in Blake's thought, and in Wordsworth's. The Preface to *Lyrical Ballads*, for instance speaks of the dangers of one kind of persuasion: a writer's 'own feelings are his own stay and support, and if he sets them aside in one instance, he may be induced to repeat this act till his mind loses all confidence in itself and becomes utterly debilitated'. Blake's 'firm perswasion' provides a subtler bridge to connect *Persuasion* with fundamental Romantic postulates than the oft-noticed democratic spirit manifested in the novel (for instance, the simple fact that all the decent characters work for a living and all the landed ones are in moral decay). Jane Stabler's '"Perswasion" in *Persuasion*' begins with Blake's encounter with Isaiah in *The Marriage of Heaven and Hell* to alert us to one of the many meanings of the word 'persuasion' in the Romantic period, that of firm inner conviction or religious belief. Jane Austen uses the verb 'to persuade' and its cognate forms throughout her fictional writing and this chapter examines the way in which the novel tests the different meanings of its title, alternating between the social arena of verbal appeals and entreaties to the private world of personal conviction: above all, the essay shows how *Persuasion* presents the act of perception as one conditioned by persuasion, and explores how this theme is experienced in the relationship between narrator and readers.

Recent readings of *Wuthering Heights* tend to fall into two categories; Marxist readings, centred on Heathcliff, and feminist ones centred on Catherine. Frederick Burwick's '*Wuthering Heights* as bifurcated novel' belongs to a third kind, more responsive to the various doublings in the novel's narrative structure. Its two narrators juxtapose two culturally divergent discourses. Its narrative time, 1801–2, overlaps only with the close of its three-generation story, but in a way that allows the events of the last three decades to have more immediacy at times than those of the early nineteenth century. Moreover, a novel in two volumes, with two heroines, mother and daughter, must in some sense be centrally preoccupied with matters of continuity and change, which might take the form of rebellion and accommodation, or might, with very different vibrations, explore the evolution from failed prototype to viable human being. One volume, as it were, ironizes the other; but which ironies are the author's? After all, its first volume ends with a startling bibliographical metaphor, asking what predicament the narrator would be in if he fell for the younger Catherine's witcheries, and the daughter turned out 'a second edition of the Mother'. Professor Burwick's essay explores the dimensions of irony created through the echoes across the generational gap of the first and second parts of the novel.

In some ways a realist rewrite of *Wuthering Heights* (at least, as that novel is read by Terry Eagleton in his own masterpiece, *Myths of Power*) *Mary Barton* suffers from a narrative voice that seems as uncertain in its sympathies as Catherine Earnshaw is in hers – passionately involved with Heathcliff, yet unable to relinquish the attachments of class. The editor's 'Negotiating *Mary Barton*' addresses this ambivalence. Too many readings of the novel address what Gaskell is expected to say, rather than what the text does say: its instabilities, though not always under control, may reflect a conscious strategy of engagement with a divided public and mask a considerable degree of communicative irony. Certainly, the novel is more historically aware than are some of the condescending constructions that have been placed upon it. What John Barton knows, the author knows; what he says, she amply corroborates; what he does, as a crime of commission, she equates – in deliberate symbolism – to the employers' murder by neglect. Where her narrator stands is quite another matter.

Modern readers have to make do with single-volume unillustrated editions of what were once lavishly illustrated three-deckers. Yet the quality of nineteenth-century illustrations, usually placed with considerable care, enriched the reader's experience. Alan Shelston's 'Three Sisters amid the Grotesque', exploring a topic that greatly fascinated the dedicatee of this book, examines the narrative function of grotesque illustration, including feminine icons and grotesque surroundings, in *The Old Curiosity Shop*, *Alice* and *Our Mutual Friend*. Henry James once complained: 'Anything that relieves responsible prose of the duty of being ... good enough, interesting enough and, if the question be of picture, pictorial enough, does it the worst of services'. A twenty-first-century reader, with the 'aesthetic' advantages of twentieth-century horrors to fall back on, who reads Dickens's account of Krook's shop and then glances at the illustrator's attempt to render the full horror of this human processing plant, may well find the illustration redundant, and its clutter too clean. Dickens's prose seems more 'pictorial'. Alan Shelston's essay invites one to ask whether we owe such a style to the coincidence of Dickens's career with the golden age of book illustration. Dickens wrote when the multi-media novel spurred authors to 'picture' their places and people. How much does this coincidence account for the disturbing pictorial dynamics that we know as Dickens's inimitable style?

The editor's second essay, 'The Androgyny of *Bleak House*' addresses what Ellen Moers has called 'the single "woman question" novel in the Dickens canon'. This work purports to be co-authored by a transcendent male observer and a domestic but illegitimate female agent, whose perspectives, it can be argued, are polarized at the outset of the novel, yet gradually merge into a speculatively desirable androgyny. Using a variety of voices from mid-century discussions of the nature of men and women, and the proper separation of their spheres, the essay suggests that the form of *Bleak House* emerges to deal with structures of feeling that may have been far from Dickens's own. Ostensibly, Dickens in *Bleak House* and Mill in *The Subjection of Women* are poles apart. Yet the two belonged to much the same networks, and Dickens is an almost unique instance of a writer who kept one foot in radical dissenting circles, while commanding a mass, middle-class audience. It has been argued elsewhere that Dora in *David Copperfield* designedly illustrates Unitarian critiques of 'toy' women, and that *Dombey and Son* covertly deploys the trope of marriage as prostitution, a trope passed down from Wollstonecraft and Godwin, through the Chartists and Unitarians.[7] His novels, that is, may be seen, as can *Household Words*, as constituting a bridge between the radical fringe to which in some respects he belonged, and the middle-class audience he could command. Certainly, the experimental structure of *Bleak House* suggests a major imaginative response to a question he could not fully resolve, yet which he anatomizes and articulates more successfully in this novel than in any other.

Nicola Trott, similarly, finds a challenge to 'separate spheres' ideology written into George Eliot's oxymoronic 'home epic', perhaps an even stronger candidate for the title of greatest English novel of the century. *Middlemarch*, once described as the novel all novels want to be when they grow up, enacts some of the displacements required of the novel when it came of age. It displaces the epic, while, at a deeper level, displacing the social and metaphysical assumptions of those who, at this date, felt nostalgia for epic grandeur and epic values. Moreover, it displaces that simple sense of reality that critics persist in seeing as characteristic of pre-Moderns. *Middlemarch* does not, of course, exemplify an age of innocence before our sense of reality became problematic: its major characters, Lydgate, Dorothea and Harriet Bulstrode, all have to learn that their 'worlds' are contingent upon other 'worlds' which cut across theirs. Their simple ideals are thwarted by an environment in which the codes of epic and religious fulfilment are supplanted by those of domestic and moral accommodation. Nicola Trott's essay is expertly cognizant of the novel's problematizing intellectual contexts, particularly the impact of the higher criticism, and of the researches of Eliot and her scientific consort, G. H. Lewes. Their interests combined the contemporaneous erosion of concepts of heroic authorship ('Homer' and the Bible become re-read in this period as deposits of collective experience) with the promotion of a social and ecological concept of human being. The novel's texture, as well as its moral probing, announces the death of the individual as an abstraction. In *Middlemarch* the pressures of such emergent structures result in a genre metamorphosis impelled by Eliot's astonishing intellectual reach.

In such a novel, capable of its own Romantic agonies, romance values simply dissolve in the crucible of fictional scepticism, as indeed they do in Conrad. As Cedric Watts put it, in introducing the 1985 Penguin edition of *Lord Jim*, Conrad's scepticism 'was an acid that burnt deeply into the ideological alloys of his age'. Classic readings of this novel attend to its narrative structure as the formal manifestation of that scepticism: the series of tragic, anguished or comic readings of Jim offered by the multiple narrative thwart the reader's attempt to arrive at any simple computation of moral defectiveness. Marlow undermines the supremely self-confident Captain Brierly – 'I had a glimpse of the real Brierly a few days before he committed his reality and sham together to the keeping of the sea'. The French Lieutenant's hollowness exposes itself in farce: 'But the honour – the honour, monsieur! ... The honour ...that is real!'. Chester's fatuous 'You must see things exactly as they are' epitomizes the problem. Gerard Barrett's essay on *Lord Jim* locates a more fundamental scepticism in the novel's medium, found both in its 'generic heterogeneity' – as at once 'an adventure story, a love story, a courtroom drama' – and, more fundamentally still, in its figurative language, which leads into 'a separate order of knowledge from that of the literal'. One could see Dickens, from whom Conrad learned the trick of instant characterization, stumbling into the same technique in *Bleak House*: those 'attendant wigs' all 'stuck in a fog bank' (chapter 1) are merely metonymies stuck in a metaphor. But Conrad's 'ineluctable' ambiguities are more radical and even more systemic. The business cards which Jim forces on visiting captains, are, Barrett suggests, 'micro-texts' which by being 'concise, clear, confident, commercial, one-dimensional and referential' epitomize the antithetical realm of Conrad's macro-text, a text in which 'ordered and predictable standards of moral and social conduct' (clearly 'there' in Dickens) are at issue.

Virginia Woolf's peculiar gift is to problematize consciousness, rendering, in Lily Briscoe's case, as Michael O'Neill puts it, not simply 'the meaning of her "impressions"', but 'of the whole business of having "impressions" at all'. Lawrence's peculiar gift – *very* peculiar in a prophet – is to allow the consciousness of his characters access to his narrative voice, so much so that they take possession of it, to the confusion of critics seeking to impose a reading of Lawrence onto Lawrence's texts. In 'The Fox', for example, crude readings tend to extrapolate all too easily from 'hero' to author. In *Sons and Lovers* it is hard to see quite how it happens, but Mr Morel becomes a centre of sympathy despite all efforts of Mrs Morel and Paul Morel and the 'point of view' to marginalize him. In 'Liking or Disliking: Conrad, Woolf, Lawrence', O'Neill takes three such modernist texts, *To the Lighthouse*, *Women in Love* and *Heart of Darkness*, which tend to be read more reductively and flatly than they deserve. The essay considers the kind of sympathy elicited in *To the Lighthouse* and *Women in Love* for characters whom critics of particular ideological bearings, and arguably, the authors themselves, insofar as we still believe in authors, see as 'bad'. All three texts 'dramatize the treacherous quicksands that beset the attempt to estimate the worth (or worthlessness) of others'. The technique that enables Woolf to trace, with unprecedented fineness, curves of complex yet recognizable feelings, approaching and recoiling from merciless judgement, 'bears witness to an ethical fineness in the technician'. It may be tempting to see Gerald Crich simply as an allegorical character 'embodying Lawrence's ideas about what was wrong with modern civilization' yet the text also invites us to experience a fascinated sympathy with a troubled individual experiencing his own hollowness. O'Neill's essay shows how the local energies of a text, thanks perhaps to the ineluctable dialogism of the novel, rarely conform to what the critic wants the work to be 'about'.

While twelve essays can hardly constitute a revised history of English fiction, these offer provocative re-readings of evolutionary moments in the body of the novel, moments, also – since narrative must be 'a socially symbolic act' – in the history of conscience and consciousness. Much of what is said in this volume has to do with the variant ways in which novelists have succeeded in devising techniques not only to critique aspects of our social behaviour, but to change it, by burrowing beneath the reader's mental skin. Art invites the reader, in Wordsworthian phrase, to confront his own 'pre-established codes of decision'; it may even bring about 'new compositions of feeling'. The writer's task, Conrad says, looking back to the manifestos of Wordsworth and of Shelley, is 'by the power of the written word, to make you hear, to make you feel – it is, before all, to make you *see*'.[8] If he succeeds, we may find also, he adds, 'that glimpse of truth for which you have forgotten to ask'. How, why, and under what pressures fictional form evolves, inevitably belongs to cultural history, whether that is seen as a history of compromise and failures, or of social evolution, or of eternal recurrence. Generally speaking, the novel (whatever we may think of the novelist) seems to be one of the good guys, tending toward a more sympathetic and self-aware humanity.

This collection has been designed to offer fresh insights into some of the major constituents of the teaching 'canon', and some which challenge admission or readmission, addressing some of the fundamental questions encountered in the study of any novel.

Who does the telling? Why is it told the way it is? What does the form mean? In what way is it innovative? What emergent social phenomena required this form of narrative? Why, in the end, does *this* novel matter? What does it invite us to 'see'?

Chapter 1

How pleasant to meet Mr Fielding: The Narrator as Hero in *Tom Jones*

W. B. Hutchings

Well, pleasant for some, less pleasant for others. *Tom Jones* used to be the first topic on the Open University's very successful A204 course, which Bill Ruddick taught in Newcastle upon Tyne for all too brief a time after his early retirement from the Manchester English department. Not renowned for being afraid to express a point of view, Open University students would be both vigorous and varied in their attitudes to the chatty and familiar voice of the narrator of *Tom Jones*. Some found him amusing and engaging, whereas others expressed irritation and even resentment. Some loved the idea of being cheerily accompanied on the stagecoach ride that is Fielding's metaphor for the temporal journey of his story. Others found that the experience had all the pleasure and entertainment of being trapped in a corner by the saloon-bar bore.

Readers who respond so negatively to Mr Fielding can be reassured by the knowledge that one of the great novelists of the twentieth century is on their side. Ford Madox Ford, in his quirky and opinionated essay on *The English Novel*, published in 1930, inveighed heartily against this most intrusive of narrative methods. Writers from Fielding to Thackeray, he said, marred their novels by 'continually brought-in passages of moralizations' and to these Fielding added 'an immense amount of rather nauseous special-pleading'.[1] Ford writes from a technician's point of view. For him, what he termed literary 'impressionism' has the desired effect of conveying the dramatic actuality of a scene or a character. All authorial intrusion should ideally be avoided, the scene being directly presented to readers as if they were themselves witnessing it. An admirer of Samuel Richardson in the familiar battle of the eighteenth-century novelists, and of the French tradition from Flaubert on, Ford objects to Fielding's loose, sloppy narrative. He is offended by the sheer lack of artistry, by Fielding's apparent refusal to treat the novel as a proper work of art rather than a self-indulgent sprawl.

Critical readers are more often offended by the narrator's tone of voice, his nudging the reader familiarly in the ribs, and insisting on his jovial presence. This intrusiveness makes the novel a lot longer than it needs to be. As Johnson said of *Paradise Lost*, nobody ever wished it longer: well, no student, certainly. But more destructive for such readers than this is the effect it has of repeatedly diverting us from what the novel is really about. It is, after all, the story of Tom Jones, an ordinary and frail man who is driven from the unsustainable world of allegory into the realism of England in the mid-eighteenth century. For Paradise Hall, read London. For Adam, read Tom. Or, for

Eve, read Sophia Western. For it is also her story, one of winning through by asserting her integrity and autonomy. This heroine converts her allegorical potential as the bearer of divine knowledge (her name is Greek for 'wisdom') into a practical application of principles to a real world, one whose reality is marked by an ethos which threatens all ideals. So why not show us these dramas and conflicts, Mr Fielding, without the unnecessary and irrelevant accompaniment of a host (to use another of his metaphors) loudly dominating proceedings from his hearth?

One solution to this problem, if only a partial one, is to exercise creative censorship. Ford proposed that one could skip the special pleading in the headings of chapters in order to get on with the picaresque story. How many readers have gone further by taking up the narrator's proffered option of omitting the opening chapters of each volume, in which Fielding steps back from the story to comment in essay form on a variety of matters which take his fancy? That at least removes some of the most obvious of the narrative interjections and speeds up the reading. It is in one of these opening chapters, that to book 5 ('*Of* THE SERIOUS *in writing; and for what Purpose it is introduced*'), that Fielding states what the reader may agree with wholeheartedly, even at this early stage:

> Peradventure there may be no Parts in this prodigious Work which will give the Reader less Pleasure in the perusing, than those which have given the Author the greatest Pains in composing. Among these probably may be reckoned those initial Essays which we have prefixed to the historical Matter contained in every Book; and which we have determined to be essentially necessary to this kind of Writing, of which we have set ourselves at the Head.[2]

He goes on to defend these parts of the book on the grounds that every work needs contrast between the serious and the comic. But he allows the reader who is satisfied that the rest of the novel already contains enough of the serious to 'pass over these, in which we profess to be laboriously dull, and begin the following Books, at the second Chapter' (1: 5.1.215).

Now all of this is hedged round with very English irony, so giving a comic air to what the narrator professes to be one of the serious sections – a further irony. Fielding, it may be, is being more elusive than at first appears. His odd confession for a writer, that he is aiming to be dull, may be viewed as welcome honesty, but really adds to our suspicion that he is playing with us. How seriously do we take that claim that he has put himself at the head of this kind of writing? Does he mean that he is the first to do it? Not true. Or that he is the best at it? Either way, is his tongue in his cheek? Consider that word 'prodigious' which he uses about his novel, with its self-consciously Latinate strutting. The tone here resembles those parts of the novel where he undermines supposed seriousness by comically deflating exaggeration. Here is Squire Allworthy greeting the dawn in style:

> It was now the Middle of *May*, and the Morning was remarkably serene, when Mr. *Allworthy* walked forth on the Terrace, where the Dawn opened

> every Minute that lovely Prospect we have before described to his Eye. And now having sent forth Streams of Light, which ascended the blue Firmament before him as Harbingers preceding his Pomp, in the full Blaze of his Majesty, up rose the Sun; than which one Object alone in this lower Creation could be more glorious, and that Mr. *Allworthy* himself presented; a human Being replete with Benevolence, meditating in what manner he might render himself most acceptable to his Creator, by doing most good to his Creatures (1: 1.4.43)

It is not easy to put one's finger exactly on the spot where simple praise turns into hyperbole. Indeed, it is possible that readers' responses might range from the mean-spirited cynic, who finds a touch of vainglory as early as the phrase 'walked forth', to the innocent admirer of purple prose, who can accept 'Firmament' and 'Harbingers preceding his Pomp' as fine pieces of mythologizing in the antique mode and 'replete with Benevolence' as a decorously appropriate phrase for this human embodiment of enlightened morality. Perhaps such innocence is less often found in today's readers than in their more classically educated eighteenth-century counterparts. But Fielding is really being highly self-conscious stylistically, for he is, as often in the novel, producing an exercise in the mock-heroic.

Mock-heroic works by uncertainty, by modulating between the twin poles of the heroic and parody. In Pope's *The Rape of the Lock*, Belinda is both a grand figure of female power and an ordinary, vulnerable and rather silly eighteenth-century woman. So here Allworthy is all worthy in his intentions, his desire to spread sweetness and light, and is at the same time sent up by a narrative which cannot take pictures of perfection seriously. For it is the narrator himself who openly punctures his own pompous balloon:

> Reader, take care, I have unadvisedly led thee to the Top of as high a Hill as Mr. *Allworthy's*, and how to get thee down without breaking thy Neck, I do not well know. However, let us e'en venture to slide down together, for Miss *Bridget* rings her Bell, and Mr. *Allworthy* is summoned to Breakfast, where I must attend, and, if you please, shall be glad of your Company. (1: 1.4.43–4)

Allworthy lives on a hill literally as well as stylistically. His house stands on the slopes of a hill, but 'nearer the Bottom than the Top of it, so as to be sheltered from the North-east by a Grove of old Oaks, which rose above it in a gradual Ascent of near half a Mile, and yet high enough to enjoy a most charming Prospect of the Valley beneath' (1: 1.4.42). His home is both temperate and moderate in its claims, subordinate to the British nature embodied in the oaks, and yet with a clear view over the lower world. Allworthy thus combines high ambition with an acceptance of the need for shelter, for moderation. In humorously acknowledging the risks of yielding to the temptations of the high style (Puttenham's English term for hyperbole is 'over reacher'), the narrator recognizes that he is in tune with his character. Like the mock-heroic, Allworthy mediates between ideal and real, between the worlds of abstract representation (All-worthy) and real humanity (Mr). The plot provides Allworthy with his own path to the top of a hill from which the descent, like Virgil's to hell in one of the eighteenth century's favourite Latin tags ('facilis descensus averno', *Aeneid*, 6.126), is dangerously easy. His authority leads him to pass judgement on those whom he does not really understand – Jenny Jones, Partridge and, above all, Tom. Those he judges are imperfect, fallible human beings. But Allworthy's judgement of them reveals his own fallibility, his inability to be all-seeing and all-knowing. And this is a fallibility which the narrator, in his sphere, shares.

This is the nub. Yes, Fielding's style draws attention to itself, as his narrator keeps on drawing attention to himself. This is literary language, this is the work of a writer, it keeps saying; just as the narrator keeps reminding us that the book is written by a human being. That human being is, like all of us, fallible in his humanity.

Consider the thesis of the opening chapter of book 10. This essay is an attack on books which represent figures of extremes, of 'angelic Perfection' or 'diabolical Depravity'. Mixed characters actually engage the reader more fully than such types, he argues, for a character who is fundamentally good and so attracts 'the Admiration and Affection of a well-disposed Mind' will, when 'there should appear some of those little Blemishes, *quas humana parum cavit natura*[3] ... raise our Compassion rather than our Abhorrence'. Mixed characters are natural, but, when represented in fiction, they are also more effective moral exemplars than 'Models of Perfection' (2: 10.1.526–7). Fielding thus seeks to counter moral objectors on their own ground, as well as to defend his practice on the grounds of realism, of truth to human nature.

The moral issue, we must admit, is assuredly moot. Johnson (*Tom Jones* is the implicit object of his concern in *Rambler* 4, published in 1750, the year after the novel) is not alone in his concern about the impact of a pattern in which a morally wayward hero is rewarded with perfect happiness. Ford, again, attacked Tom Jones as 'lewd, stupid and treacherous' and accused Fielding of hypocrisy in making him his hero (*The English Novel*, 92). However, Fielding's conviction is carried into effect in the neatest possible way. His narrator, even as he puts forward this argument, shows that he too is not without a little human blemish.

For there is one thing guaranteed to make him lose his cool, and that is a critic. He is not alone among authors in this, of course, many of whom perceive critics as blood-sucking leeches. But our narrator is particularly obsessed, and shows it repeatedly. In this chapter he lectures 'a little Reptile of a Critic' (2: 10.1.525) on the need to restrain any desire to censure a part of the book until the whole design is apparent. The chapter is entitled, in admonitory vein, '*Containing Instructions very necessary to be perused by modern Critics*', not an attitude adapted to mollifying the opposition. Nor is this an isolated example of such antagonism. The novel has scarcely begun before we find him justifying his intention to digress simply with the assertion that he is 'a better Judge than any pitiful Critic whatever'. Such critics, he declares, should 'mind their own Business, and not ... intermeddle with Affairs, or Works, which no ways concern them' (1: 1.2.37). The opening chapter of book 5 discourses on the need for critics to know their place, as the clerks rather than the legislators of mankind, taking down rules as dictated by authors. He laments the process of time by which 'the Clerk began to invade the Power and assume the Dignity of his Master'. Being 'Men of shallow Capacities', these critics 'mistook mere Form for Substance', and hence produced laws which reflect notional doctrines rather than the spirit of creative flexibility (1: 5.1.211). This sets the pattern for the subsequent discussion of the role of critics. It is simply that, with reiterated attacks, the narrator's tone has become noticeably sharper and less forgiving by book 10.

Our narrator, then, is very much a man of flesh and blood. His irritability is itself proof of this, as it is of his all-too-human sensitiveness. He is prickly on the subject dear to his heart, his writing, and his vanity is easily touched. That word 'prodigious' which we quoted earlier may have a tongue-in-cheek air about it, but it also reflects a continuing tone of vaunting pride. Critics may carp, but he actually does the business, is his refrain. Just as he later (14.1) argues that only those who have experienced life can truly write about it, so only those who write novels, it would seem, have the right to act as critics.

The narrator in *Tom Jones*, then, is – like the man on the Clapham stagecoach – one who demonstrates and represents the book's central view of human nature and fictional characters. They are mixed beings, made up of traits which are now appealing and amusing, now irritating and tiresome. And we readers, too, are mixed and variable human beings, and so disagree about which of the narrator's traits is to be tolerated or admired, disliked or loved. The narrator is himself an ordinary man, and so a representative hero, and each of us is his representative reader. No wonder we cannot agree about him.

Fielding constructs this narrator in various ways. We have seen how he is self-conscious about how he writes and the value he attaches to his writing. He is always conscious, too, of the existence of the reader, directly addressing us at all stages of the story. His attitude is friendly and open, flattering us with such appellations as 'my sagacious Friend' (for example, 1: 1.3.38). But when reader and style come together in his mind, he can often be pretty condescending. For example, Deborah Wilkins, Mr Allworthy's servant (described, rather to the disquiet of some of us, as both 'elderly' and 'in the 52d Year of her Age' [1: 1.3.39–40]) sets out to discover which of the brazen hussies of the village is the mother of the foundling:

> Not otherwise than when a Kite, tremendous Bird, is beheld by the feathered Generation soaring aloft, and hovering over their Heads, the amorous Dove, and every innocent little Bird spread wide the Alarm, and fly trembling to their Hiding-places: He proudly beats the Air, conscious of his Dignity, and meditates intended Mischief. (1: 1.6.47)

Well, here is another instance of Fielding enjoying the pleasures of mock-heroic humour. Deborah could appear in Pope's *Dunciad* as another of that poem's humorous grotesques inhabiting the cultural wastes of Grub Street. Fielding notes the game he is playing by telling us in the title to the chapter that '*Mrs. Deborah is introduced into the Parish, with a Simile*'. But he takes the game a stage further. He acknowledges again that the reader is, of course, 'sagacious', but still proceeds to explain his own simile:

> It is my Intention therefore to signify, that as it is the Nature of a Kite to devour little Birds, so it is the Nature of such Persons as Mrs. *Wilkins*, to insult and tyrannize over little People. This being indeed the Means which they use to recompense to themselves their extreme Servility and Condescension to their Superiors; for nothing can be more reasonable, than that Slaves and Flatterers should exact the same Taxes on all below them, which they themselves pay to all above them. (1: 1.6.47–48)

Yes, well, we could have worked that out for ourselves, couldn't we? Indeed, our vanity responds that we wouldn't be reading his novel in the first place if we really needed help with such elementary images, or to have the moral explicated quite so fully and deliberately for us. We ordinary readers who do not wish to be called 'critics' have our pride, too, after all. Looking back on it, we might now feel, isn't there a touch of condescension in that word 'sagacious'? The hyperbole (why not just 'intelligent' or even 'wise'?) begins to look suspiciously like the kind of mock-heroic playing we have noted elsewhere. All good stylistic fun, then, or dreadful patronizing? Pleasant or unpleasant, as the case may be. And perhaps our responses reveal a bit about ourselves, too.

The narrator, then, is a real presence who embodies and demonstrates the novel's central perspective on human nature and its fictional representations. This is not to make a simple confusion between the historical Henry Fielding and the narrative voice of *Tom Jones*. As we shall see, there are clear links between them. But Fielding has taken the artistic decision to dramatize his narrator distinctively. Such a method draws attention to the fictional nature of the work. This is a 'history', as the title-page assures us, but it is one written by 'an author', as the opening words of the very first chapter say. If this undermines right from the start the story's pretensions to 'reality', the presence of the narrator, by contrast, assures us of the book's true reality. He is real, and is the living embodiment of the book's humane vision. With this assurance, we can accept the 'realism' of the book for what it is. It is not a history in any naively authentic sense, but it identifies itself as virtual history by the extent to which the moral and social pattern prescribed by the narrator accords with readers' perception of the moral and social world they inhabit.

The novel is essentially a public form of literature, evoked in *Tom Jones* by Fielding's metaphor of the author as innkeeper, offering all persons his entertainment for them to approve or condemn as they judge (1.1). It is public because its topic is society, human nature in all its 'prodigious Variety'. As all are welcome at the inn, so Fielding's novel offers a varied menu to match all tastes. The range extends from the squirearchy to the peasantry, from the country of Somerset to the city of London, from the servant class to the aristocracy. *Tom Jones*'s breadth makes it one of the earliest examples of the 'state of England' novel, that which observes and presents a spectrum of contemporary society.

Observation with such extensive view requires an observer, and so is subjective, the result of one person's vision. Objectivity is the result of a communal act of observation, a pooling of our perceptions towards a series of general truths. 'General' here is meant in its proper, Johnsonian, sense as the opposite of 'particular', not as the opposite of 'precise'. Whereas the particular is limited to its own individual interests and prejudices, the general is that which is shared in common. This is what Dr Johnson's Imlac means when he says that the business of a poet is to remark 'general properties' (*Rasselas*, chapter 10). We, the readers, are essential because we judge the general validity of the narrator's observations by comparison with our experience. We shall all have our own particularities derived from our own fallibility, but between us we come to some kind of agreement – tentative, provisional – about the general pattern of social behaviour we see in the novel. Despite all the differences of view about the narrator, that was what used to happen in those A204 seminars.

The best advice to give to readers who get irritated by Fielding's opening chapters is the reverse of what he proposes. Omit the rest of each book, and read just the opening essays together. Do this, and we have an essayist, whose character is defined by the attitudes and opinions he embraces. The writing is in the tradition of those eighteenth-century essays presented from a fictional viewpoint (Mr Spectator, Mr Rambler) which live by the extent to which they evoke or challenge our experience. Mr Spectator glories in the experience of observing the Royal Exchange in all its public and multinational business, as many a Londoner would have done (*Spectator* 69). Mr Rambler challenges us to judge whether our experience tells us that the punishment of capital offences for theft is actually proving a deterrent to criminal activity (*Rambler* 114). As he is engaged in the process of writing a novel, our essayist is naturally primarily concerned with the nature of fiction and the response of readers to his work. These opening chapters constitute a manifesto for the kind of novel *Tom Jones* is. So in book 2 the prefatory essay accepts and celebrates an author's need to select, for there will inevitably be large parts of the characters' lives which must remain 'Blanks in the grand Lottery of Time'. So some chapters will 'contain only the Time of a single Day' while others will 'comprise Years' (1: 2.1.76–7). In terms of intensity of experience and in our memory, our lives are not measured out in coffee-spoons. Other essays, notably those to books 4 and 8, examine the kind of fictional truth the novel presents, as opposed to 'those idle Romances which are filled with Monsters' (1: 4.1.150). The book 8 essay develops a careful and sophisticated theory of probability as the main criterion: probability of event, of belief, of that which is within the capacity of an ordinary mortal:

> But we who deal in private Character, who search into the most retired Recesses, and draw forth Examples of Virtue and Vice, from Holes and Corners of the World . . . it becomes us to keep within the Limits not only of Possibility, but of Probability too. (1: 8.1.402)

Equally significant is the amount of space Fielding devotes to defining the role and responsibilities of the author. Book 9's is the key essay here, asserting as it does the need for an author to possess powers of judgement and knowledge of a cross-section of people:

> Again, there is another Sort of Knowledge beyond the Power of Learning to bestow, and this is to be had by Conversation. So necessary is this to the

> understanding the Characters of Men, that none are more ignorant of them
> than those learned Pedants, whose Lives have been entirely consumed in
> Colleges, and among Books: For however exquisitely Human Nature may
> have been described by Writers, the true practical System can be learnt
> only in the World. (1: 9.1.492)

Experience is the key-note, and experience is emotional as well as physical:

> Nor will all the Qualities I have hitherto given my Historian avail him, unless
> he have what is generally meant by a good Heart, and be capable of feeling.
> The Author who will make me weep, says *Horace*, must first weep himself.
> (1: 9.1.494)

The desired author here resembles the principal character of the novel our author is writing. Having a 'good heart' despite all his errors and misadventures is Tom's principal characteristic and his saving grace.

Those who take issue with the implied morality of this novel will rightly point to the dangers inherent in such a value without an explicit moral code for guidance. However, it is only fair to Fielding to note that his devotion to judgement means that he does not evade some, at least, of the consequences of this hearty approach to morality. It is, after all, Tom's magnanimous relief at Allworthy's recovery from life-threatening illness that is indirectly responsible for his own dismissal from the estate. His joy takes him to celebration, and celebration to an imprudent amount of wine. Unfortunately, Blifil and Thwackum observe his chance encounter with Molly Seagrim in the woods in his flushed state (5.10), and later use their knowledge to Tom's disadvantage (6.10).

That Fielding is aware of the need for the narrator to exhibit moral responsibility is made clear by the careful positioning of book 9's essay. We are near the mid-point of the novel's eighteen books and of Tom's journey from country to city. Book 8 ends with the interpolated story of the Man of the Hill, which adumbrates in a number of ways Tom's own future, his descent into the moral wasteland of London and the treachery of the world. The crucial difference between Tom and the Man of the Hill lies in the finale to each narrative, the lesson that each draws from his experiences. The older man retires into a state of misanthropic solitude, convinced of the complete corruption of humankind and its unworthiness of its creator. Tom certainly acknowledges the existence of evil, but argues that the Man of the Hill generalizes incorrectly 'by taking the Character of Mankind from the worst and basest among them' (1: 8.15.485). He has retreated to the top of a hill because he thinks that humankind is at the bottom, an extreme and unbalanced position unlike that of Allworthy's (and so Tom's) house. Tom proposes that one must accept personal responsibility for one's actions rather than blame everything on the viciousness of others. He comments that the Man of the Hill has been not only unfortunate, but also incautious in the placing of his affections. Such an observation applies equally to Tom, in the past and in the future, proof both that Tom's outlook is sound and that he has yet to learn to apply notion to action. The result of this human tendency to imprudence is that wickedness can arise as often from accident as from design. As Tom says, 'many a Man who commits Evil, is not totally bad and corrupt in his Heart' (1: 8.15.486).

With these conclusions book 8 ends. Book 9 begins with the essay on the nature and responsibilities of an author, and the first action of the book constitutes an emblem of Tom's own progress and decline into the relative morality of the real world. From the top of Mazard Hill, Tom and the Man of the Hill look first back towards the south, and Tom exclaims:

> 'I was endeavouring to trace out my own Journey hither. Good Heavens! What a Distance is *Gloucester* from us! What a vast Tract of Land must be between me and my own Home.' 'Ay, ay, young Gentleman,' cries the other, 'and, by your Sighing, from what you love better than your own Home, or I am mistaken.' (1: 9.2.495)

This is the land of lost content, of home, youth and love. They then walk to the other side of the hill, looking north-west:

> Here they were no sooner arrived, than they heard at a Distance the most violent Skreams of a Woman, proceeding from the Wood below them. *Jones* listened a Moment, and then, without saying a Word to his Companion (for indeed the Occasion seemed sufficiently pressing) ran, or rather slid, down the Hill, and without the least Apprehension or Concern for his own Safety, made directly to the Thicket whence the Sound had issued. (1: 9.2.495)

Tom's reaction, immediate and unthinking, is typical in its lack of concern for himself and its resulting lack of control over himself. Whereas the Man of the Hill remains sitting on the top of the hill, remote and unconcerned, Tom commits himself to an act of complicated virtue: the rescue of the damsel in distress lands him in a situation which exposes him to his habitual imprudence. Tom's encounter with the woman is set in a 'Thicket', evoking the scene of that former disastrous loss of sexual control when Tom, drunk with joy at Allworthy's recovery, retires with Molly 'into the thickest Part of the Grove' (1: 5.10.257). The woman he now rescues is Mrs Waters, alias Jenny Jones, the supposed mother of the foundling, and the events which follow at the inn at Upton initiate the moral crises of the second half of the book.

Fielding thus demonstrates mixed humanity as inevitably caught in morally problematic situations. Tom's vices are not the opposite of his virtues, but are bound up with them. His instinct to rescue a distressed fellow human being – so superior in its moral agency to the Man of the Hill's passive indifference – is also the instinct that draws him too closely to the warmth of humanity. A lack of prudence is both admirable and reprehensible.

Throughout the narrative of this chapter Fielding, as ever, keeps the reader fully aware of his narrator's controlling presence. He begins the chapter with a typical piece of mock-heroic:

> *Aurora* now first opened her Casement, *anglicè*, the Day began to break, when *Jones* walked forth in Company with the Stranger, and mounted *Mazard-Hill*. (1: 9.2.495)

By playing with the different possibilities of language, from the Latinate to the English, from myth to real landscape, Fielding shows language to be a human tool, capable of reflecting individual idiosyncrasy. The narrator repeatedly intrudes with direct or sly comment as well as stylistic self-consciousness. Ensign Northerton, the aggressor, realizes with surprise that his adversary is someone whom he had earlier encountered, 'but I conceive his Pleasure was rather less on this Occasion' (1: 9.2.496). On their way to Upton, Tom offers Mrs Walters his coat to cover her torn clothes, 'but, I know not for what Reason, she absolutely refused the most earnest Solicitations to accept it' (1: 9.2.498). Tom thus proposes to walk in front of her so that his eyes do not 'offend' her, and the narrator compares the couple to a modern Orpheus and Eurydice, albeit a more artful Eurydice and a highly susceptible Orpheus. The entire episode is overtly presented and shaped by the narrator. His interpretative commentary invites the reader's own judgement on a modern hero, one who is no classical paragon of virtue, but whose youthful impetuosity both renders him attractive and exposes him to danger.

Fielding, like many eighteenth-century writers, was a trained lawyer, professionally concerned with judgement. He studied in the Middle Temple, was called to the Bar in 1740, and was appointed Justice of the Peace for Westminster in 1748. Soon after the publication of *Tom Jones* in 1749, he was made Justice of the Peace for the whole of Middlesex. He wrote pamphlets on crime and poverty, and he and his blind half-brother John drew up a plan for a police force for London. In *Tom Jones*, the judicial system appears both literally and as a running metaphor for how we judge human actions and motivation. Allworthy, as we have noted, is both the type of the benevolent Justice of the Peace whose aim is the greater happiness of society, and a prime example of how humanity, with the best of intentions, can be wrong. Justice, even if impartial, is blind to truth. He is Fielding's testimony to the value, necessity and fallibility of human judgement.

Imperfection is shown throughout the all-too-human world of the novel. For example, in book 7, Mrs Honour, Sophia's maid, is confronted with the choice of whether to remain faithful to her mistress and accompany her on her flight from her father's house, or to transfer her fidelity to Squire Western and inform him of his daughter's plans. On the one hand, the prospect of a handsome reward from Western and the danger of a journey with Sophia weigh heavily. 'She was, however, too upright a Judge to decree on one Side before she had heard the other.' So she acknowledges that the prospect of accompanying Sophia to London has its attractions, and that Sophia is more likely to be generous with her rewards than is the surly squire. 'She then cross-examined all the Articles which had raised her Fears on the other Side, and found, on fairly sifting the Matter, that there was very little in them.' At this point, 'both Scales' of judgement are in 'a pretty even Balance' (1: 7.8.353–4). She then recollects that Sophia will not be able to reward her fully until she comes of age, a fact which tilts the balance ominously against fidelity. The case is actually decided by a completely irrelevant event. Rivalry between Honour and Mrs Western's maid, who assumes superiority over her, erupts in a quarrel which culminates in Honour proudly asserting her independence from Mrs Western. On hearing of the quarrel, Squire Western, who is, like Allworthy, a Justice of the Peace, swears that he will have Honour sent to Bridewell. But, fortunately,

Western's clerk, who 'had a Qualification, which no Clerk to a Justice of Peace ought ever to be without, namely, some Understanding in the Law of this Realm' (1: 7.9.357), quietly tells his master that a even a servant cannot be sent to prison unless she has broken the law. Mrs Western disputes this, but has to settle for merely dismissing Honour, who thus ends up doing the right deed for the wrong reason: she remains faithful to Sophia as a result of her pride and jealousy. Honour's fallibility is recognizable and, to a sympathetic judge, understandable.

This use of legal processes and legal metaphors clearly links the narrator of *Tom Jones* with the historical Henry Fielding. To the extent that the novel is imbued with the profession of its creator, it obviously owes a great deal to Fielding's experience. But the narrator of *Tom Jones* is not just a disguised Henry Fielding. In his repeated interventions in the narrative, he declares that a narrative must have a point of view, an angle from which it is written. The kind of narrator he is – and this is Fielding's choice and artistry – represents and embodies what the operation of justice in the novel demonstrates: as we are all fallible, the need for judgement must always be tempered with a recognition of human frailty. There are no heroes in the absolute sense in the real and relative world of eighteenth-century England. There are just human beings. Both the fictional 'hero' and the real narrator of *Tom Jones* reflect this awareness. Our judgements as readers are likewise vulnerable to error and prejudice. True judgement is only possible through a general sweep of humane collective activity, in which we learn to accept that our responses must be tempered by a broader acceptance of diversity. That's why the modern legal system has juries and universities have seminars.

Chapter 2

'Where then lies the difference?': The (Ante)Postmodernity of *Tristram Shandy*

Jayne Lewis

> The common men, who know very little of fortification, confound the ravelin and the half-moon together, – tho' they are very different things; – not in their figure or construction, for we make them exactly alike in all points; – for they always consist of two faces, making a salient angle, with the gorges, not straight, but in form of a crescent. – Where then lies the difference (quoth my father, a little testily) – In their situation, answered my uncle *Toby*: – For when a ravelin, brother, stands before the curtin, it is a ravelin; and when a ravelin stands before a bastion, then the ravelin is not a ravelin; – it is a half-moon.
>
> —*Tristram Shandy*

Before entertaining the weighty matter of what makes a ravelin a ravelin, I want to raise a different question. Let us assume, first of all, that the English novel has had a life, one that, having officially begun at some point in the eighteenth century, persists up through the present moment. The novel naturally looks different at different phases of its life: Samuel Richardson's epistolary and sentimental *Clarissa* (1747–48) creates a world singularly unlike the teeming, indignant verbal metropolis of Charles Dickens's *Bleak House* (1852–53), and neither narrative bears much obvious resemblance to Virginia Woolf's lyrical, associative *Mrs Dalloway* (1925). As our own century turns, the novel now wears a new, postmodern mask epitomized in the paratactic, linguistically self-conscious, compulsively ironic pages of Jeanette Winterson or Julian Barnes. Tracking such differences helps us to make sense of the English novel's life – to tell a coherent story about its transformations from time to time, and thus to discern its continuity over time.

What then to do about *Tristram Shandy*? Laurence Sterne's novel of 1760–67 is itself the first-hand story of a 'Life', but from its first page it mocks our easy assumption that the life of the English novel has unfolded in an orderly series of stages, each characterized by a unique set of attributes. In its own day, *Tristram Shandy* was often regarded as a raunchy anomaly, and most Victorians failed to appreciate it at all. But early in the twentieth century, modernist writers like Woolf and James Joyce (whose *Finnegans Wake* begins with a punning homage to it) saw their own strategies of representation mirrored in a work which travels only via the eccentric pathways of the associative mind. At the same time, Sterne's fragmentary, digressive, often parodic narrative technique provokes many readers these days to cite *Tristram Shandy* as evidence that the novel was postmodern even before it was modern.[1] As if to mirror such uncanny resemblances, Tristram Shandy's own 'Life' declines to present itself as a straightforward story of 'progressive' development. At the very least, Tristram declares, 'my work is digressive, and it is progressive too.'[2] Compounded of these 'two contrary motions', and lacking either a proper beginning or a definite end, that 'work' amounts to an unregenerate pastiche of fragments, interruptions, gaps and digressions. Human life, it seems to say, is not the tidy train of changes we make it out to be; nor is the life of the novel.

Tristram Shandy himself is famously anxious to outrun the sort of time that moves in an inexorable straight line from birth to death. Volume 7 has our tubercular, erratic hero galloping furiously off to France in a desperate attempt to outstrip death, that 'long-striding scoundrel of a scare-sinner, who is posting after me' (7.7.585). As if to support Tristram's flight from changeful and sequential time – from what we might call history – the very plot of *Tristram Shandy* steadfastly refuses to behave like a plot: albeit at times to Tristram's frustration, Sterne's narrative routinely eschews the 'progressive movement' that can only end in the grave. Instead it interrupts itself, digresses from itself, and more than once stands stock still amid a chaos of words, images, opinions and obsessions of every shape and stripe.

Here then are two of the most puzzling features of Sterne's novel: its uncanny resemblance to the postmodern fictions that would not materialize until two hundred years after its birth, and the fugitive, often eerily immobilized vision of individual human life that *Tristram Shandy* – like Tristram Shandy – embodies. These quirks of Sterne's narrative disrupt our habits of thinking developmentally, or even chronologically, about both personal and literary history. Together, moreover, they beg a question similar to the one posed in the second of the novel's nine volumes by Tristram's 'systematical' father, Walter (1.21.76). The elder Shandy has been enduring a rambling disquisition on military technology by his brother Toby, whose long-ago service at the Battle of Namur resulted not just in an unspeakable injury to the groin but also in an unquenchable penchant for bringing every conversation around to the subject of arms. When Toby, typically, tangles himself up in a description of half-moons and ravelins, Walter demands to know 'where then lies the difference' between these seemingly indistinguishable engines of war (2.12.129). His urgency mimics ours to know the nature of *Tristram Shandy*'s difference from postmodern fiction, or indeed to know where in Tristram's story we can find the stable markers of progressive change that make human life conceivable to itself.

As it happens, my uncle Toby's gentle answer to Walter's query – that the differences between things lie 'in their situation' – also lends itself to the question of what *Tristram Shandy* has to say about both personal and literary history. For it is only by turning from the intrinsic features of Sterne's narrative to its 'situation' in an eighteenth-century English culture concocted of equal parts scepticism and sentiment, and at last to its place *vis-à-vis* the reader it alternately chastises and cajoles, that we can begin to gauge its relationship to 'history'. Only then, in turn, can we appreciate *Tristram*

Shandy's particularity, discerning in this novel the traits that, in Sterne's own words in a letter to a friend, promise to 'Identify it from all Others of the [same] Stamp', postmodern or otherwise.[3]

The historicity of *Tristram Shandy*

When the first two volumes of *Tristram Shandy* appeared in London on the first day of the year 1760, few of its readers could think what to do with them. 'This is a humorous performance, of which we are unable to convey any distinct ideas to our readers', fumbled the *Critical Review*, while the *Royal Female Magazine* found Sterne's novel in 'contempt of all the rules observed in other writings, and therefore cannot justly have its merit measured by them.'[4] Partly in oedipal revolt against a father who was 'one of the most regular men in everything he did' (1.4.6), Sterne's Tristram vows early on that, in telling the story of his life, 'I shall confine myself neither to [Horace's] rules nor to the rules of any man that ever lived' (1.4.5). Schooled in neoclassical values of literary construction and trained by the architects of the new genre of the novel to expect either a Fieldingesque 'comic epic in prose' or the 'writing to the moment' that Richardson had recommended, eighteenth-century readers often threw up their hands at the very transgressions – against syntax, logic, genre and taste – which their postmodern counterparts have lately recognized and embraced.

There are many ways of classifying these transgressions, but here it will be useful to understand them as affronts to a model of history that was calibrated in Sterne's own century and, as opposed to ancient, decided to call itself modern. For one thing, borrowing from the narrative practices of enlightenment historiographers who presented the past as a 'chain' of linked occurrences inherently available to narrative,[5] any number of eighteenth-century novels purport to chart the progress of individual lives, and thus cast themselves as the 'History' of one English person or another – Tom Jones, Betsy Thoughtless, even Richardson's inimitable 'young lady', Clarissa Harlowe. *Tristram Shandy*'s title page, by contrast, promises only the eponymous hero's 'Life and Opinions', and neither the shape of these nor their relationship to each other is specified. Accordingly, by the end of the second volume Tristram has hinted broadly at the event of his birth but has not yet entered the world ... nor will he for quite some time. As he notes with dismay midway through his first volume, 'I have been at it these six weeks, making all the speed I possibly could, – and am not yet born' (1.14.42).

'It', here, is the vexatious time that writing takes, and Tristram's frequent, frustrated references to 'it' further skew what one critic has termed 'the time-sense' of his narrative, foreclosing any chance there might have been for us to receive the scrambled chapters of his life story in coherent chronological order.[6] Because we learn so much about what happens to Tristram's pen over the course of 'this rhapsodical work' (1.13.39), we learn remarkably little about what has happened to Tristram himself. It is true that he is eventually born, though not without a disastrous encounter with a pair of forceps; when he is five years old, a window sash falls on him with mortifying results; he is eventually breeched; and in adulthood he takes a feverish and lubricious tour of France. Beyond these incidents, though, we gain little sense of what we might call Tristram's 'history', for all that he classifies himself as a 'historiographer' (1.14.41). What we do discover comes to us largely by chance, via anecdote and innuendo, or squeezed in between other people's often equally fragmented histories – here 'the history of my Uncle Toby's Campaigns' and there that of his 'Amours' with the Widow Wadman, here Slawkenbergius's raunchy *roman à nez* and there the pathetic story of LeFever.

In place of a sequentially ordered record of the 'train of events' (1.19.64) that Tristram claims befell him and thereby made his life what it is, Sterne puts the most accident-prone of narratives. Every sentence of Tristram's story risks deflection by some opposing story: well might he opine that 'the life of the writer, whatever he might fancy to the contrary, [is] not so much a state of *composition*, as a state of *warfare*' (5.16.447). Despite profuse dedications to contemporary persons and liberal mention of contemporary events, Tristram's style of narration seems to catapult *Tristram Shandy* from its own place in literary history, marking its author's anachronistic affinity with the many postmodern narrators who likewise refuse to bind themselves either to modernity's sequential order of telling or to its pretence that there is no ever-widening chasm between words and the world they presume to represent.[7]

His name might hearken back to medieval romance, but like his postmodern counterparts, Tristram ricochets from opinion to incident to conversational snippet and back again, his tale governed by no law beyond the teller's peculiar impulses of association. His very first chapter for instance begins with Tristram's reflections upon his own conception, only to veer sharply into free thoughts upon the tyranny of chance and thence to the popular theory of the animal spirits, ending with a brief cryptic exchange in which Tristram's mother reminds his father to wind the clock – a chore we only later learn is the signal for conjugal relations in the Shandy household. The clock doesn't get wound for quite some time, narratively speaking, and this is fitting, since it is precisely the sort of time kept by clocks (and of course conventional histories) that Tristram eschews in favour of a narrative style that mimics his childhood bent toward an 'unaccountable obliquity [...] in my manner of setting up my top' (1.3.4).

Carried out in digressions so prolific that there is little hope of telling them apart from the main thrust of Tristram's 'unaccountable' account, this 'obliquity' makes it impossible to experience either Tristram's 'Life' or his life as the 'train of events' he makes it out to be. What is more, it becomes impossible to distinguish 'The Life' from the life, the verbal representation from its presumably historical object. As the difference between the narrative of Tristram's life and the life itself proves harder and harder to measure, Sterne's novel again entices us to classify it as postmodern *avant la lettre*. Certainly it shares with fiction of our own day a movement away from – if not outright against – history, with history understood both as a form of sequential narration that reinforces our sense of chronological time *and* as the world of lived experience that presumably exists apart from symbolic constructs such as novels.[8]

At the level of what little plot *Tristram Shandy* possesses, it is possible to see this flight from history as a flight into consciousness. Consciousness here is governed by arbitrary habits of association; in the mind, Sterne's hero observes, thoughts seem to follow one another in 'a regular succession' but in fact do so only 'like the images in the inside of a lanthorn turned round by the heat of a candle' (3.9.225), thereby actually evading the chronological imperative. The mind moves but goes nowhere, and it is thus dangerously, if comically, inclined to obsession. In one of Tristram's most famous and pervasive metaphors, obsessions are hobbyhorses, and every Shandy rides one. So, Tristram charges, does each of his readers; indeed, he demands, 'Have not the wisest men in all ages, not excepting *Solomon* himself, – have they not had their HOBBY-HORSES?' (1.9.12). Available across 'all ages', and anyway objects whose progress is always illusory, hobbyhorses do more than stand in for mental custom. They also betray Tristram's, if not Sterne's, apparent belligerence toward both historical movement and historical life. So too does the miniature battlefield that Trim and Toby build in the Shandy garden, thereby shrinking military history to an unchanging simulacrum of itself. The toys and games of childhood strewn throughout *Tristram Shandy* – the playground, the hobbyhorse, even the elliptical top that Tristram's literary style so uncannily resembles – at once signal and fulfil a deeper desire to escape from conventional history, both discursive and lived.

Through these same devices, however, Sterne also satirizes the wish to be anywhere but in linear time. The rider of a hobbyhorse will for instance set off at an autistic clip that borders now on masturbation, now on mania.[9] Take Uncle Toby. A soldier, we're reminded, 'seldom looks further forward than the end of his musket, or backwards beyond his knapsack' (8.19.687). Long after his own life as a soldier has ended, Toby is still 'no chronologer' (5.14.443). He is stuck instead to his hobbyhorse, the Battle of Namur, which historical occurrence we ourselves know not from any chronicle of its progress but instead as a compulsive repetition in Uncle Toby's own mind. When Toby's hobbyhorse trots him out of history, it also removes him from both social and political community, while at the level of communication simply preventing him from being rationally understood by anyone other than his faithful corporal Trim. Even as Uncle Toby is the door through which the history of nations enters *Tristram Shandy*, his hobbyhorse threatens to exclude him from narratability, from shareable experience, and at last from time.

Toby strands himself outside history in one way, Tristram the narrator in another. He refers to his own hobbyhorse – his novel – in the language of onanistic play: 'Are we for ever to be twisting, and untwisting the same rope?' he demands of his story line, 'for ever in the same track – for ever at the same pace?' (5.1.408). As Tristram's pen fails to move either forward or backwards, moments of arrested motion begin to look less like traces of biological life than like intimations of death: 'So much of motion, is so much of life [...] to stand still is [...] death and the devil' (7.13.593). Yet this is precisely the effect of Tristram's digressions, 'for if [the author] begins a digression, – from that moment [...] his whole work stands stock-still' (1.22.81). If Tristram's mother stoops to a keyhole to eavesdrop on one of her husband's conversations, she is sure to be stooping still many pages later; Toby begins knocking the ashes out of his pipe to finish many chapters on. More blockage than tamer of time, digression at last brings language itself to a halt: near the end of the novel (if such end there can be said to be), Tristram prepares elaborately to digress, only to realize that 'in talking of my digression – I declare before heaven I have made it' (9.15.767).

If the hobbyhorse embodies agitation without forward motion, then Shandian narrative shows itself to be an animal of the same species, and the reprieve its digressions win from history often sounds like a death sentence. Tristram, for example, prides himself on 'hav[ing] so complicated and involved the digressive and progressive movements, one wheel within another, that the whole machine, in general, has been kept a-going; – and what's more, it shall be kept a-going these forty years' (1.22.82). Yet as it jolts and shudders along, the 'machine' of the novel develops countless gaps and fissures that look more like symptoms of a morbid pathology than evidence of perpetual mobility. Every dash is potentially as much a crypt as it is a lively interruption, liable to sabotage the book of life that Tristram has set out to write – that 'civil, nonsensical, good humoured *Shandean* book, which will do all your hearts good' (6.17.525). Which is not to say that Tristram can think of another way to write 'history'. 'A historiographer' can never 'drive on his history, as a muleteer drives on his mule – straight forward ', he assures us. Instead, 'he will have fifty deviations from a straight line to make' (1.14.41).

Such observations remind us that, as a 'historiographer', Tristram is not merely digressive; he is self-consciously, philosophically so. Instead of successive instalments in his personal history, he spews out a chapter of buttons, a chapter of whiskers, a chapter of chances, a chapter of sleep, and a chapter of things, then makes an ironic effort to mollify his readers by diagramming his own 'transverse zig-zaggery' (3.3.189) for them. As far as these readers are concerned, such compulsive 'deviations from a straight line' guarantee the ironically frenzied immobility that so ambiguously delivers *Tristram Shandy* from history. Tristram, though, theorizes his 'deviations' as the effects of chance. How could he not, having received his own name by accident and against his father's best-laid plans? Mangled in the nose by forceps and in more delicate regions by the window sash, he lives to justify his father's epithet: 'child of decrepitude! Interruption! Mistake!' And like their progenitor Tristram's words fall victim to every 'misfortune or disaster in the book of embryotic evils' (4.19.354); they cannot in turn but suffer the very same 'fatality [that] attends the actions of some men: Order them as they will, they pass thro' a certain medium, which [...] twists and refracts them from their true direction'. Doomed never to move in any 'direction' for long, the verbal structure of *Tristram Shandy* replaces ordered history with chaos. Indeed, history only makes itself known through catastrophe: Small wonder that Sterne's novel apparently lends itself more generously to postmodern categories of analysis – chaos theory, say – than to the modern systems emergent in its author's own day. Certainly if there is a physics at work in *Tristram Shandy*, no one would claim that it is Newtonian.[10]

Modernist admirers of Sterne, busy developing their own stream-of-consciousness techniques and exploring the inherent isolation of the individual mind, meanwhile understood *Tristram Shandy*'s inability to get on 'in a tolerable straight line' (6.40.570) as a psychological function, a dramatization of the mind's natural habits of association. Sterne after all consciously indebted himself to John Locke's influential late seventeenth-century theory of 'human understanding' as a map of associated ideas whose coordinates are first engraved by experience. By and large, Sterne seems to delight in the possibilities for play that the associative model creates, and Tristram and his family are all antic experiments with that model. In the course of these experiments, however, the Shandys – Walter and Toby, Walter and his wife – reliably fail to understand or even accurately perceive one another because their minds have evolved such idiosyncratic habits of association that communication and self-revelation are often impossible. From this point of view, Sterne's novel would seem to be more a parody of Locke's theory than a simple application of it. If Lockean psychology was to become the modern rule, *Tristram Shandy* looks for all the world like a precociously postmodern satire upon it.[11]

To the extent that their comic exaggeration lends Sterne's novel much of its air of postmodernity, it is appropriate that within that novel the mind's habits of association furnish a vehicle of deliverance from historical time. In Volume 3, for example, Walter Shandy and his cronies have been waiting for Tristram to be born, though they certainly have not been doing so for nearly as long as Tristram's reader has. Walter consults his watch and observes that although 'it is two hours, and ten minutes, – and no more [...] since Dr. *Slop* and *Obadiah* arrived' to deliver the baby, to his 'imagination it seems almost an age'. Toby's explanation for this effect is apt: ''Tis owing, entirely, [...] to the succession of our ideas' (3.18.222). As we've now seen, this nonlinear 'succession' is manifested narratively in Tristram's digressions, and as a sociological principle in the wide-ranging and inconclusive conversations of which this exchange is one part. In all of these guises, the sort of mental 'succession' that is no succession at all distorts the historicity of *Tristram Shandy*, permitting the novel to retreat from conventional (and communal and even critical) measures of temporal change.

In place of these, Tristram offers his own self-reflexive history. Indeed, our 'historiographer' turns out to think of Locke's *Essay concerning Human Understanding* as a 'history-book' – a 'history-book, Sir, [...] of what passes in a man's own mind' (2.2.98). What passes in the mind is, in turn, always present in the mind – less passing through it than transpiring there perpetually. Just so, thanks to the principle of association, the mind in Locke is a spatial structure, analogous to a room or, in Locke's own favorite metaphor, a page. In this model, history's signal trait, duration, is more an occupying idea – a fixture – than a property of the mind, which structure is in turn best represented on the spatial field of the page. Tristram adapts this feature of the Lockean paradigm to his own book. He exploits both that book's physical properties and the unique temporality of the reading and writing experiences to produce his own version of 'history' – his anti-history, in a word.

The fictionality of *Tristram Shandy*

If all of Uncle Toby's associations wend their way toward war, Tristram's hobbyhorse is, of course, his book, and in the eternal present that writing takes, he rides it furiously.

We can now take a closer look at what it is he is riding, or writing, or, in the sly, lascivious double-speak of the novel, otherwise getting off to 'a good rattling gallop' (4.20.356). It's not hard to do so. For while many eighteenth-century novelists issued statements as to what they felt they were doing in their work, none seriously rivalled Tristram's obsessive habit of reference to the sheer literary status of his 'Life and Opinions'.

These references take several forms. We've seen already that *Tristram Shandy* is in fact made up of everyone's story but Tristram's. Considered as a book, it moreover consists, literally, of bits and pieces of other books, which range from childbirth manuals to ledgers, from sermons to legal documents. Parodies pile on top of plagiarisms of writers from Burton to Montaigne to Cervantes, and over all hovers the ghost of the *Tristrapaedia* wherein Walter Shandy, we are told, once set out to document his son's life. *Tristram Shandy*'s amplified intertextuality keeps the novel's own textual status squarely before us; at the same time, Tristram's tendency to blur the differences between his book and those of others permits sceptical commentary on the shady relationship between books and the lives, worlds and histories that ostensibly transpire outside them. Walter Shandy's abandoned *Tristrapaedia*, for example, is presumably *Tristram Shandy* in another, exponentially more 'systematical' key. Yet like Tristram's book it too has fallen prey to all the ills the page is heir to, failing either to overtake or to partake of historical life. After three years of writing, we learn, Walter had 'scarce completed one half of his undertaking' and moreover 'the first part of the work' has been rendered entirely useless by Tristram's own breakneck pace of transformation: 'every day a page or two became of no consequence' and the hapless author 'advanced so very slow with his work' while 'I began to live and get forward at such a rate' (5.16.449).

Though he is not displeased to have thwarted his father's stab at authorship, Tristram too feels life race on while his own pen eddies vigorously: 'Write as I will and rush as I may into the middle of things, [...] – I shall never overtake myself' (4.13.342). Unlike the elder Shandy, the younger commits himself all the more to the space of the page (where one can move forwards or backwards, though by and large only seemingly), in preference to its historical occasion (where one can only move forwards, but at least can be said actually to do so). As if to turn the father's predicament on its head, the son's narrative thus 'frisk[s] and curvett[s]' while next to nothing actually happens in it. Tristram exults under the unique temporal conditions of purely textual 'Life'. Volume 7, for instance, takes him to France, where though ailing in the flesh, he professes to find himself in 'such a situation, as no traveller ever stood before me; for I am this moment walking across the market-place of Auxerre with my father and my uncle Toby, in our way back to dinner – and I am this moment also entering Lyons with my post-chaise broke into a thousand pieces – and I am moreover this moment in a handsome pavillion built by Pringello, upon the banks of the Garonne, which Mons. Sligniac has lent me, and where I now sit rhapsodizing all these affairs' (7.28.622). Such passages remind us that, considered as physical objects, books have a peculiar power to gather multiple and disparate points of time into a single space. No less than the hobbyhorsical brain, the page thus supplies a vehicle of escape from historical time. In turn, it seems possible to exchange the historical world that books ostensibly represent for the comparatively non-historical world of books themselves.

Tristram (and Sterne behind him) for this reason never allows us to forget that we are reading a book, or that he is writing one. He often does so simply by foregrounding the materiality of the literary text, ever reminding us that *Tristram Shandy* is literally no 'Life' but only a collection of typographical marks on a page. Although Yorick's sermons, riddled with retractions and deviations, fall out of someone else's book and are cut into strips, just as Tristram accidentally burns some of his own manuscript, written texts are also imagined as replacements for the fragile human body that produces them. 'Writing is but a different name for conversation', Tristram maintains in one place (2.11.125), adding elsewhere that 'to write a book is for all the world like humming a song' (4.25.374). Yet a book is also uniquely a book, and Sterne exploits every conceivable typographical device in order to tell us so, cramming his text with black or marbled pages, deliberately misplaced chapters, gaps, fields of asterisks, dashes, diagrams, misplaced prefaces and dedications that pop up long after the book has begun. Our author's manic 'experiments upon chapters' (4.25.372) thus demonstrate the book's vulnerability to the same accidents that plague the rest of the material world. At the same time, they register literary self-consciousness at its most hyperactive, forbidding us to forget that the world of *Tristram Shandy* is an artificial one, a manmade construct whose hero and presumed author is himself a fiction.

Indeed, through the forms of self-reflexivity we've now considered, Sterne encourages us to regard 'Tristram Shandy' less as a person than as a book. In doing so, he anticipates postmodern rebellion against conventional (modern) ideas of the author as a historical agent – a unified, originating individual behind his or her text. Historically speaking, of course, *Tristram Shandy* is the work of a consumptive Irish-born clergyman who published the novel in instalments over the last eight years of his life, either breaking off because of ill health or corroborating Tristram's speculation, upon discovering that a chapter of his manuscript has gone missing, that a 'book is more perfect and complete by wanting the chapter, than having it' (4.25.372).[12] But contemporary readers almost always treated *Tristram Shandy* as if it had been written by 'Mr. Tristram Shandy' himself. One even pronounced that individual 'a writer infinitely more ingenious and entertaining than any other of the present race of novelists'.[13]

Tristram's predicament anticipates the question that has been raised in our own day by Michel Foucault: 'What', we are made to ask, 'is an author?' Foucault's postmodern suggestion is that 'the author' is nothing more than a 'function' of the words on a page.[14] Sterne's proto-postmodern position would seem to be the same. Certainly, just as Tristram experiences himself as the product of a series of accidents over which he has no control, so does he seem to exercise no control over his own text, which frequently appears to be writing him, rather than the other way around. 'Ask my pen, – It governs me, – I govern not it' (6.6.500). So whereas we might imagine Tristram, as one recent reader does, telling stories to establish his own coherent identity, he is always in danger of becoming the (very incoherent) story he tells, or doesn't tell.[15] To the extent that *Tristram Shandy* is demonstrably fragmentary, so is Tristram Shandy, and this places his 'Fragment of Life' in a most awkward situation with respect to history.[16] Tristram himself is aware of it. He justly reckons that his critics will 'damn me biographically, rendering my book, from this very moment, a profess'd ROMANCE' (74). Likewise, when he predicts that 'my opinions will be the death of me' (207), he certifies, however ironically, his own death into the text of those very 'opinions'.

Nevertheless, reports of this death are easily exaggerated. For if the author is dead, he is yet, in the course of the narrative, dying. As such, he stays bound into a particular historical trajectory. Tristram knows this: 'Time wastes too fast: every letter I trace tells me with what rapidity Life follows my pen' (9.8.754). In the event, such indelible traces of irreducibly historical life shape *Tristram Shandy* quite as inexorably as do Tristram's proleptically postmodern efforts to escape that life. We saw that in Sterne's novel books themselves are both mutable historical objects and a means of defeating chronological time. We also saw that, derived from Locke's 'history-book', Sterne's concept of consciousness was both historically determined and immune from traditional strains of temporality. Such compromises conspire to make *Tristram Shandy* different from the postmodern narratives which otherwise share both its textual self-consciousness and its attitudes toward history, its antic experimentation with conventional methods of ordering the world. It is now time to look more closely at the nature of that difference.

The difference of *Tristram Shandy*

'Modern' versions of literary and personal history were of course only beginning to crystallize in Sterne's eighteenth century. They were, moreover, predicated upon contemporary attitudes toward language and embodiment – attitudes which, unlike other authors of his own day, Sterne flatly refuses to assimilate to a progressive historical narrative. The result, however, is not the purely prescient postmodernity it is so easy to attribute to Sterne's novel. Nor does Sterne's novel look suddenly, after all, like an irreducible artifact of its own era. Both and neither of these things, *Tristram Shandy* is perhaps best regarded as a dramatic examination of what in fact accounts for difference – between words, persons, and historical moments.

First, words. Sterne's novel is obviously made up of words – quite a lot of them, in fact. These words, as we've seen, are self-consciously produced by a fictional human being, Tristram Shandy, as a means of accounting for his own historical being. Since Tristram never actually existed, his ruse of creating, in his book, a world insulated from historical contingency is remarkably successful. Its irony is that Tristram's words, like those of everyone else in the novel, actually *do* fall victim to accidents which confer historical reference, if not status.

Tristram Shandy is chock-a-block with voluble speakers whose relationship to words is instructive in this regard. Walter Shandy expounds theory after theory, while Uncle Toby's 'life ', we learn, 'was put in jeopardy by words' (2.2.101). As of course is that of the ill-fated Yorick, who (as Sterne was too) is a preacher who makes his living by the word. Tristram's own sentences are littered with telling colloquialisms ('in a word', 'by my word') and his formal reflections upon words take up inordinate space and time. At first, words in *Tristram Shandy* seem therefore to spin a self-consciously manmade web of signs, each divorced from its referent, its differences from other words all exposed as arbitrary. Sterne even spotlights this arbitrariness by leaving gaps which the reader may fill with a word of his or her choosing. Commenting on one such gap, he typically invites his reader to 'take the dash away, and write Backside, – 'tis Bawdy. – Scratch Backside out, and put *Cover'd-way* in, – 'tis a Metaphor' (2.6.116). Just so, Tristram mischievously uses the word 'nose' to suggest another, at least equally protuberant organ. The word 'whiskers' can't be trusted not to refer to the nether regions; the too scrupulous Abbess of Andouillets and her travelling companion split a curse word between them to drive a mule forward; names like the original, auspicious Trismegistus metamorphose ominously into Tristram. 'Well might *Locke* write a chapter on the imperfections of words', Tristram muses ruefully, invoking Locke's ultimately tragic longing to make language conducive to 'human understanding', a bridge between the idiosyncrasies of individual, associative minds (V.7.429)

Yet in the end it is these very 'imperfections' which keep *Tristram Shandy* from inhabiting an ungrounded, wholly symbolic world. For, as in precisely the instances just mentioned, it is only when words are misunderstood or mangled or exchanged for other words that they have effects. These effects prove sometimes dire and sometimes comical, but in every case they are causally and sequentially – historically – linked to something else. And they also link human beings to one another. Words thereby prove substantial and sustaining precisely because of their 'imperfections', not in spite of them. Hence Toby's 'Amours' with the Widow Wadman proceed because language is inadequate to convey his plight; its failures bind him back into community and at last into forward-moving history. Meanwhile, on every page of his 'Life', Tristram accepts a unique and courageous 'situation' with respect to words. By opening himself literally to their accidental tangents, he both absorbs and exemplifies the problem of difference that words embody. He makes himself a not-quite-living example of the extent to which difference itself is at once invented (hence arbitrary) *and* nonetheless of material, historical significance.

The language of *Tristram Shandy* produces and sustains history in spite of itself. For Sterne links words finally not to that which is purely symbolic, but rather to that which is productive and receptive of the symbolic. Most obviously, this is the human body itself, whose reality, at once so precarious and so irrefutable, profoundly shapes Sterne's text. Sterne himself was slowly dying of consumption and pleurisy during the years he was composing his novel and sickly Tristram compulsively marks his own body's disintegration into its constitutive parts. While as we've seen Tristram aims to write his way outside the predicament of his own contingent existence in time, what he finally does is to affirm the historically bound body's primacy as a means of conveying – and comprehending – this very attempt.

From the start, Tristram gives his reader 'my word' that human affairs are all motivated by 'animal spirits' which, 'when they are once set a-going [...] away they go cluttering like hey-go-mad' (1.1.2). Their antic energy in turn pulses through every page of *Tristram Shandy*; indeed, if characters are distinguished by their habits of association, they are equally known to us as nervous systems, often finer tuned than does them good, but invariably linked to one another in one quivering diapason of feeling. The Shandys and their friends – even the abstruse philosopher Walter – are all creatures of emotion and sensation even before they are creatures of language. Tristram's work accordingly registers every tremor of a sick man's hand, every tear sliding down every cheek, every jump of nerve and every sigh. At the same time, his notorious (and often puerile) double-entendres keep up a constant *vibrato* of sexual titillation that further grounds his text in tremulous flesh. The surprisingly effectual Corporal Trim's rank speaks volumes; Walter Shandy is meanwhile ridiculous because he denies the corporeal foundations of human being and its representation. Determined 'to force every event in nature into an hypothesis', he will always seek a 'laconick way of expressing – but of libelling at the same time, the desires and appetites of the lower part of us'.

For his part, Tristram rejects his father's legacy of abstraction by taking the rambunctious world of the 'animal spirits' as his matrix. He thereby animates the words that make up his narrative, compelling us to experience those words as more than empty signifiers, and indeed as more than discrete signs. On the contrary, the human body irresistibly pulls words into history and its inherent narratives, bounded as these are by the *finis* of certain death. Indeed, Tristram frequently pictures words themselves as behaving the same way bodies do: an innocent word like 'whiskers', for instance, is likely to be corrupted from its association with hairs less in sight. For Sterne, such associations are more than mere occasions for laughter. They are also conditions of understanding, and albeit playfully he confirms Locke's own theory that verbal signs are comprehensible only to the extent that they are grounded in sense impressions. Tristram thus typically jeers at the author who stacks 'a number of tall, opake words, one before another, in a right line, betwixt your own and your readers [sic] conception, – when in all likelihood, if you had looked about, you might have seen something standing, or hanging up, which would have cleared the point at once' (3.20.235).

Tristram, to a fault, refers an enormous amount of his own discourse to 'something standing, or hanging up', which is how Sterne heaped charges of indecency upon his own head. But leaving aside authorial weakness for phallic double-entendres, in *Tristram Shandy* the human body entire frames linguistic reference at least as much as does the associative human mind: 'What little knowledge is got by mere words', Tristram marvels. 'We must go up to the first springs' (9.20.773). Unlike the mind, moreover, the font of 'first things' refuses even the illusion of deliverance from historical time – from chronologies and chains of circumstance, from story. For Tristram imagines the world of 'uncrystalized flesh and blood' (1.23.83) as an integrated, extensive structure, narratively ordered and visibly vulnerable to time: 'There are some trains of certain ideas which leave prints of themselves about our eyes and eye-brows; and there is a consciousness of it, somewhere about the heart, which serves but to make these etchings the stronger – we see, spell, and put them together without a dictionary' (5.1.413).

Tristram is of course intensely aware of his own physical being, which he ruefully regards as the root of tragedy: about to recount (at last) the story of his disastrous birth, for instance, he classifies his as 'the most pensive and melancholy frame of mind, that ever sympathetic breast was touched with – My nerves relax as I tell it. – Every line I write, I feel an abatement of the quickness of my pulse.' But the 'delicate and fine-spun web' (2.19.175) of the human frame also proves an unexpected source of continuity and community, of triumph over the isolation of the self. Toby's plight, of course, is only slightly less tragic than Tristram's but while his body is shattered (by, we might say, history) and his vocabulary thereby depleted, he lives in a world of plenitude by virtue of his exceptional capacity for feeling: his heart is 'subject to sudden overflowings' (8.19.693) and tears are ever 'trickling down his cheeks'. Tristram in his turn is brought back into history through his own capacity for sympathy with Toby. The story of his 'amours', Tristram admits, 'had the same effect on me as if they had been my own – I was in the most perfect state of bounty and good will, and felt the kindliest harmony vibrating within me' (9.24.781).

It is, of course, all very well to note the remarkable degree to which the language of *Tristram Shandy* invokes the world of sensation, of continuity, of history. 'True *Shandeism*', Tristram after all informs us, 'opens the heart and lungs, and like all those affections which partake of its nature, it forces the blood and other vital fluids of the body to run freely through its channels' (4.32.401). Its avowed 'Shandeism' reintegrates Sterne's novel with history even as Tristram seeks the ahistorical, self-referential sublime that has ironically become a hallmark of postmodernism. Still, it might be objected, Shandeism is only described for us: it is scarcely as if Uncle Toby or the hapless Yorick, or the pathetic Le Fever, or the sickly Tristram, or the consumptive Sterne is physically sandwiched between the covers of the book, thus dragging it into the time-bound and corruptible world its author would like to transcend. In a different sense, however, Sterne's system of bodily references does ground his text in a particular historical moment. When he wrote *Tristram Shandy*, that is, the prevailing narrative style of the English novel was that of the sentimental novel, as pioneered by one of Sterne's harshest critics, Richardson. Richardson and his followers made the arousal of feeling literature's *raison d'être*. They crafted a vocabulary of tears and sighs and made a capacity for sympathy the standard of virtue.[17] Sterne himself published a short volume satirizing sentimental convention in the last year of his life, exaggerating its constitutive tears and tremors in the discordant story of Yorick's travels in France.

Satire aside, the literature of sensibility still contributed a set of assumptions crucial to *Tristram Shandy*, and of these the most central was its obsessive consciousness of the presence of the reader, on whose emotional arousal the authority of sentimental narrative depends. Just so, from the start Tristram's reader is at least as intrinsic to his narrative as Tristram himself, providing a substantial and immediate life upon which his own 'Life' is always grounded. As if to secure this grounding, regardless of circumstances,

Tristram's imagined reader is a shape shifter, sometimes male and sometimes female ('Madam'), sometimes antagonistic and sometimes sympathetic, sometimes titled ('Your Worship') and sometimes not, sometimes abstract and sometimes as concrete as then-secretary of state William Pitt himself. This infinity of identities ironically preserves the reader as a stable (if perforce imaginative) space beyond Tristram's written 'Life'.

Sterne, via Tristram, starts off by classifying *Tristram Shandy* as a 'Fragment of Life', and as we've seen, this 'Fragment' consists entirely of other, smaller fragments, both linguistic and experiential. While its fragmentation seems to place Sterne's novel outside a conventional narrative of personal and literary history, it can also be seen as the quality that most fully embeds *Tristram Shandy* in history. For Sterne – or at least Tristram – expects his reader to complete the fragments, contextualizing them within a whole that is both historically specific (the reader is acknowledged to occupy a particular point in linear time) and eternally present (the reader can live at any point in time). It is in this spirit that Tristram assures 'the inquisitive' that 'to them I write, – and by them I shall be read, – if any such reading as this could be supposed to hold out so long, to the very end of the world' (1.21.74). It is this 'inquisitive' reader whom Tristram invites to all the Widow Wadman to be 'paint[ed] on your own mind' (6.38.566), and it is this reader who supplies the 'underwritten fragment' that appears in the salacious 'chapter on Whiskers'. When Tristram mentions that a 'book is more perfect and complete by wanting a chapter than by having it' (6.25.372), he is not so much rationalizing the disappearance of several manuscript pages as he is signalling his own work's completion in his reader. In other words, the dashes, gaps and lapses that litter the reader's visual field may easily be construed as bids for an empty, anti-historical status that ironically anticipates postmodern conventions of representation. But just as Tristram resolutely imagines 'imperfec[t]' words as completed only in relation to a body linked sympathetically to other bodies, so does the fragmentary structure of his book leave space for his reader to animate it. Sterne's compulsively summoned 'Sir' or 'Madam' can be sympathetic, or inquisitive or even recalcitrant; the point is that he or she *is*, and it is in relation to him or her that Sterne's book guarantees its historical specificity, its difference both from other books and from itself.

Midway through *Tristram Shandy*, our narrator refuses to 'finish [a] sentence' before he has commented on 'the strange state of affairs between the reader and myself, just as things stand at present – an observation never applicable before to any one biographical writer since the creation of the world, but to myself' (4.13.341). *Tristram Shandy*'s own historical distinctiveness, like Tristram Shandy's, depends at last not on its 'biographical' veracity – its status as history – so much as on its situation *vis-à-vis* the reader. Just as Tristram reads his father's *Tristrapaedia* and, 'to render [it] complete', fills in its missing chapter (5.26.459), so Sterne constantly summons his reader, making his or her presence the true matrix of his text. For it is he, or she, who will bring the historically detached linguistic play of his novel to a halt, anchoring it at last in history while at the same time permitting escape from that very history. Rooted in the sentimental practices of Sterne's own historical moment, *Tristram Shandy* achieves an ironic apotheosis. For its home is at last neither the associative mind that shuts out the historical world nor the self-conscious, parodic pages that pretend to hover outside history. Sterne's novel belongs, finally, to the temporally unlimited and yet inescapably historical space of its own reception.

Chapter 3

Old Mortality: Editor and Narrator

Mary Wedd

It used to be customary for Scott enthusiasts to say to reluctant beginners, 'Leave out the first chapter or two and plunge in where the story starts'. This is not bad advice but the reader who returns to the beginning, once hooked by the story, often finds added enlightenment there. For example, the early chapters of *Waverley* dealing with the hero's education and upbringing, help to account for and prepare us for the vacillation suggested by his name. Angus Calder, in his admirable 1975 edition of the Penguin *Old Mortality*, suggests that the newcomer should 'vault over' not only his own Introduction but ' the rather tedious Cleishbotham and perhaps even the interesting Pattieson, and begin at once with Chapter 2', from which 'the narrative which follows ... is one of the leanest, swiftest and starkest constructions in the whole of fiction'. So it is, illustrating, as Calder brilliantly expresses it, 'the sustained pain of persistent moral choice in an amoral environment', surely a pattern for our times. But the method by which this is achieved is one of ubiquitous irony, particularly in the mismatch between what the characters think they are doing and what they are really doing. It is a matter of point of view.

The opening of the story illustrates this at once. To Lady Margaret Bellenden the most important thing in the world was her loyalty to the feudal hierarchy, her own place in it and the Stuart king at the head of it. 'Take but degree away, untune that string / And hark what discord follows.' She has a point: Morton cannot instil any kind of discipline into the Covenanters, 'this disunited and undisciplined army'.[1] But equally it is true that Charles II, as governments will, in order to get support made a promise which he broke as soon as he had attained his end. Moreover, the Covenanters were indeed cruelly persecuted. The fair-minded Lord Evandale says that the 'politicians and prelates' have driven them to their present alienation (12.198). All this is lost on Lady Margaret. The greatest honour of her life was when she entertained the king once to breakfast at Tillietudlem, which she never fails to mention. The narrator adds that, though the monarch embraced his hostess on this occasion, he greeted her maids with equal enthusiasm.

She sees herself as a person of importance but the irony is that she is only the impoverished widow of a knight, who cannot even muster the obligatory armed men and whose necessity to enlist Goose Gibby renders her a laughing-stock. Similarly, Mause, with whom she has had a warm relationship, imagines she serves a Higher Authority and by her Covenanting zeal endangers not only her mistress's credibility but her own and Cuddy's future. Her eviction by Lady Margaret discredits the system of society the one believes in, while reducing to absurdity the other's confused religious allegiances. Both characters are subjects for humour but in both also, misguided though they may be, a certain dignity shines through, just as the destruction of their interdependence heralds the wider and more devastating conflict which follows and of which they are a kind of parody. Both think they are upholders of a noble faith, yet both are really figures of fun.

A worse discrepancy is apparent in the two main bodies of the participants in the story, whose fanatical belief in the rightness of their cause is nullified by the barbarism with which they try to enforce it. As Scott himself expressed it, 'they were both a set of cruel and bloody bigots, and had, notwithstanding, those virtues to which bigotry is sometimes allied.' Yet, just as each party is allowed its 'virtues' despite its horrors, so too the often humorous depiction of each gives added irony by the contrast between their absurdity and their ruthlessness. As A. N. Wilson says of Scott's Covenanters, 'One of the most impressive things about them is that they are at once comic and truly terrible'.[2] Similarly the savagery of Claverhouse, which had rendered him in folk-memory as little short of the Devil himself, is not minimized but he is allowed the charm often exercised on their own kind by those who regard their disadvantaged inferiors as barely human. He feels little regret, he says, 'for sweeping from the face of the earth some few hundred of villain churles, who are born but to plough it', while, like Froissart, he would feel sorrow for the death of a 'gallant and high-bred knight' (35.271). Between the two factions is the humane and tolerant Morton who, as moderates usually are, is right but powerless.

So what is the point of view of the teller of this equivocal tale and who does Scott wish us to regard as the narrator? Not the Landlord whose name heads the collection and whose character is drawn in the introduction to *Tales of My Landlord* preceding the first of them, *The Black Dwarf*, whose one volume was combined with the three of *Old Mortality*. In 1816 Scott, for his own purposes which included a change of publisher, wanted a different pseudonym from 'The Author of Waverley' and planned instead *Tales of My Landlord* 'Collected and Reported by Jedidiah Cleishbotham'. So is this 'Parish Clerk and Schoolmaster of Gandercleugh' the true narrator? His description of the Landlord and of himself makes clear that neither of them is. One must never underestimate Scott's pleasure in amusing himself, even at his own expense; this is one of the qualities that make *The Antiquary*, for example, such a joy to read. As John Sutherland points out, 'Scott had been hugely amused in 1812 by the comic apparatus to Washington Irving's *History of New York* (1809) by "Diedrich Knickerbocker"', and Jedidiah Cleishbotham is a similar creation.[3] He makes clear that the pub where 'on the left-hand side of the fire' he might be found 'winter and summer, for every evening in my life, during forty years bypast, (the Christian Sabbaths only excepted,)' provided the ideal centre, 'the navel' of Scotland. (What *did* he do after Church on Sunday evening? Wind up Mr Shandy's Clock?) It was unnecessary, then, for him to add to his former visits, to Edinburgh twice, to Glasgow three times. He believed that all life came to him in his armchair. Nevertheless, he disclaims any authorship. 'I am NOT the writer, redactor, or compiler, of the Tales of my Landlord; nor am I, in one single iota, answerable for their contents, more or less.' The self-important 'Flog-bottom' and the landlord, who is poacher-cum-illegal-distiller, are not capable of telling such a tale in such a way. The Burns quotation and the epigraph from *Don Quixote* indicate that the inn is but a recording centre and repository for the *Tales*. Can it be that the teacher of the school's *lower* classes, who yet had the temerity to correct the headmaster's construing of Latin, and who 'delighted in the collection of olden tales and legends' could be the author of a book about which even John Sutherland has to admit: 'One admires and shudders'?[4]

Peter Pattieson, who had died young, is criticized by his 'superior and patron' because he, 'in arranging these Tales for the press, hath more consulted his own fancy than the accuracy of the narrative; nay, that he hath sometimes blended two or three stories together for the mere grace of his plots'. This objection is still made when Scott alters historical details for the sake of his artistic pattern, but in this book the two invented scenes of the siege of Tillietudlem and the death of Burley are essential pillars sustaining the construction of the novel, while the general picture is demonstrably true to the reality of the times as seen by contemporary sources. Cleishbotham thinks Pattieson would have been wise to have asked him 'to have carefully revised, altered and augmented, at my judgement and discretion', but Peter had more sense, forbidding any such thing and his wishes had been respected. This, however, did not preclude numerous footnotes, signed 'J.C.'! 'J.C.' felt that 'I have proved that I could have written them, if I would ...'. Pattieson tells how he met Old Mortality in the graveyard, as Lockhart tells us Scott himself did at Dunnottar, and gleaned from him much about 'the exploits of the Covenanters', but he was aware that the old man's anecdotes were 'distorted by party prejudice'. So Old Mortality was not the true narrator either. If he had been, neither McCrie nor Hogg would have had cause to complain. But Pattieson says of the events, 'I have endeavoured to correct or verify them from the most authentic sources of tradition, afforded by the representatives of either party'. He describes his efforts to ensure 'that I might be enabled to present an unbiased picture of the manners of that unhappy period, and, at the same time, to do justice to the merits of both parties' (1.13). So, gradually, the images of Pattieson and Scott himself, as the Editor Cleishbotham was not allowed to be, coalesce into the objective narrator, who creates the wonderful balance between opposites and the realistic picture of idealism yoked to atrocity which characterizes this book. Perhaps, then, the slippery character of the narrator serves to warn the reader of the equivocal nature of the story and to prepare him for the bitter ironies to follow.

As David Hewitt has shown, the character of Peter Pattieson serves to create the illusion of 'oral tale-telling'. It is an illusion only, because it is undercut by the fact that, as the notes show, 'the real sources are overwhelmingly literary'.[5] Lockhart says, 'Old Mortality ... is remarkable as the *novelist's* first attempt to re-people the past by the power of imagination working on materials furnished by books'. Yet the emphasis on an oral tradition gives the narrative a feeling of 'living history'. The teller of the story, Peter Pattieson, has met Old Mortality, who, though now dead, had kept the memory of 'that unhappy period' alive. The opposing myths as passed down to future generations are equally extreme in their prejudice and the tellers of them are unreliable narrators. 'What is truth? said jesting Pilate; and would not stay for an answer.' How then to indicate these things yet distance the 'Editor' or true narrator so that he can depict both points of view and claim the support of written documents of the actual period of 'the killing time', while himself indicating a third point of view? Though Scott may have wished to suggest that by the end of the Tale the Revolution of 1688, as would later the Union of 1707, had marked the end of such conflict in Scotland, he knew – who better? – that the Jacobite risings were still to come. 'Bloody bigots' are always with us and the book remains entirely relevant for us today. One does not have to look far for internecine strife, often based on religious differences, and world-wide there are numerous instances of equal savagery and barbarism. It is what William Golding calls 'off-campus history', which does not easily die for it is 'felt in the blood and bones' and is, as he surmises, wholly 'pernicious'.[6] The editors of the World's Classics edition conclude that Scott 'felt, however obscurely, that the Scottish past was of such importance that he put all of himself, memory, intelligence, and energy, into a committed act of exorcism and evocation'.[7] That may indeed be true but, whether he knew it or not, he gave us an object-lesson for all countries and all ages. The particular became universal.

In our era of holier-than-thou political correctness, Scott has become fair game because of his snobbery. Even these editors, who are careful to warn the reader 'to read with an awareness of a double historical perspective' whereby 'the presentation of the seventeenth century is filtered through the preoccupations and anxieties of the early nineteenth century', are inclined to criticize Scott for making his '"serious" characters speak in standard English while minor or comic characters are allowed convincing Scots, sometimes, as in the case of Mause, surprisingly moving and eloquent'. They do acknowledge that this is an over-simplification, that indeed the interplay of Scots and standard English in the book is very complex, but they betray the fact that they are uncomfortable with what they see as Scott's snobbery. Today a survivor from the earlier years of the twentieth century can remember when 'the Squire's children', at the village school before going off to their preparatory schools, were virtually bilingual, talking broad dialect at school and switching it off in favour of standard English when they left the school gates. Similarly, there is a strong tinge of Scots even in Lady Margaret's 'upper-class' speech, while with Mause she slips naturally into full-blown vernacular. Nor is it just to condemn Scott for adhering to a class system which was general among his peers right up to the outbreak of the Second World War. One might as well blame Shakespeare for stressing the importance of a strong monarch and a stable hierarchy in Elizabethan or Jacobean England. Though the modern reader cannot excuse Scott's die-hard political views, in relation to Peterloo for example, in this book he treats with equal irony the extremes on both sides. One can understand his sharing the prevalent fear of revolution then, though not his advocating of methods which in *Old Mortality* he deplores. As Douglas Mack says, 'The seventeenth-century conflicts in *The Tale of Old Mortality* were of much more than antiquarian concern in 1816'.[8] So they are now.

Morton, who often seems to speak for Scott, the Editor, has similar arguments with representatives both of the Covenanters and of their opponents. Balfour, hot-foot from the murder of Archbishop Sharpe, expresses a doubt which overtakes 'the faithful' at times as to whether what they have done has been truly by divine inspiration or the work of the devil. This conflict dogs him to the end, yet it remains true that merely killing the enemy is not enough for the Covenanters; there has to be an element of sadistic torture in it too. Morton replies to Balfour, 'I own I should strongly doubt the origin of any inspiration which seemed to dictate a line of conduct contrary to those feelings of natural humanity, which Heaven has assigned to us as the general law of our conduct' (6.43). Scott, the lawyer, often stresses in the book the need to keep the laws and the awful consequences of lawlessness. Elsewhere Morton speaks passionately of 'my chartered rights as a freeman' (14.124). Balfour is soon back to his normal belief that it is the duty of the Covenanters 'when we have drawn the sword to smite the ungodly with the edge, though he be our neighbour, and the man of power and cruelty, though he were of our own kindred and the friend of our bosom'. Whatever happened to 'Love thine enemy' or 'Thou shalt love thy neighbour as thyself'? It is noticeable that the Covenanters, though they can quote both Testaments as it suits them, tend to favour the Old. The irony in Balfour's speech is that, in condemning 'the man of power and cruelty' he is unaware that he is coming closer than neighbour or kindred – he is condemning himself. Morton sees this clearly. 'These are the sentiments ... that your enemies impute to you, and which palliate, if they do not exculpate, the cruel measures which the Council have directed against you' (6.43). Unlike the Covenanters, Morton had learnt that 'goodness or worth were not limited to those of any single form of religious observance' (13.109). The terrible irony in this is that, later, when Morton is in the hands of Macbriar and his followers and waiting for the clock to wear away the Sabbath so that they can kill him, 'on the brink between this and the future world', he turns, like them, to religious thoughts, but because he speaks 'half aloud' a petition from 'the Book of Common Prayer of the Church of England', they decide to execute him immediately (33.264).

Claverhouse is depicted as just as ruthless and cruel. When he hears that 'A large body of whigs are in arms among the hills', he rejoices: '"When the adder crawls into daylight," he added, striking the heel of his boot upon the floor, as if in the act of crushing a noxious reptile, "I can trample him to death"' (12.105). His equivalent of the distinction the Covenanters make between religious sects is that between gentlemen and the expendable others.

> 'You are right,' said Claverhouse, with a smile; 'you are very right – we are both fanatics; but there is some distinction between the fanaticism of honour and that of dark and sullen superstition.'
> 'Yet you both shed blood without mercy or remorse,' said Morton, who

could not suppress his feelings.

'Surely,' said Claverhouse, with the same composure; 'but of what kind? – There is a difference, I trust, between the blood of learned and reverend prelates and scholars, of gallant soldiers and noble gentlemen, and the red puddle that stagnates in the veins of psalm-singing mechanics, crack-brained demagogues, and sullen boors; – some distinction, in short, between spilling a flask of generous wine and dashing down a cann-ful of base muddy ale.'

'Your distinction is too nice for my comprehension,' replied Morton. 'God gives every spark of life – that of the peasant as well as the prince; and those who destroy his work recklessly or causelessly, must answer in either case. What right, for example, have I to General Grahame's protection now, more that when I first met him?' (35.270–71)

The answer, of course, is that class-bonding which was taken for granted until recently. Claverhouse has discovered that Morton is 'a gentleman' and 'officer material', perhaps eventually for his own side.

It is also true that Morton is not 'the same when I first met you that you are now'. He has matured from his experiences. 'Henry Morton was one of those gifted characters which possess a force of talent unsuspected by the owner himself' (13.109). When he returns home after absence at the war, Alison does not at first know him in his battle-dress but also his whole demeanour has changed.

Upon approaching Milnewood, Henry's knock upon the gate no longer intimated the conscious timidity of a stripling who has been out of bounds, but the confidence of a man in full possession of his own rights, and master of his own actions – bold, free, and decided....

'Where is my uncle, Alison?' said Morton, smiling at her alarm. 'Lordsake, Mr. Harry, is this you?' returned the old lady. 'In troth, ye garr'd my heart loup to my very mouth – But it canna be you your ainsel, for ye look taller and mair manly-like than ye used to do.' (27.215–16)

Morton protests at Claverhouse's view of the superiority of 'the fanaticism of honour', yet when he is Claverhouse's prisoner he owes his life to it and is even allowed to keep his sword because it is 'the distinguishing mark of a gentleman' (35.270). In the army's Gestapo-like 'black book' of the disaffected, Morton is condemned as having 'high-flown and dangerous notions about liberty of thought and speech' (35.273). So it is with oppressive regimes the world over.

The savage cruelty of the Covenanters is matched by the soldiers under Claverhouse. One has only to read the description in Chapter 35 of the triumphant procession after the Battle of Bothwell Bridge. Though this actual procession seems not to be historical, the details are. The impact of the whole is epitomized in this.

The next object was two heads borne upon pikes; and before each bloody head were carried the hands of the dismembered sufferers, which were, by the brutal mockery of those who bore them, often approached towards each other as if in the attitude of exhortation or prayer. (35.275)

In the next chapter we witness in detail the torture of the 'Scottish boot' perpetrated on Macbriar, who refuses to betray Balfour even to the point where his agony renders him unconscious. He is restored to life only to hear his death-sentence. He gives his persecutors 'the benefit of seeing how a Christian man can suffer in the good cause'. He was 'executed within half an hour, dying with the same enthusiastic firmness which his whole life had evinced' (36.282–3).

Adherents of both sides show exemplary courage in the face of death:

> The Cameronians, so lately about to be the willing agents of a bloody execution, were now themselves to undergo it. They seemed prepared alike for either extremity, nor did any of them show the least sign of fear, when ordered to leave the room for the purpose of meeting instant death. (34.267)

The attitude towards death of those who like to think of themselves as heroes has not altered since Beowulf: 'Every one of us must endure the end of life in the world; let him who can, gain fame before death; that is best for a noble warrior after he is dead' (1386–9 translated). Claverhouse's version is identical:

> 'It is not the expiring pang that is worth thinking of in an event that must happen one day, and may befal us on any given moment – it is the memory which the soldier leaves behind him, like the long train of light that follows the sunken sun – that is all which is worth caring for, which distinguishes the death of the brave or the ignoble. When I think of death, Mr. Morton, as a thing worth thinking of, it is in the hope of pressing one day some well-fought and hard-won field of battle, and dying with the shout of victory in my ear – *that* would be worth dying for, and more, it would be worth having lived for.' (34.268)

This is a striking piece of dramatic irony. The reader knows, as Claverhouse did not then, that this was to be exactly his fate when he triumphantly won the Battle of Killiecrankie but was killed in the moment of victory. Incidentally, this left the Jacobite army without an adequate leader and, in the story, led to Lord Evandale's departure, to replace him, and his death. It is characteristic of the confused moral climate that he remains loyal to the king while disapproving of his actions.

Immediately after Claverhouse's speech on death, by a twist in the dramatic irony, Meiklewrath in his spectre-like dying pronouncement also foretells what was later to come true:

> 'Behold the princes, for whom thou has sold thy soul to the destroyer, shall be removed from their place, and banished to other lands...' (34.268)

So much for the Stuarts. As for Claverhouse himself, his values are condemned:

> 'Wilt thou trust in thy bow and in thy spear, in thy steed and in thy banner? And shall not God visit for innocent blood? – Wilt thou glory in thy wisdom, and in thy courage, and in thy might? And shall not the Lord judge thee?' (268.24)

Moreover, the reader knows, in a final ironic clincher, that Claverhouse would not be immortalized in folk memory by a 'long train of light' but under the abhorred name of 'Bluidy Clavers'.

In these crucial scenes the 'Editor' allows the characters to speak for themselves, taking up the function of 'narrators' but he manipulates them so that, unknown to them, they are expressing ironic comments on both what they are saying and on the action itself. It is not only the main protagonists who comment on the conflict. To each party there are parallel figures among the everyday folk, and the Scots dialect that they use wonderfully expresses every human emotion from the comic to the tragic. There are trimmers in both classes, such as Niel Blane the innkeeper and Morton's uncle 'to whom the least lamb in his own folds at Milnewood is dearer than the whole Christian flock' (5.35). They have their eye on the main chance and are ironic counterparts to the moderate, Morton. But for strong commonsense and easy-going tolerance one must look to Cuddie, who deplores the interdenominational feud. 'I see nae sae muckle difference atween the twa ways o't as a' the folk pretend' (7.56). For indignation at the destructiveness of the conflict one may turn to Ailie Wilson, who says of Mause, 'to set up to be sae muckle better than ither folk, the auld besom, and to bring sae muckle distress on a douce quiet family!' (8.73). Incidentally, one senses that Ailie is drawn straight from life and with affection. It is a touching moment when at last she recognizes Morton after his return from the continent: 'God guide us! It's my ain bairn!' (39.316).

At the moment of horror, when Cuddie sees the danger Morton is in from Meiklewrath and his companions and rushes off to the army for help, he expresses the situation unforgettably in his own terms: 'They'll kill him, the murdering loons, and think they're doing a gude turn' (33.261). Cuddie and Jenny seem to be a kind of touchstone of good sense and ordinary affections in a crazy world. The honourable behaviour of Morton and Evandale to one another demonstrates a different pattern for adherents of opposing sides, just as the love between Edith and Morton does, and Elizabeth Maclure, though she lost both her sons in the war, was, like Edith Cavell in a later conflict, willing to save the life alike of friend and foe. The message of the New Testament was not lost on her.

The patterning of the book is exemplary. I doubt if the excellent but inexperienced Pattieson could have compassed it. Douglas Mack has shown how the volume divisions of the original publication – now again to be traced in the Edinburgh Edition and the 1999 Penguin – 'shape the narrative into large coherent sections' leading up to and away from the battles of Loudon Hill and Bothwell Bridge.[9] Where Scott departs from strict history it is to contribute to this succession of climaxes, as in the siege of Tillietudlem and the death of Burley. From Scott's novels the reader takes away and remembers certain vivid scenes; the unhistorical confrontation of Morton and Burley in the cave in *Old Mortality* is one of these and triumphantly justifies its inclusion. Was Morton's jump 'across the fearful chasm' to 'the projecting rock on the opposite side' perhaps suggested to Scott by the similar feat at Killiecrankie which is still commemorated by the place known as 'Soldier's Leap'?

Scott's self-conscious excuse for the time-lapse at the beginning of chapter 37 (volume 4, chapter 7) tends to reinforce the reader's doubt about the structural legitimacy of this device, but in fact it works well. As Kenneth M. Sroka puts it, '*Old Mortality*'s two-part structure is not its fatal flaw, a flagging of inspiration, or a disruption of what is done so well earlier on, but rather a functional statement about the nature of the story, an aesthetic parable'.[10] After the disruption of society and the many deaths, ordinary people who have survived pick up the pieces of their lives and carry on as best they can. There is nothing else for them to do. Sroka draws a distinction between the first part, which illustrates the mutability and 'mortality' which is the stuff of history, and the second part which by skipping a decade allows us to focus on 'the private fortune' of the hero and other survivors, and the use of memory and repetition to oppose 'fiction' to 'history'. We are back to the function of the narrator or story-teller, who is free to manipulate the sense of time and timelessness.

Aesthetically, the final scenes with the (fictional) death of Burley and the dying Evandale joining the hand of Morton to that of Edith, though she is at the moment unconscious of his presence, are a perfect ending. There the story-teller says he had intended to conclude. But back we go to the frame. There is no sense that in this novel, as Scott acknowledged of *The Black Dwarf*, he had 'bungled up a conclusion'. We easily forgive him such devices as his killing off the five brothers in *Rob Roy*, for example, so that the hero can inherit, but here, where excuses are not needed, Peter Pattieson makes the mistake of going to tea with Miss Martha Buskbody. As her name suggests, she is 'cumbered about with much serving' and gets her living by dress-making. She, it seems, represents the low-brow reader of popular fiction – the equivalent in our day would be someone who had the television on in every free hour – and she wants to know what happened next and to have the story properly rounded off. It takes a brave man – or woman – to acknowledge sharing her curiosity, but undoubtedly some of us do, and Scott knew this very well. In this *Conclusion* he is having fun again, at his own expense as well as Miss Buskbody's.

What is it that the narrations at the beginning and at the end of the book have in common? Surely it is that we are in the world of ordinary, everyday people in times of peace and the rule of law contrasting with the tortured life of the main story which has now passed into folklore, Peter Pattieson's 'olden tales and legends'. With the exception of the portrait of Old Mortality himself, the treatment of the characters and the milieu of the frame, though lightened by Scott's humour, is close to satire. The rascally landlord, the flogging Headmaster who spends all his leisure time in the fireside seat at the pub, the dressmaker who has read 'through the whole stock of three circulating libraries' and insists on a happy ending and 'the marriage of the principal personages', however 'harrowing to our nerves' the main course of the story, what are we to think of these? The flaccidity and complacency of these characters, though in a way comforting compared with the terrible intensity of barbarian conflict, do not do much to repair our view of human nature. Like the two sides in the war, both states of being are deplorable. Certainly these people 'respectably' earn their living and seriously harm no one but they have not half the spirit of Cuddie, who is the instrument of restoring Tillietudlem to Lady Margaret, or of Jennie with her hot brose. Even Peter Pattieson himself, the pick of the bunch who ostensibly tells the tale, gives the most depressing account of the

46 MARY WEDD

trade of a teacher and is destined to die young. The 'Editor' takes pains to demonstrate the vacuity of these people's lives. Is this perhaps Scott's final irony, that, when 'the killing days' are over, those who enjoy peace and relative prosperity do so little with them?

Author's acknowledgement

My thanks to Professor Fred Burwick who made me a present of this subject. Bill Ruddick and I shared a love of Scott's work and it was Bill who first first introduced me to the Scott Conference at Aberdeen and elsewhere. I am grateful for this opportunity to contribute to the book in his honour.

Chapter 4

Mathilda – Who Knew Too Much

Frederick Burwick

In August, 1819, while Percy Bysshe Shelley was finishing *The Cenci* (1819), a drama of a daughter's rape and subsequent revenge against her brutal and tyrannical father, Mary Shelley began writing *The Fields of Fancy*, later to be titled *Mathilda* (1819).[1] In this first-person narrative, a young woman tells the story of her relationship with her father. When Mary Shelley completed the novel, she sent it to her father, William Godwin, who was supposed to submit it to a publisher. He not only refused to submit it, he blocked any further attempt at publication by declining to return it to her.[2] The novel remained unpublished until 1959 when it was edited by Elizabeth Nitchie from the manuscript in the Bodleian Library, Oxford.[3] Nitchie recognized, as Godwin most probably had before her, that the novel was filled with autobiographical details that reflected the strained relationship between the author and her father.[4]

To provide her characters with a literary education relevant to their situation is a recurrent attribute of Mary Shelley's novels. Informing plot and structure by means of this self-reflexive intertextuality, she gives her central character an opportunity to study the literary tradition in which she has placed him or her. Thus the Creature in *Frankenstein* acquires an education in reading Milton's *Paradise Lost*, Goethe's *Werther*, Plutarch's *Lives*. In *The Last Man*, the progress of events is suspended while Lionel peruses Daniel De Foe's *Journal of the Plague Year* and 'the masterly delineations' of Charles Brockden Brown's *Arthur Mervyn*.

Although Mathilda tells her story after her father's suicide, her familiarity with the literature of incest was not acquired in retrospect. It had already been absorbed as part of her literary education at the time of her father's return. The significance of Mathilda's familiarity with the literature of incest might be interpreted as a deliberate preparation for an event that she anticipates, as if she had a premonition that her father would one day reveal his sexual desire for her. Mary Shelley's fictional character reveals that from age sixteen she has been expert in the literature of incest. She knows and quotes major literary works on father-daughter incest: John Fletcher's *The Captaine* (1647) and Vittorio Alfieri's *Myrrha* (1789). From Giovanni Bocaccio's *Decameron* (1349–51), she also cites the tale of 'Tancred and Ghismunda', in which the daughter justifies her sexual desires by declaring to her father, 'I am as you made me, of flesh and blood', and like her father she is 'overflowing with desire for love and passion'.[5] In contrast to the incest plot developed in *Cenci*, Mary Shelley has her heroine cite works in which not the father but the daughter is the instigator of the illicit passion.

In referring to this novel as 'prophetic', Mary Shelley reveals the extent to which she continued to identify with her tragic heroine three years after the novel had been sent to her father. Her explanation of the 'prophetic', however, turned attention away from her past to the circumstances that followed upon her completion of the novel in 1819. She relates her own sense of loss on the drowning of Percy Bysshe Shelley to Mathilda's grief on the death of her father. The parallels she draws to Shelley's drowning in August 1822, three years after the completion of the novel, may be relevant only in so far as they prompt her to reveal that she felt an identity with Mathilda and had imbued her fictional character with certain autobiographical aspects of herself.

The twelve chapters of *Mathilda* may be divided into two parts: the events leading up to her father's confessing his passion (chs 1–6); and her failed attempt to prevent his suicide and her own self-torment that blights her relationship with Woodville (chs 7–12). At the beginning of her tale, Mathilda describes herself as a 'female Oedipus'. The first three chapters relate the idyllic love of her father for the beautiful Diana, Diana's death and her father's anguished departure, and her own subsequent childhood with her aunt. In her idealization of her parent's love, Mathilda seems unconscious of the dysfunctional immaturity of their relationship. Her father 'was educated by a weak mother with all the indulgence she thought due to a nobleman of wealth'. He and Diana 'had been playmates from infancy', and their play is soon charged with passion: 'At eleven years of age Diana was his favourite playmate but he already talked the language of love. …they became every day more ardent and tender. It was a passion that had grown with his growth; it had become entwined with every faculty and every sentiment and only to be lost with life.'

At the close of the second chapter, Mathilda confesses that under the aloof care of her aunt, she grew up 'a dreamer'. Her favourite vision was her reunion with her father, 'the idol of my imagination'. In her visions, 'I was to be his consoler, his companion in after years'. They would one day meet, and his first words would be, 'My daughter, I love thee.' The next three chapters, which commence when Mathilda has reached the age of sixteen, narrate her reunion with her father and the death of her aunt. As the third chapter opens, she still lives only for her reading and her 'fantasy companions'. Then her father returns, and 'all around me was changed from dull uniformity to the brightest scene of joy and delight'. When she moves with him to London, as recounted in chapter 4, she attracts a suitor. Her father's previously open and friendly disposition abruptly darkens, and he takes her from London and returns to the family estate. Here she likens her fate to that of Proserpine:

> The day before we had passed alone together in the country; I remember we had talked of future travels that we should undertake together – there was an eager delight in our tones and gestures that could only spring from deep and mutual love joined to the most unrestrained confidence; and now the next day, the next hour, I saw his brows contracted, his eyes fixed in sullen fierceness on the ground, and his voice so gentle and so dear made me shiver when he addressed me. Often, when my wandering fancy brought by its various images now consolation and now aggravation of grief to my heart, I have compared myself to Proserpine, who was gaily and heedlessly

gathering flowers on the sweet plain of Enna, when the King of Hell snatched her away to the abodes of death and misery. Alas! who so lately knew of nought but the joy of life; who had slept only to dream sweet dreams and awoke to incomparable happiness, I now passed my days and nights in tears. I who sought and had found joy in the love-breathing countenance of my father now when I dared fix on him a supplicating look it was ever answered by an angry frown.

As her story is related in *Lemprière's Classical Dictionary* (1788),[6] Proserpine was so beautiful that her own father 'became enamoured of her, and deceived her by changing himself into a serpent, and folding her in his coils'. She is subsequently raped by Pluto, who carries her off to the underworld. Jupiter intercedes and commands that she be allowed to return from the infernal regions and spend six months of each year on earth. In identifying with Proserpine, Mathilda apparently does not imagine herself seduced by her serpent father, or ravished by Pluto, his 'infernal' alter-ego. The allusion to Proserpine, some years later to be the subject of a play by Mary Shelley,[7] may well have been intended only to contrast a time of joy and time of sadness. Yet the reader's confidence that the allusion is without its usual sexual references is undermined by further literary allusions to incest which immediately follow.

As Mary notes in her journal, she was reading the plays of Beaumont and Fletcher at the very time she was writing *Mathilda*.[8] In Fletcher's *The Captaine*, Lelia, 'a cunning wanton widow', receives a soldier and is overwhelmed with lust. Even after he has revealed himself as her father, she does not temper her desire. 'I have turn'd the reverence of a child', she tells him, 'Into the hot affection of a lover.' When he accuses her of 'sins/ Unnatural', she seeks to convince him that incest is a natural passion:

> 'tis not against nature
> For us to lie together: if you have
> An arrow of the same tree with your bow,
> Is't more unnatural to shoot it there
> Than in another? 'Tis our general nature
> To procreate, as fire's to consume. (IV.v.206–11)

In the scene in which Mathilda laments her father's apparent rejection of her (ch. 4), Mary has her character quote Lelia:

> Day after day passed marked only by my complaints and often I lifted my soul in vain prayer for a softer descent from joy to woe, or if that were denied me that I might be allowed to die, and fade for ever under the cruel blast that swept over me
>
> > for what should I do here,
> > Like a decaying flower, still withering
> > Under his bitter words, whose kindly heat
> > Should give my poor heart life? [I.iii.237–40]
>
> Sometimes I said to myself, this is an enchantment, and I must strive against it. My father is blinded by some malignant vision which I must remove. And

then, like David, I would try music to win the evil spirit from him; and once while singing I lifted my eyes towards him and saw his fixed on me and filled with tears; all his muscles seemed relaxed to softness. I sprung towards him with a cry of joy and would have thrown myself into his arms, but he pushed me roughly from him and left me. And even from this slight incident he contracted fresh gloom and an additional severity of manner.

In addition to quoting Fletcher's incestuous Lelia, Mathilda in the very next paragraph announces her admiration for Alfieri's tragedy of a daughter's incestuous love for her father. Apparently oblivious of the shocking implications of declaring to her father amidst 'company with several other persons' that she considers *Myrrha* 'the best of Alfieri's tragedies', she nevertheless describes his reaction, struggling 'with some concealed emotion', as a symptom of 'the diseased yet incomprehensible state of his mind':

On this occasion I chanced to say that I thought Myrrha the best of Alfieri's tragedies, as I said this I chanced to cast my eyes on my father and met his for the first time the expression of those beloved eyes displeased me, and I saw with affright that his whole frame shook with some concealed emotion that in spite of his efforts half conquered him as this tempest faded from his soul he became melancholy and silent. Every day some new scene occurred and displayed in him a mind working as [it] were with an unknown horror that now he could master but which at times threatened to overturn his reason, and to throw the bright seat of his intelligence into a perpetual chaos.

One year before she commenced writing *Mathilda*, Percy Bysshe Shelley wrote to her about her translation of *Myrrha* (22 September 1818).[9] Mathilda's, and Mary Shelley's, familiarity with the play adapted by Alfieri from Ovid's *Metamorphoses*, makes it evident that his was the work on which she had been engaged. Myrrha is the daughter of King Ciniro, towards whom she feels an irrepressible desire. Her attempt to suppress her unnatural sexual longing disrupts her mental and emotional equilibrium. She exhibits radical mood swings. She consents to marry Pereo, the suitor her parents have selected for her, but in an hysterical fit at her wedding she curses him. Pereo commits suicide. Questioned by her father, she confesses her passionate love for him. Seeing his shock, she seizes his sword and plunges it into her breast.

A year passes with Mathilda and her father living in relative isolation. His good spirits are only partially restored. In chapter 5, now seventeen years old, Mathilda senses that her father is troubled by some dark secret which he struggles to keep concealed from her. She is relentless in urging him to reveal his secret. If 'I might speak', he cautions her, 'then you would be implicated in my destruction'. She pledges that the wings of 'our mutual love' will soar above any 'chasm' that his secret might open up, 'and we shall love each other as before, and for ever'. It would be 'happier', he replies, 'if in your frantic curiosity you tore my heart from my breast and tried to read its secrets ... as its life blood was dropping from it'. Mathilda herself wonders at the 'pertinacious folly' of her persistence. 'I demand that dreadful word', she urges him, 'though it be as a flash of lightning to destroy me, speak it'.[10] Finally, he succumbs to her urging. He speaks the words of her childhood dream of their reunion: 'My daughter,

I love you.' No sooner does she perceive that this is an unfatherly love, than she imagines a vampire of despair released within her being: 'I felt her fangs upon my heart.'[11]

Her father's confession of his guilty attraction is the crisis toward which Mathilda's narrative has thus far developed. The first half of the novel comes to a close, in chapter 6, with her distraught mental plight and her father's departure. She declares that he is dead to her. Yet even while she is imagining the possibility of him lying in his coffin, she grows anxious at the possibility that her 'beloved and most wretched father' might in fact die. She hopes that he may spend another sixteen years of absence wandering the wilds until his vile passion be expunged from his mind and body, so that he might return and embrace her with 'sinless emotion'. Her curse is one of purification and redemption: 'This is my curse, a daughter's curse: go, and return pure to thy child, who will never love aught but thee.' Yet that mild curse is retracted when she hears his footsteps at her bedroom door. She stifles her sobs and pauses 'breathless' as he lingers outside her room. 'Why approach my chamber? Was not that sacred?' She now wishes him gone forever. She falls into a disturbed slumber. In her dream she sees him seated under a tree at the seaside dressed in white robes. As she approaches, he flees. He nears a cliff above the sea. She hastens her steps, and clutches at his robe before he plunges from the precipice.

The second half of the novel begins with his farewell letter and suicide (ch. 7) and studies Mathilda's grief and guilt. The letter tells her that he had adored her, as Dante worshipped Beatrice,[12] with a 'sinless passion', until he witnessed her in London beset by admirers. The realization 'that you might love another with a more ardent affection than you bore me', he declares, awoke 'the fiend' of sexual desire within him. When she reads his letters she realizes that her dream had been a premonition of his resolve. She orders a carriage and knows that she must follow the road that 'led *towards the sea*'. Seeing a lone tree which she recognizes from her dream, she declares to her steward, 'Mark. Gaspar, if the next flash of lightning rend not that oak my father will be alive.' In that very moment a bolt lightning strikes and the oak is blasted from sight. 'Of, God!' she wails, 'Is this thy decree.' The pursuit continues. They reach the spot where her father has left his horse and 'walked on – *towards the sea*'. They reach the precipice. On the shore they spy a cottage. They knock. The cottagers open and show the draped bed where the corpse of her father lies.

'He loved me with a guilty passion', she acknowledges at the beginning of chapter 8. She tries to resume her life in London, and for a while she thinks her emotional 'convalescence' advances. Then she becomes aware of how deeply her father's guilt has penetrated her own being: 'I must shrink before the eye of man lest he should read my father's guilt in my glazed eyes: I must be silent lest my faltering voice should betray unimagined horrors.' Mary Shelley's depiction of psychological damage is acutely alert to the symptoms of the sexually abused young girl. Mathilda returns to her aunt's Scottish estate. Since to pretend that this incestuous lust had never happened is to live a lie, she resolves to live an even greater lie: to feign her own suicide, to assume a new identity. The disguise is but another 'degradation of falsehood', and she must 'look back with disgust at my artifices and contrivances'. In seeking to escape into nature, she likens herself to Coleridge's Ancient Mariner finding his own blessing in blessing the water snakes (lines 272–87).

But the retreat into nature does not work its absolution. At the opening of chapter 9, she has passed two years on the Scottish heath. She is now 19 years old, and self-recriminations continue to persecute her. Appropriating one of Shelley's metaphors, Mathilda declares herself as 'tender as the sensitive plant'. And drawing from Shelley's poem, 'On the Head of Medusa', she likens herself to that petrific and petrifying being. If it were not for her cold and stultifying nature, she might have found friendship when she meets Woodville. Because he too has suffered, they might 'be fitted to a mutual consolation', were it not for the fact that his was 'a natural grief' that may 'purify the heart', and hers of the unnatural kind that destroys 'the heart's core'. Her story of Woodville and Elinore tells of a more delicate love than that of her father and Diana, two playmates whose love matured into 'ardent and tender' passion. But like that love it is blighted by death: Elinore grows sick and dies. Six months after Elinore's death, Mathilda meets Woodville. He confides in her, tells her of his grief, yet realizes that she will allow no one into her confidence (ch. 10). The more open that he is with her, the more peevish she becomes in response. He is 'gentle and sympathizing'; she is 'captious and unreasonable, unfit for the slightest novelty of feeling'.

In chapter 11, it becomes clear how disturbed Mathilda has become. 'I had become arrogant, peevish, and above all suspicious.' To humour her out of her melancholy, Woodville visits her cottage. Since hope is dead to them both, Mathilda reasons, they both should die. 'It was madness', she realizes, but she nevertheless sets the stage for a mutual suicide: 'I procured Laudanum and placing it in two glasses on the table, filled my room with flowers and decorated the last scene of my tragedy with the nicest care.' When he arrive she insists that he be a true friend and not 'refuse to accompany me on this dark journey'. At the time of her father's confession she had felt the phantom of despair sink her 'fangs upon my heart' (ch. 5). Now she declares that she herself has become that phantom: 'I have learned the language of despair: I have it all by heart, for I am Despair.' Woodville seeks to persuade her to banish her thoughts of suicide: 'as you have played Despair with me I will play the part of Una with you an bring you hurtless from this dark cavern.' Mathilda is momentarily consoled. But she cannot repress the condemnation that she has levelled against herself: 'I believed myself polluted by the unnatural love that I inspired.'

At the beginning of chapter 12 she bids her last farewell to Woodville. She pictures herself as Dante's Mathilda, gathering flowers at the edge of a dark brook in purgatory.[13] Losing her way on the heath, she sleeps on the open ground. Again echoing the words of Coleridge's Ancient Mariner (line 300), she declares that 'When I awoke it rained'. What for the Mariner was a saving rain of grace is for Mathilda a rain that brings fever and consumption. She resigns herself to a more 'innocent death' than she would have achieved with the overdose of laudanum. Four years have passed since her father returned to her, three years since 'my folly destroyed the only being I was doomed to love'. She dies with the expectation that she 'shall meet him in another world'.

The novel which Mary Shelley began in August was completed in November 1819. In her journal the following February, she records making final corrections before sending the manuscript with the Gisbornes to be delivered to her father in England.[14] Godwin had the novel in hand by May 1820, but he refused to forward it to a publisher. Worse, he refused to return it to his daughter. He even refused to communicate with the Gisbornes, whom Mary had sent to intercede in her behalf.[15] Her own father effectively censored the tale of a father's psychological trespass that Mary Shelley had sought to make public.

Just as Mathilda's dream foretold the fate of her father, Mary Shelley was convinced that her own novel, commenced in August 1819, had prophesied the fate of her husband, who three years later drowned at sea. When the news of the squall on Bay of Spezia reached her, Mary and Jane Williams set out in a cross-country coach ride *'towards the sea'* with the same desperation that had been ascribed to Mathilda: 'It must have been fearful to see us – two poor, wild, aghast creatures – driving (like Matilda) towards the *sea* to learn if we were to be for ever doomed to our misery.'[16] Mary Shelley also recorded her grief in her journal: 'Oh my own beloved – let me not be so deserted – It seems to me that while I live & talk & act – all this may go on & you not be here. But you ought to be acquainted with every mental exertion – or I am indeed alone. There is much anguish in this. Before when I wrote Mathilda, miserable as I was the *inspiration* was sufficient to quell my wretchedness temporarily – but now I have no respite.'[17] The death of her son William had rendered Mary 'miserable' at the time of composition. Because her father had blocked the publication, *Mathilda* remained a private and personal document, and she came to regard it not only as reflection of her own past but also as ominous prophecy of her future. As she confided to Maria Gisborne, 'Matilda foretells even many small circumstances most truly – & the whole of it is a monument of what now is.'[18] The novel had become 'autobiographical' with a vengeance. The events that she had narrated as fiction seemed to intertwine with her own life and to dictate her actual fate.

Incest, a recurrent motif in Romantic literature, was especially prominent in the works of Percy Bysshe Shelley, not only in *Cenci*, as already mentioned, but also in 'Alastor' and *Laon and Cythna* (*The Revolt of Islam*). Lord Byron's notorious affair with his half-sister Augusta Leigh brought incest into a more immediate presence in the Shelley circle, especially since Byron was engaged in an affair with Mary Shelley's half-sister, Claire Claremont. For her part, Claire considered Byron a man who readily indulged incest. 'Did you ever read the history of the Cenci's?' she asked Byron at the time when Shelley was working on his play. She called it 'a most frightful & horrible story', and went on to say that 'I am sorely afraid ... that in the elder Cenci you may behold yourself in twenty years ... but if I live Allegra shall never be a Beatrice.'[19]

To say that Mary Shelley's *Mathilda* is autobiographical is not to incriminate William Godwin in an overt act of incest. Richard Holmes phrased it well when he called it 'a private and self-exploratory novel' and 'a therapeutic instrument'.[20] Because Godwin had exploited Shelley financially, had assailed his character with negative remarks, had persisted in trying to control and manipulate his daughter, Mary had good reason to reflect on a father's trespassing the boundaries of love. As is evident in the novel, there is more to Mathilda's father than just the fictional representation of Godwin. Mary Shelley has identified him as well with Percy Bysshe. Lionel's description of his parents in the opening pages of *The Last Man* will remind us that Mary Shelley does not avoid the representation of inept and irresponsible fathers. The account of the daughter's naïve fantasies and the father's misplaced sexual desires are but half the story Mary has told in this novel. The other half describes the lasting psychological damage: 'I believed myself to be polluted by the unnatural love I had inspired.' The guilt she bears cripples her capacity to feel sympathy or love.

Chapter 5

'Perswasion' in *Persuasion*

Jane Stabler

> The Prophets Isaiah and Ezekiel dined with me, and I asked them how they dared so roundly to assert that God spoke to them; and whether they did not think at the time that they would be misunderstood, & so be the cause of imposition.
> Isaiah answer'd: 'I saw no God, nor heard any, in a finite organical perception; but my senses discover'd the infinite in every thing, and as I was then perswaded, & remain confirm'd, that the voice of honest indignation is the voice of God, I cared not for the consequences, but wrote.'
> Then I asked: 'Does a firm perswasion that a thing is so, make it so?'
> He replied: 'All poets believe that it does, & in ages of imagination the firm perswasion removed mountains; but many are not capable of a firm perswasion of any thing.'
> —William Blake, *The Marriage of Heaven and Hell* [1]

William Blake's encounter with Isaiah in *The Marriage of Heaven and Hell* alerts us to one of the many meanings of the word 'persuasion' in the Romantic period, that of firm inner conviction or religious belief.[2] The prophet suggests that to perceive through all the senses (not just the finite, organical ones), is to discover the infinite and that poets share this ability to create by belief. We know that Jane Austen's Christianity was extremely important to her ('I am by no means convinced that we ought not all to be Evangelicals, & am at least persuaded that they who are so from Reason & Feeling, must be happiest & safest.').[3] In her last completed novel, Austen explores the imaginative and religious dynamics of persuasion both in the unfolding plot and the texture of her narrative.

In the introduction to a new Penguin edition of *Persuasion* Gillian Beer suggests that as persuasion can 'slide across into seduction', the art of persuading is 'fraught with moral dangers'.[4] Beer draws attention to Samuel Johnson's dictionary definitions of the term, unfolding his indications that while allowing oneself to be persuaded may be a way of yielding to better judgement, a person who persuades may be an 'importunate adviser'.[5] From her letters we know that Jane Austen was involved in frequent minor domestic dramas of persuasion as well as the more serious question of how to advise her niece on a possible engagement. 'Miss Payne called in on Saturday & was persuaded to stay [sic] dinner', Austen told her sister, summarizing an exchange of gentle social pressure (*Letters* 186). We do not know how long it took to convince Miss Payne to stay, but the necessity of swaying people towards an acceptance of benevolence places a burden on the recipient which, at the very least, engages both parties in a decorous battle of wills. Austen recorded her activity on the winning side of one of these struggles when she wrote to tell her sister that

> Harriot was at first very little inclined, or rather totally disinclined, to profit by her ladyship's attention; but at length, after many debates, she was persuaded by me and herself together to accept the ticket. (*Letters* 109)

The issue here was whether Harriot should go to a ball or not. It sounds trivial but, as Austen remarked shrewdly, 'Little Matters' are 'highly important' (*Letters* 156). In *Northanger Abbey* we see how the supportive or congenial dynamics of persuasion within the family circle may acquire more threatening characteristics when Catherine's own brother 'openly [sides] against her' on the matter of the drive to Clifton as she is 'attacked with supplications':

> 'I did not think you had been so obstinate, Catherine,' said James; 'you were not used to be so hard to persuade; you once were the kindest, best-tempered of my sisters.'[6]

James's words allow us to hear directly the manipulative potential of persuasion: Catherine's very identity is being challenged (or 'attacked', to use Austen's powerful word) to satisfy the interests of people for whom she cares.

Johnson's 'importunate adviser' describes very well the persistent or troublesome pressure from an intimate companion which creates dramatic tension in all of Austen's novels: we think of Mrs John Dashwood begging her husband to reconsider his generosity to Elinor and Marianne at the start of *Sense and Sensibility*, or Edmund trying to draw Fanny into the theatricals in *Mansfield Park* against both their better judgements, or Darcy in *Pride and Prejudice* telling how he remonstrated with Bingley about his attachment to Jane Bennet.

For Captain Wentworth and Henrietta Musgrove as well as many readers of Jane Austen's *Persuasion*, Lady Russell is the daunting apotheosis of this power which blends social hierarchy with force of personality: 'I have always heard of Lady Russell, as a woman of the greatest influence with every body!', Henrietta gushes, 'I always look upon her as able to persuade a person to any thing! I am afraid of her, as I have told you before, quite afraid of her, because she is so very clever.'[7] Lady Russell's strong self-possession exists on a cusp between benign and harmful influence, and has the effect of highlighting the fragility of other selves. As Blake's Isaiah remarks, 'Many are not capable of a firm perswasion of anything'.

When Wentworth attributes Anne's breaking-off of their engagement to 'over-persuasion' – 'She had given him up to oblige others. It had been the effect of over-persuasion. It had been weakness and timidity' (62) – he oscillates between blaming the overbearing influence of Lady Russell and the too-easily-swayed nature of Anne. Before she meets Wentworth again, Anne has grown to believe that 'she should yet have been a happier woman in maintaining the engagement, than she had been in the sacrifice of it' (33). Austen seems unwilling to allow either Anne or Wentworth the last word on this decision. When they are reconciled at the end of the novel there is still more anguished scrutiny of Anne's earlier choice: Anne hovers delicately between a repudiation and a defence of her younger self: 'If I was wrong in yielding to persuasion once, remember that it was to persuasion exerted on the side of safety' (230). Wentworth does not respond directly to this point. A little later in the same chapter, Anne again attempts to clarify her position:

> 'I was perfectly right in being guided by the friend whom you will love better than you do now ... Do not mistake me, however. I am not saying that she did not err in her advice ... I certainly never should, in any circumstance of tolerable similarity, give such advice. But I mean, that I was right in submitting to her, and that if I had done otherwise, I should have suffered more in continuing the engagement than I did even in giving it up, because I should have suffered in my conscience.' (232)

Anne's complete conviction ('I was perfectly right') here approaches moral homily. Her emphasis on the integrity and, paradoxically, the independence of her conscience has a strong undertow of Evangelical Christian idealism, defined by Marilyn Butler as 'a private spiritual state which is elevated and intense'.[8] This moral stance is consistent with, for example, Anne's strict disapproval of Mr. Elliot's Sunday travelling and her efforts to rouse herself (and Captain Benwick) from brooding self-immurement. The social effects of personal belief are indicated by Butler's point that, as the Evangelicals were 'dedicated critics of moral backsliding among the governing classes', Evangelical Christianity helped to buttress conservative middle-class identity in the Romantic period.[9]

Wentworth's response to Anne's speech, 'Not yet', tells us, however, that he has listened only as far as her prediction that he will like Lady Russell better in the future. He does not (and probably cannot) accept the view that Anne was right to give way when she did. His silence at both of the moments when Anne argues for the breaking of the first engagement shows us that he remains firmly unpersuaded. Although Wentworth could perhaps deduce it from Anne's adherence to the principle of duty, she does not admit to him what Austen allows us to know, 'Anne could just acknowledge within herself such a possibility of having been induced to marry [Mr Elliot], as made her shudder at the idea of misery which must have followed. It was just possible that she might have been persuaded by Lady Russell!' (199). Marilyn Butler detects a 'failure to define the tempter-figure' in *Persuasion* (Butler 280), but it is possible that Anne's internalization of Lady Russell's influence is a more subtle form of temptation than the allure of an eligible man.

Anne's more robust defence of her submissive behaviour once she is secure in a reunion with Wentworth forms an interesting contrast with her earlier belief that she would have been happier if she had disregarded familial duty. If we return to the period of Anne's desolate Wentworthlessness we find that Jane Austen places Anne's being 'persuaded to believe the engagement a wrong thing' (31) very near to her being 'persuaded ... she should yet have been a happier woman in maintaining the engagement' (32–3). The difference between these two positions is not just one of time (eight years have passed), but of different sorts of dialogue. In the first instance, Anne has been subject to Lady Russell's verbal appeals and exhortations; in the second we are given the growth of silent conviction within an individual.

A great deal of critical attention has been devoted to the novel's treatment of solicitation and entreaty, the social arena of persuasion explored by Dr Johnson. The passage from William Blake at the beginning of this essay, however, may help us to see how the dynamics of social influence and personal conviction intermesh in the novel. Blake brings the two worlds together when he asks the prophet whether he worried about being misunderstood and 'the cause of imposition' (or mass deception).[10] Whereas Blake's religious conviction is identical with imaginative leap, in Austen's novel the cast of thought which defines religious belief is at odds with personal imagination or flights of fancy. A letter to Cassandra Austen in 1817 summarizes the way in which Austen sees these two forms of persuasion as opposing forces:

> You are all over Imagination. – The most astonishing part of your Character is, that with so much Imagination, so much flight of Mind, such unbounded Fancies, you should have such excellent Judgement in what you do! – Religious Principle I fancy must explain it. (*Letters* 334)

For Austen, religious persuasion works on the side of 'Judgement', not with 'Flight of Mind'. In Austen's writing, therefore, the complexities of mental inclination are as fraught as the social dynamics of persuasion. In Anne Elliot's story, the dramas that are set in motion by persuading or being persuaded by another party are infinitely complicated by the trajectories of inner persuasion. Barbara Hardy's view that *Persuasion* is Austen's 'only novel where the theme of imagination is neither pervasive nor prominent' overlooks the way in which imaginative conviction is embedded in the title and texture of the work.[11]

The idea that each individual has a conditioned outlook on the world and that these personal beliefs shape perception was not new in Jane Austen's time. In *An Essay Concerning Human Understanding* (1690), John Locke had suggested that experience shapes the individual: 'Custom settles habits of thinking in the understanding, as well as of determining in the will' (2.33.6).[12] The difficulty of obtaining certain knowledge makes it unavoidable that '*men be persuaded of several opinions whereof the proofs are not actually in their thoughts*' (4.16.2). Locke's philosophy had a profound influence on the eighteenth century, enabling, for example, the work of David Hume. Hume's *Treatise on Human Nature* (1739) developed Locke's quasi-sceptical approach and recognized that observation was contingent upon the customary outlook of the observer. Hume saw 'internal sentiment' as capable of 'gilding or staining all natural objects' and raising 'a new creation'.[13] His ideas were condemned as wicked and irreligious, but eighteenth-century debates about the construction of taste reveal that relativism was accepted by many at a local, if not a global level. As Austen remarks in *Persuasion*: 'Every body has their taste in noises as well as in other matters' (128).

In *The Life and Opinions of Tristram Shandy* (1760–67), Laurence Sterne identifies the dominant desires and anxieties of characters which set them off on trains of thought unintelligible to all but the most sensitively attuned interlocutor. The narrator's uncle is obsessed with the moment in the siege of Namur which resulted in a war wound in his groin: since this accident uncle Toby's conversation has circled around the science of siege warfare. These preoccupations (and the equally obsessive theoretical ones of his brother) are carefully explained and labelled by Sterne as 'hobby-horses'. By making them into lovable (if exasperating) foibles, the reader can enjoy the comedy of uncle Toby about to embark upon his favourite topic and being deflected by the narrator's father:

> when my uncle Toby discovered the transverse zig-zaggery of my father's approaches towards it, it instantly brought into his mind those he had done duty in, before the gate of St Nicolas; – the idea of which drew off his attention so entirely from the subject in debate, that he had got his right hand to the bell to ring up Trim, to go and fetch his map of Namur, and his compasses and sector along with it, to measure the returning angles of the traverses of that attack, – but particularly of that one, where he received his wound upon his groin.
> My father knit his brows, and as he knit them, all the blood in his body seemed to rush up into his face – my uncle Toby dismounted immediately.[14]

Sterne's narrative commentary tells us exactly when a character mounts or dismounts his particular hobby-horse. This careful guidance of the reader is characteristic of eighteenth- and nineteenth-century fiction as novelists explored the ways in which imagination shapes perception. Writing a century after Sterne, George Eliot wanted to help her readers gain 'a clearer conception' of what bound them all together.[15] In *Middlemarch* (1861) she shows how the characters' fanciful ideas about themselves and each other people maim their chances of happiness. Dorothea Brooke is symbolically short-sighted and, like King Lear, she has to learn to 'see better' and to acknowledge the extent to which self-interest is capable of clouding perception. Eliot offers us cool, detached measurements of Dorothea's progress. We are told when Dorothea begins 'to see that she had been under a wild illusion', and that she needs to imagine her husband's 'equivalent centre of self, whence the lights and shadows must always fall with a certain difference'.[16] Standing back from the second unhappy marriage in the novel, Eliot tells us that Rosamond and Lydgate, 'each lived in a world of which the other knew nothing' (195). Lydgate's 'alternate vision', his ability to 'see beyond ... infatuations' (182) makes him much more troubled than Rosamond who is 'little used to imagining other people's states of mind' (834). The story line of *Middlemarch* builds towards a series of climactic verbal persuadings, but these take place against a history of inner persuasions which have to be overcome. Throughout the book only Eliot's moral percipience gauges all these web-like intersections, allowing the reader to 'see beyond the misery of it' (869).

The novel's preoccupation with relativity of perception continued well into the twentieth century and may be seen in an extreme form in Alain Robbe-Grillet's *La Jalousie* (1957). In this experimental *nouveau roman* a narrating voice driven by (we assume) sexual jealousy supplies a series of fragmented perceptions and partial views of the other male and female figures in the book. These scenes are linked by association with a possible affair which may exist only in the imagination of the perceiving intelligence:

> She takes refuge now ... in the corner of the room, which also makes the south-west corner of the house. It would be easy to watch her through one of the two doors, that of the central corridor, or that of the bathroom, but the doors are of solid wood without the arrangement of slats (*système de jalousies*) which lets you see through. As for the blinds (*jalousies*) over the three windows, each one now no longer allows any view.[17]

The narrator's interest in the precise geometry of objects and shadows makes Robbe-Grillet's fictional world view curiously like Sterne's. Robbe-Grillet puns on the word *jalousie* which in French means jealousy and venetian blind; the emotional and isolated condition of the speaker create a similarly incomplete view of events. These three novels from three centuries are predicated upon different ways of telling the reader about consciousness. Sterne's narrator is comically and continuously obsessed with efforts to make his reader understand him; George Eliot's intelligence oversees the narrative events of *Middlemarch*, offering clear vistas which stretch away from the embroiled struggles of her characters; Alain Robbe-Grillet extends the psychological reach of the novel by confronting the reader with primarily visual information which the reader must piece together. Jane Austen does not commit her narrative to any single one of these modes, but uses a fluid combination of all three.

Persuasion exploits comedy of obsession in Sir Walter's and Elizabeth's fixation with family rank, Mary's hypochondria and Mrs Musgrove's lamentations for her dead son. Sir Walter's 'hobby-horse' is laid out for us at the start of the novel where we are told that 'for his own amusement' he 'never took up any book but the Baronetage' (9).[18] Austen alerts us to this rank-oriented outlook and then leaves us to realise its crushing limitation: 'looking on the broad back of the dowager Viscountess Dalrymple', Elizabeth 'had nothing to wish for which did not seem within her reach' (175). Before we meet Mary we are told that her consciousness is dominated by 'always thinking a great deal about her own complaints' (36) and 'fancying herself neglected and ill-used' (39). This information enables us to decode the accusation in her first words to Anne, 'So, you are come at last' (39). Austen's treatment of Mrs Musgrove's bereavement also uses a blend of authoritative overview and vignette. We hear from Louisa that her mother is 'thinking so much of poor Richard' (51) and within a paragraph Austen steps in to tell us that the 'real circumstances' of the case are that he was 'a very troublesome, hopeless son' (52). When, in a later scene, Mrs Musgrove begins to reminisce about her son to Wentworth, the reader is prepared for her train of association, but Wentworth 'not having Dick Musgrove at all near his thoughts' cannot at first follow what she is saying (67).

Austen's omniscience anticipates the precision of Eliot, but not her wide compassion; the swipe at Mrs Musgrove's 'large fat sighings over the destiny of a son, whom alive nobody had cared for' (68) is a notorious example of authorial contempt. While the predictable responses of Sir Walter, Elizabeth, Mary and Mrs Musgrove display the working of internal persuasion at its crudest, Austen supplies a range of more complex (and more likeable) characters whose vision is compromised by their habits of thought. Lady Russell, we are told, 'had prejudices on the side of ancestry ... which blinded her a little' (17). Anne recognizes and fears this 'shade of prejudice' against Wentworth late in the novel (169). Visual perception is not the only sense to be impaired by inner persuasion. Lady Russell's liking for Bath means that she does not hear the 'heavy rumble ... bawling ... and ceaseless clink' which Austen records (128). Lady Russell regards Anne's dislike for the city, however, 'as a prejudice and mistake' (20): one person's prejudiced opinion is another's reasoned certainty.

Admiral Croft's removal of the multiple looking-glasses from Sir Walter's dressing-room at Kellynch-hall shows he is not as vain a man, but Austen demonstrates that he is still capable of self-preoccupation. At the social gathering when Mrs Musgrove sighs over her lost son, Admiral Croft approaches her 'without any observation of what he might be interrupting, thinking only of his own thoughts' (68). This description could be Austen's voice, or it might be coloured by Mrs Musgrove's view of events, but in either case it suggests relativity of perception. The subsequent discussion is another example of personal conviction shaping vision. Admiral Croft and Wentworth disagree about accommodating women on board ship: the Admiral insists that '"when he [Wentworth] has got a wife, he will sing a different tune"' (69), and Wentworth replies, equally dismissively, that this is just a habitual married response. In the same conversation, Mrs Croft admits that when she was left on shore one winter she had 'all manner of imaginary complaints' (70). Her argument in favour of women travelling on board ship is usually read as a courageous defence of female liberty, but its counter-side is that Mrs Croft has the same capacity as Mary Musgrove to be self-deluded and self-obsessed.

Charles Hayter is a reasonable enough man, 'very amiable' and 'pleasing', Austen tells us (73), but his affection for Henrietta makes him 'not well inclined towards Captain Wentworth', and so determined to bury himself in the newspaper to avoid speaking to Wentworth that he is unable to see how much distress the clambering little Walter causes Anne (79). The fluctuating relationship between Henrietta and Charles Hayter is the subject of much speculation between Mary and her husband and the occasion for another disclosure of inner persuasion. Charles disagrees with his wife because 'he saw things as an eldest son himself' (75). Mary does not perceive the reason, but she imputes prejudice: 'I am sure you would have thought as I did, unless you had been determined to give it against me' (76). Wentworth himself confesses to damaging self-persuasion: 'I shut my eyes, and would not understand you, or do you justice', he tells Anne when they are finally able to share their personal perceptions with each other (233).

All these instances of self-delusion are entirely unreflecting, or realized only in retrospect, but *Persuasion* also summons a more complicated example of the tendency to construct events imaginatively. When Anne and Captain Harville debate the respective nature of male and female constancy, Harville supplies a powerful and moving testimonial for naval domestic devotion:

> 'if I could but make you comprehend what a man suffers when he takes a last look at his wife and children, and watches the boat that he has sent them off in, as long as it is in sight ... if I could convey to you the glow of his soul when he does see them again; when, coming back after a twelvemonth's absence perhaps, and obliged to put into another port, he calculates how soon it be possible to get them there, pretending to deceive himself, and saying, "They cannot be here till such a day," but all the while hoping for them twelve hours sooner'. (221)

The image of the sailor 'pretending to deceive himself' is an example of inner persuasion as a kind of drama rather than a delusion; it shows how complex personal motivations can be and the extent to which they compete with the world of objective fact.

Austen's omniscient voice emerges from these blinkered perceptions to clarify and accelerate narrative progress. Such an intervention is necessary as she assembles all her characters in Bath. The reader is told that Anne is about to see Wentworth before the encounter is described ('the very next time Anne walked out, she saw him' [164]). This moment of directive overview is significant because it highlights the extreme partiality of Anne's consciousness: 'For a few moments she saw nothing before her. It was all confusion. She was lost' (165). There are moments in *Persuasion* when despite the third-person narration, the reader faces visual blanks or blind spots like those in Robbe-Grillet's *La Jalousie*. These moments show the daring and experimental way in which Austen filters events through Anne's perception as in the confused stream of consciousness which relays her first re-encounter with Wentworth. Such moments leave the reader to determine whether what has been told to us is a matter of certain knowledge or the creation of Anne's imagination.

Anne is established as a good, mentally stable character and much has been written in appreciation of the access we have to her subjectivity, but critics have been too ready to adopt her as a completely reliable narrator. Gilbert and Gubar suggest that 'all the characters present [Anne] with their personal preferences rationalized into principles by which they attempt to persuade her ... everyone but she is convinced that his or her version of reality is the only valid one'.[19] In this reading, Anne is the only character capable of enlightened perception, while all other characters ride their own hobby-horses or gaze through Venetian blinds of their own construction. Other critics have elided Anne's and Austen's narrative authority. Tony Tanner's suggestion that Anne has to 'negotiate a plurality of partial discourses' develops the idea of her superior interpretative ability: 'She, and she alone, always speaks truly'.[20] Wayne C. Booth contrasts *Emma* with *Persuasion*: 'In *Emma* there are many breaks in the point of view, because Emma's beclouded mind cannot do the whole job. In *Persuasion*, where the heroine's viewpoint is faulty only in her ignorance of Captain Wentworth's love, there are very few'.[21] W. A. Craik follows Booth's view, 'Anne is just as right as her author. When Anne forms opinions, she has no prejudices to mislead her like Emma ... and so she sees quite clearly'.[22] Tara Ghoshal Wallace argues that Anne's insecurity about Wentworth is not a failure to decode signs, but due to Wentworth giving her misleading information.[23] M. J. Scott writes of Anne as 'an oracle' who stands above other characters 'in a world where knowledge is partial'.[24] Anne is indeed presented as a super-sensitive consciousness with omniscient authorial aspirations who 'longed for the power of representing to them all what they were about' (80). But she is also capable of misinterpretation through being too wedded to her own interest.

As we have seen in the presentation of the other characters, *Persuasion* presents the act of perception as one conditioned by inner conviction. With Anne, however, Jane Austen leaves the reader an unprecedented amount of freedom to work out the extent to which her view of events is biased. Yasmine Gooneratne has analysed Anne's 'delicate mist of inward preoccupation ... in the novel's final pages' and it is certainly true that in the latter stages of the novel Anne's focus on Wentworth leads her to mistake the actions of other characters such as Mr Elliot and Mrs Clay.[25] It is possible, however, that Anne's 'inward preoccupation' might lead us to question everything we are told in the novel.

Anne's capacity to invent what she sees is manifest in the humorous moment in Pulteney-street where she is 'perfectly conscious' that Lady Russell is 'intently observing' Wentworth only to be told that it was not the 'personal grace' of the Captain, but the quest for some drawing-room curtains – 'the handsomest and best hung of any in Bath' (169-70) that preoccupied her companion. Anne is aware of the human potential to shape a convenient version of reality: 'What wild imaginations one forms, where the dear self is concerned' (189), she admits when she realizes that Mr Elliot has heard about her from Mrs Smith rather than Captain Wentworth's brother. Although she comes very quickly to understand her mistake, we should not forget that Anne is as ready as other characters in the book to interpret the world following her fancy. In this way she repeats errors made by Emma Woodhouse and Catherine Morland, although she is never explicitly corrected in the way that these characters are.

Much less obvious than her blunder with the curtains or her assumption about who has been talking about her is Anne's misreading of events in the early days of Wentworth's visit to the Crofts at Kellynch-hall. Anne watches everyone closely, particularly Wentworth: 'how were his sentiments to be read? Was this like wishing to avoid her? And the next moment she was hating herself for the folly which asked the question' (61). We are told that Anne knows Wentworth well: she can detect his 'momentary' and 'transient' flicker of amusement when he contrasts Mrs Musgrove's view of 'poor Richard' with his own (67).

> 'Poor dear fellow!' continued Mrs Musgrove, 'he was grown so steady, and such an excellent correspondent, while he was under your care! Ah it would have been a happy thing, if he had never left you. I assure you, Captain Wentworth, we are very sorry he ever left you.'
>
> There was a momentary expression in Captain Wentworth's face at this speech, a certain glance of his bright eye, and curl of his handsome mouth, which convinced Anne, that instead of sharing in Mrs Musgrove's kind wishes, as to her son, he had probably been at some pains to get rid of him; (67).

But in the matter of Wentworth's relationship with Louisa and Henrietta, Anne's perceptions are not always identical with Austen's. Anne takes a perverse pleasure in 'watching the loves and jealousies of the four':

> She did not attribute guile to any. It was the highest satisfaction to her, to believe Captain Wentworth not in the least aware of the pain he was occasioning. There was no triumph, no pitiful triumph in his manner. He had, probably, never heard, and never thought of any claims of Charles Hayter. He was only wrong in accepting the attentions – (for accepting must be the word) of two young women at once. (80)

Austen narrates this section about and through Anne's thoughts. Anne's even-handedness is revealed as being more equal to some than others. It was 'the highest satisfaction' to 'believe Captain Wentworth...'. By using the verb 'believe', Austen suggests an act of self-persuasion on Anne's part, and this is emphasized by the slightly anxious repetition 'There was no triumph, no pitiful triumph in his manner'. Does this mean there was no triumph at all, or that Anne is forced to concede some triumph, but not a 'pitiful' variety? (We need to remember that she has already admitted the possibility of Wentworth being 'a little spoilt by such ... admiration' [71].) The possibility that Anne is deluding herself about Wentworth's involvement with the Musgrove girls builds in the next sentence which offers the significantly qualified conviction that 'He had, probably, never heard, and never thought of any claims of Charles Hayter'. The 'probably' is telling evidence of a drama of inner persuasion. If we retain a memory of this scene as we read further into the chapter, we find that Anne's interpretation of events is completely contradicted. Her mistake is revealed as we overhear Wentworth cheerfully telling Louisa: 'the hints you gave just now ... did but confirm my own observations, the last time I was in company with him, I need not affect to have no comprehension of what is going on' (85). In other words, Wentworth has been able to deduce Hayter's attachment to Henrietta while 'accepting' Henrietta's attentions. If we need any further evidence that 'encouraging' would be a better word than 'accepting', Wentworth admits to Anne at the end of the novel that he had been 'trying whether I could attach myself to either of the girls' (229). At the time, Anne wants to believe otherwise and so she persuades herself (and possibly the reader) to see things a little differently.

Austen does not step aside to tell us that Wentworth's casual confession reveals Anne to have been slanting things in Wentworth's favour. The snatch of speech we hear is a small detail, easily overshadowed by the emotional implications of his discourse on the hazel-nut. In this speech (much to Anne's mortification), Wentworth salutes Louisa's 'character of decision and firmness' by praising the inner strength of the nut:

> 'a beautiful glossy nut, which, blessed with original strength, has outlived all the storms of autumn ... My first wish for all, whom I am interested in, is that they should be firm.' (86)

Only Austen and the reader realize that Anne more truly embodies this kernel of value 'in her November of life'. On the way back from Winthrop, however, the focus of Anne's consciousness has changed. She now disregards Henrietta and Charles: 'The minutiae of the business Anne could not attempt to understand' (87), and devotes all her imaginative energy to the other relationship: 'Every thing now marked out Louisa for Captain Wentworth; nothing could be plainer' (87–8). Wentworth's earlier revelation is, nevertheless, an interesting moment. It shows us that Anne's careful observations and considerations of the events which make up the narrative are inflected with personal bias. More importantly, it tells us that the narrator is content to let this bias lie buried if it is not picked up by the reader.

If we regard Anne's perception more warily after this episode, we might be inclined to question her belief that Louisa 'put more forward' for Wentworth's notice – a detail which follows from the recognition that he 'was more engaged with Louisa than with Henrietta' (82). Likewise, although we are told that Wentworth has determined to visit Captain Harville and provides a 'description of the fine country about Lyme', Louisa is subsequently presented as 'the most eager of the eager' to arrange the visit to Lyme (92). When the party decides to take one last walk on the Cobb, we are told there was a 'general wish' to do this, but it is implied that Louisa's being 'so determined' is the decisive impetus (106). It is possible that in all these cases, we witness Anne's partiality shielding Wentworth and her jealous imaginative emphasis on Louisa's 'very resolute character' (113). After the walk to Winthrop, we see Louisa bolstered with Wentworth's commendation: we are told that 'besides the pleasure of doing as she liked', Louisa is 'now armed with the idea of merit in maintaining her own way' (92). Although Wentworth's endorsement of Louisa's 'present powers of mind' (86) in part explains the way she later 'bore down all the wishes' of other people (92), Anne shields Wentworth from the responsibility of encouraging her wilfulness.

It would, of course, be possible to go too far with this re-reading of Anne's narration. If we found ourselves questioning whether Louisa jumped down the steps on the Cobb because she was 'determined' (Anne's view), or because she felt 'armed' by Wentworth's 'idea of merit' (not recalled at this point by Anne), the moral lesson of the accident – about the dangers of persisting in headstrong behaviour – would disintegrate. What I want to suggest is that Austen does invite us to question the way in which we are 'bound' to Anne's consciousness (to use Booth's word), and that the educative 'telling' of *Persuasion* is therefore more open to question than in any other of her novels.

The narrative strategy of *Persuasion* invites the reader to enter, but also to be capable of assessing the consciousnesses of all its characters. We are supplied with information about experience, environment and the personal catastrophes which dominate their habits of mind by an authoritative omniscient (and sometimes spiteful) narrator. The verbal exchanges which are then reported directly and indirectly allow us to test characters against our inside knowledge of their persuasions. In some cases, these convictions are explicitly challenged and adjusted: 'There was nothing less for Lady Russell to do, than to admit that she had been pretty completely wrong, and to take up a new set of opinions and of hopes' (234–5).

At other times, Austen invites the reader to address his or her own cast of thought as *Persuasion* contests the master narrative which has shaped English culture. In the discussion with Captain Harville, Anne questions the extent to which male interpretations have dominated history: 'Men have had every advantage of us in telling their own story. Education has been theirs in so much higher a degree; the pen has been in their hands' (221). Harville half anticipates Anne's point against misogynistic proverbs ('you will say, these were all written by men'), and the disruption of this old way of looking at the world is dramatized beautifully when we are told that, while he was striving to listen to Anne, Wentworth's 'pen had fallen down'. It is an almost silent ceding of authority to Anne, a tribute to her revisionary 'governance' (227): 'I can hardly write', his letter admits, 'I am every instant hearing something which overpowers me' (223). In the case of the immovable characters like Sir Walter and Elizabeth, Austen moves into the present tense to tell us that 'a change is not very probable there' (235): such character types will never drop their prejudices and are unable to reflect critically on their own construction of events.

Austen has been criticized for mixing one-dimensional characters with the deeper complexities of Anne's consciousness in *Persuasion*. But it is vital that we see Anne not as a 'perfectly right' approximation to Austen's almost 'perfectly right' consciousness, but as a character who can slip into those distorting habits of mind which are exhibited by the other characters. Despite Anne's vigilance, as we have seen, her vision is sometimes a little skewed. Her misreadings are quietly passed-over, but the fact that she makes them tells us that her consciousness is not a clear window on the world, and that a purely objective vision is not possible, though it may be morally desirable.

By leaving just a few flaws and gaps in an otherwise comprehensive narration, the book can take us by surprise. *Persuasion* shows us that everyday perception involves the working of imagination in a way which is contiguous with Anne's image for the growth of opinion: 'We each begin probably with a little bias ... and upon that bias build every circumstance in favour of it which has occurred within our own circle' (221). The novel tells us that reading is a continual negotiation of these distorting perspectives even though this runs the risk of making us sceptical about Austen as a teller too. In the last pages of the story, however, Austen asks us to suspend scepticism, and to enter into a final act of persuasion. Despite the ethical hazards of holding to partial views of the world, Austen admits the attraction of irrational fancy and, in the end, Anne's creative realization of the man she loves becomes reality. We are fortunate to have both the first draft and the revised ending to the novel so we can follow the author's change of heart. The original ending of *Persuasion* forces Anne to refute the rumour that she will marry Mr Elliot when Wentworth asks her on behalf of the Crofts whether she wishes them to vacate Kellynch. In the revised ending, Austen allows imaginative conviction to shape events. Anne matches Blake's prophet when she expresses her faith in infinite potential free from any finite organical perception. Whereas men require 'an object', she says, women have the power of 'loving longest, when existence or when hope is gone' (222). Although it is against probability and some of the evidence, Captain Benwick falls in love with Louisa and Wentworth is able to see himself as a true lover:

You do believe that there is true attachment and constancy among men.
Believe it to be most fervent, most undeviating in
F.W.

Firm perswasion that a thing is so has made it so.

Chapter 6

Wuthering Heights as Bifurcated Novel

Frederick Burwick

> 'Let me beware of the fascination that lurks in Catherine Heathcliff's brilliant eyes. I should be in a curious taking if I surrendered my heart to that young person, and the daughter turned out a second edition of the mother.'
>
> —Lockwood, *Wuthering Heights*[1]

1. Tellers

When two or more witnesses give their account of an event, the story never comes out the same. The differences, as Browning fully realized in *The Ring and the Book* (1868–69), provide for powerful ironic tensions. Over and over again, in Browning's poem, the story is told of what happened on the fatal night when Count Guido Franceschini went in search of his seventeen-year-old bride Pompilia who, in the company of the handsome young priest Giuseppe Caponsacchi, had run away from his ancient villa and returned home to her parents in Rome. And in every telling there is another version of the motives and the consequences. Although Browning allows the Pope to serve as arbiter, he also effectively undermines confidence in testimony. Even Guido's final confession leaves the reader with uneasy qualms about the claims of truth and justice.

What is expected of a reader who observes that one truth-claim modifies or compromises another? Is the task to decide which version is more deserving of credence? And how is the reader to respond to an account delivered with full expectation that it will be disbelieved? As Clayton Koelb has shown in *The Incredulous Reader*, dialogical opposition can fold untruth within truth, disbelief within belief, in a virtually endless regress.[2] When Pirandello, in *It is so! (If you think so)* [*Così è (si vi pare)*] (1917), takes up the problem of competing claims to truth, he gradually pushes the claims into such extreme contradiction that if one version is true the proponent of the other is not simply mistaken, or lying, but mentally unbalanced. The claims of Signora Flora and Signor Ponza baffle the efforts of the gossips in a small Italian town, and with them Pirandello's theatre audience, to determine whether Ponza is deranged and cruelly conceals his wife (according to the tale his mother-in-law tells), or Signora Frola suffers from the delusion that her daughter is still alive, refusing to believe that Ponza has remarried (as Ponza tells the story). Signora Ponza fully understands the bond of affection and mutual dependence that has grown up between Signora Frola and Ponza as each attempts to humour the supposed delusion of the other. When she at last appears in the final scene, everyone, gossiping neighbours and audience alike, expect the truth to be revealed. Instead, they find that she humours them both, declaring herself to be both the daughter of Signora Frola and the second wife of Ponza. When the local Prefect demands that she must be 'either the one or the other' she answers that she is 'whom you believe me to be'. The two versions of the story are incompatible, yet, as the stage manager declares when the curtain falls, both are true. 'Are you satisfied?' he asks, and bursts out laughing.

The bifurcated novel and the twice-told tale not only allow for variations, contradictions and paradoxical tensions, they also thematize the very act of story-telling. Whereas other modes of narrative necessarily rely on a presumed reality outside of the novel that is mimetically reflected in the telling, the twice-told tale reflects itself. One version of the tale inevitably stands in some kind of mirror-relation to the other. The reader readily observes the differences, but may well be baffled in trying to explain whether one or both of the mirrored images is distorted. Charles Brockden Brown's *Arthur Mervyn* (1799), Mary Shelley's *Frankenstein* (1816), E. T. A. Hoffmann's *Kater Murr* (1820/21), and James Hogg's *Confessions of a Justified Sinner* (1824) are four novels of the earlier nineteenth century which develop their irony through vari-eties of structural bifurcation. All may have been available to the author of *Wuthering Heights* (1847), whose own richly experimental novel works with intricate permutations of multiple narrative, unreliable narration, and two-volume structure.

In this bifurcated narrative the social, psychological and economic manipulation of one generation, Catherine and Heathcliff, at the hands of Hindley Earnshaw, is wilfully re-enacted, by the latter, upon the offspring of all three. The story of Heathcliff's tempestuous and blighted passion for Catherine Earnshaw in the first volume of the novel is first perversely replicated in the second. In volume 1, Heathcliff's love for Catherine is deemed impossible by the Lintons and the Earnshaws, and thwarted by Catherine's perverse decision to marry Edgar Linton in order to enrich Heathcliff. In some readings this choice is 'forced' by social and patriarchal pressures. In volume 2, a second generation of characters who bear the psychological imprint of their parents, become puppets in the hands of a tormented puppeteer who manipulates their lives to revenge the frustration and blight of his own life. Heathcliff takes his revenge by forcing Catherine's daughter, Cathy Linton to marry her sickly cousin, Linton Heathcliff, son of his own marriage to Isabella Linton. At the close, however, the pattern is reversed, with the widowed Cathy choosing to marry Hindley's son, Hareton Earnshaw, and thus revert to her mother's maiden name.

Deciding who, if anyone, is morally responsible for this tragic cycle of events is made next to impossible by the novel's multiplicity of agent-narrators. The primary agents of the story – Catherine Earnshaw, Heathcliff, and Cathy Linton – not only experience and articulate their histories in quite different ways, but these histories are for much of the time mediated by an ambiguous agent-narrator, Nelly Dean, who is as much the manipulator as the reporter of events, and whose insights into the central characters of her story are clearly and demonstrably unstable. In addition to the narrative doubling involved in the shift from Lockwood's detached yet naïve narrative to Ellen

Dean's informed yet opinionated one, the reader has also to negotiate contributory narratives by the long-dead Catherine Earnshaw, in her diaries, by Heathcliff (both in his childhood and shortly before his death), by Isabella in a letter, by Cathy Linton in conversation with her nurse, and by the stout servant Zillah.

The reader of *Wuthering Heights* may at first suppose that Lockwood is to be the narrator of this novel: for three chapters, indeed, he performs this role, and this device has much to do with the novel's ultimate significance. Almost all that follows is in some sense foreshadowed in the three-chapter prelude, even though Lockwood is in no position to tell us anything of its primary events. He takes us across the threshold between foppish Southern existence and the earthier ways of the Yorkshire moors; between present and past; between waking and dream, civilized and natural. His first task is to take us from Thrushcross Grange, where he is tenant, to Wuthering Heights where his landlord lives. These are, bizarrely, the only two houses in the novel, and the contrast between them is brought out with obvious symbolic intent. For one thing, the physical setting itself defines the tensions of wealth and class. The Earnshaws' working farmhouse is on the heights, the provincial designation *wuthering* suggesting the exposure of the place to the tumult of storms. Within Wuthering Heights, from start to finish, power relations seem to be in chronic flux: neither Joseph nor Zillah appear to function as domestics, they function as quasi-autonomous power figures in their own right – and Joseph, it seems, has always done so. Lockwood's initial description of the house conveys a place of power and disconcerting spatial perspectives: innumerable dogs haunt unnumbered recesses; immense pewter dishes tower row after row; servants emerge from the depths. In what is presumably a relatively small house (it seems to be very short of bedrooms) there are unplumbed depths into which the kitchen, for instance, has 'retreated'. Thrushcross Grange is not, initially described at all, even though it is where Lockwood is living. We see it first throughout the awestruck eyes of Catherine and Heathcliff as children, and as the residence of the wealthy and elegant Lintons. Its symmetrical, high-windowed architecture, chandeliers and walled park suggest the wealth and settled culture of Augustan England, where servants know their place.

When the narrative commences, however, both properties are in the possession of Mr Heathcliff of Wuthering Heights. This Liverpool foundling, abused and insulted by both houses in his childhood, has, by way of revenge, married the daughter of one house (Isabella Linton) and acquired the properties of both. As Marxist critics properly point out, the engine of this novel of 'passion' is property, and the most telling enunciation of Heathcliff's brutal campaign of revenge is expressed entirely in such terms:

'I want the triumph of seeing *my* descendant fairly lord of their estates! My child hiring their children to till their fathers' lands for wages'. (2.6.208)

On his first visit to meet his landlord, Lockwood has a cold and curt reception. Heathcliff intervenes only with contemptuous amusement when he sees his guest beset by a pack of snarling dogs. When Lockwood declares Wuthering Heights 'a perfect misanthropist's heaven' and Heathcliff 'a capital fellow' with whom to share 'the desolation', he is not only profoundly mistaken in imagining himself and Heathcliff to be comparable beings, but is also (unwittingly) making the first Marxist joke.

On his second visit to Wuthering Heights, when a snowfall renders it impossible for Lockwood to find the paths back across the moors, the servant Zillah offers him what turns out to have been the bed shared in childhood by Heathcliff and Catherine Earnshaw some twenty-four years before. In the woodwork is scratched a series of names: 'Catherine Earnshaw, here and there varied to Catherine Heathcliff, and then again to Catherine Linton' (1.3.17), clearly the work of a young woman attempting to choose her partner and her identity. The reader cannot know it, any more than Lockwood can, but Brontë has here encrypted both plots in her two-generational novel. For this is the story, in volume 1, of a young woman called Catherine Earnshaw who spurns the name Catherine Heathcliff because it would degrade her, and destroys herself by becoming Catherine Linton. At the start of volume 2, in a nervous illness brought about by this inauthentic choice, she gives birth to a daughter called Catherine Linton. This daughter, having lost her mother at birth, is later forced to become Catherine Heathcliff, before choosing to become Catherine Earnshaw—and take her mother's place at the Grange. The first generation tale, concerned with the rebellion of the passionate and unconventional Catherine and Heathcliff, is for many readers and some critics the one that matters: it evokes an archetypal adolescence, the ultimate rebellion against the adult world. The subsequent tale, concerned with the eventual union of Cathy and Hareton, and their earned liberation from Heathcliff's scheme of revenge, may, nonetheless, hold the novelist's deeper purposes.

Before sleeping, and unable to make anything of this cryptic love-knot of names, Lockwood reads in the journal of the first Catherine Earnshaw an account of how she and Heathcliff experienced the combined tyranny of Hindley Earnshaw, Catherine's elder brother, and the grim servant Joseph, who subjected them to endless sermons. Lockwood falls asleep and dreams of being taken by Joseph to a similar sermon at the local chapel, where he defends himself stoutly when set upon by the congregation: his dreamwork compensates amply for his actual humiliation by the dogs and rescue by Zillah. So this first dream arises in a perfectly ordinary way out of elements in his experience and his reading. Next, however, he has a very different dream, not rooted in his own experience. Thinking that a branch is rattling against the window, he breaks the glass in his attempt to unhook the casement. As he reaches out, his fingers close on a small ice-cold hand, and a weeping voice begs to be let in, saying that she is Catherine Linton, and has been a waif for twenty years. 'Why did I think of *Linton*? I had read *Earnshaw* twenty times for Linton' (1.3.23). When the nocturnal presence tries to climb through the broken casement, Lockwood screams. Heathcliff enters in a state of agitation, forces open the window (which has not in reality been broken: Catherine has manifested herself only in Lockwood's dream) and begs the spirit to return from the stormy darkness. The function of Lockwood's two dreams is triple. First, they establish a link between the foppish Lockwood and the rough occupants of Wuthering Heights. In his dreams Lockwood is capable of as much aggression as Heathcliff, and more cruelty. Second, they exhibit the transfiguring effect of Wuthering Heights –

foreshadowing, for example, how the timid Isabella, in chapter 13, will, within moments of arriving in Wuthering Heights, covet Hindley Earnshaw's weapon, reflecting 'how powerful I should be, possessing such an instrument'. Her metamorphosis is anticipated in the transformation of the passive Lockwood, in his dreams, into someone capable of combatting an entire congregation, or of rubbing a child's wrist on a broken window pane. Third, they initiate the plot.

At the beginning of chapter 4, a convalescing Lockwood turns to his housekeeper Ellen (Nelly) Dean, to satisfy the curiosity Catherine's spectre has aroused, about the events of that night and the occupants of Wuthering Heights: Catherine, that is to say, has commanded Lockwood to learn her story. He will learn eventually that the figure he so unaccountably dreams, and who thus sets the story in motion, has been dead for eighteen years, and that at the time of her death she was not a child, but a married woman. In Lockwood's second dream she uses her married name, but appears as an eternally homeless child, 'waifed' by her decision to become Mrs Linton not Mrs Heathcliff. We might reasonably expect that Lockwood's first introduction to the events of the past will be from Nelly. In practice, however, Lockwood's first experience of Joseph in his prime, and of Heathcliff in his childhood, and of relations between Hindley and Catherine, comes though the medium of Catherine the Elder – who is dead. The most vivid facets of the narrative of the 1770s will be divided between Catherine (whom we read face to face) and Heathcliff (reported by Nelly). The childhood of both is thereby made, in many respects, more present to us than the present life (in 1801–2) of any of the characters. Moreover, Catherine is an agent in Lockwood's direct experience before Nelly has said a word. So the feeling of most readers that the story of Catherine and Heathcliff is somehow a transcendent one – transcending normal experience, and to do with things out of space and out of time, having reference to a metaphysical realm of ideal love – is as much the effect of the narrative structure as it is of anything the characters themselves say. It is the capacity of the 'heroine' of the book to transcend the narrative to which she belongs (that is, Nelly's reminiscences of life almost twenty years back) and feature as an agent in the narratives of 1801–2 (including of course Heathcliff's final share of the narrative at the end of the novel) that gives a sort of transcendent authority to her speech. Whereas Mr Earnshaw, Mr and Mrs Linton, Hindley, Frances, Isabella, and Linton Heathcliff cease to act as agents when they die, the testimony of the prosaic, imperceptive and unimaginative Lockwood persuades us that Catherine does not. Lockwood does not know it, and will never understand it, but his encounter with this sprite or child-woman is a major interpretive crux: does Catherine Earnshaw represent an ideal extra-social passion, the very embodiment of romantic love, or simply an inability to grow up?

The story-telling, however, is now handed over to another no less fallible narrator. Lockwood's fallibility arises from his ignorance of all social mores in this community; he is, as chapters 2 and 3 make clear to the point of comedy, wholly out of his depth. Nelly Dean's fallibility is more problematic. How reliable is she? Is she merely a reporter or is she a major agent? Should we accept her judgements or reject them because (a) she doesn't understand what's going on, or (b) she is prejudiced and moralistic? As Carl Woodring points out ('The narrators of *Wuthering Heights*', 1957), she keeps secrets, tells tales, intercepts letters, tries to encourages Heathcliff to run away, and indeed gives him the idea he might be master of Wuthering Heights. In chapter 5 she can be seen as instigating the growing childhood rivalries she narrates. In chapter 9 she could short-circuit the entire plot by warning Cathy that Heathcliff has overheard her remark that marriage to Heathcliff would be degrading (though the reader might have mixed feelings about such an outcome). In chapter 10 she engineers the confrontation between Edgar Linton and Heathcliff which she deplores, and which is, in some degree responsible for the subsequent illness of Catherine. In volume 2, having allowed the relationship between Cathy and Linton Heathcliff to develop, contrary to Edgar Linton's wishes, she reflects on her own complicity, 'passing harsh judgment on my many derelictions of duty; from which, it struck me then, all the misfortunes of all my employers sprang. ... I thought Heathcliff himself less guilty than I' (2.13.277).

When Nelly lies, meddles or manipulates, she usually tells us when she is doing so. In one sense this openness and self-criticism (Nelly is almost the only character in the novel able to contemplate that she might be in error) encourages the reader to believe Nelly's narrative, but the knowledge that she lies must affect our reading of her moral judgements. At the same time we encounter deeper problems still: one is that as a *reflecting moral agent,* breaking her own strict codes, Nelly is more guilty than Heathcliff as an *impulsive natural force*. Another is that Nelly, though closer to events, may understand her story as little as Lockwood does. Indeed it is not at all clear that anyone in this novel understands anyone else. The multiplicity of expert opinion and testimony within the novel places the reader in the position of saying 'yes, but' to almost every judgement offered on the conduct of Catherine and Heathcliff by Nelly, Edgar, Isabella, Zillah. At times, indeed, the novel invites its readers to become advocates for behaviour (that of Catherine and Heathcliff) which probably almost everything in our socialized psyche (or superego) would normally reject almost as emphatically as Nelly does. Nelly may be properly read as embodying moral averageness rather than villainy, but that very averageness pushes us towards endorsement of the morally 'reprobate'.

2. Tellings

In *Wuthering Heights*, major events concerning both of the central characters in the first generation are open to radically different readings. In chapter 11 a violent confrontation occurs between Edgar Linton, whom the romantic heroine Catherine Earnshaw has married, and Heathcliff, whom (in the eyes of virtually all readers) she ought to have married. According to Nelly's narrative the confrontation comes about because Catherine has locked her delicate husband in a kitchen with Heathcliff, hurled abuse at him, and expressed the desire that Heathcliff 'may flog you sick for daring to think an evil thought of me' (1.11.115). Yet Nelly has herself prompted Edgar to surprise Catherine and Heathcliff, and a disastrous fight is only narrowly averted by another of Nelly's lies. When she is later called to attend Catherine, who 'did not know my share in the disturbance', Nelly confesses that 'I was anxious to keep her in ignorance' (1.11.116). In Catherine's account, however, the confrontation is partly Isabella's fault, for falling in love with Heathcliff, and partly Edgar's for being abusive, complaining, mean and jealous. Up to now, Catherine explains to Nelly, Edgar

> 'has been discreet in dreading to provoke me; you must represent the peril of quitting that policy, and remind him of my passionate temper, verging, when kindled, on frenzy—I wish you could dismiss that apathy out of your countenance, and look rather more anxious about me!'
> The stolidity with which I received these instructions was, no doubt, rather exasperating, for they were delivered in perfect sincerity; but I believed a person who could plan the turning of her fits of passion to account, beforehand, might by exerting her will, manage to control herself tolerably even while under their influence. (1.11.117)

Nelly's recognition of Catherine's 'perfect sincerity', and of the exasperation she herself might be causing the heroine, is striking. By everyday standards, Nelly's judgement that wives should not expose their husbands to ridicule and violence is understandable; so is is her view that Catherine's whole mode of existence is self-serving and manipulative. Equally, however, the novel suggests that Nelly is ill equipped to understand Catherine's ideals, her illness, her temperament, her passion – or indeed the author's poetry.

The most romantic declaration in the novel, in chapter 9, passes over Nelly's head: "What were the use of my creation if I were entirely contained here?" asks Catherine.

> 'My great miseries in this world have been Heathcliff's miseries [...] my great thought in living is himself. If all else perished, and *he* remained, I should still continue to be; and if all else remained, and he were annihilated, the Universe would turn to a mighty stranger. I should not seem a part of it. My love for Linton is the like the foliage in the woods. Time will change it, I'm well aware, as winter changes the trees—my love for Heathcliff resembles the eternal rocks beneath—a source of little visible delight, but necessary. Nelly, I am Heathcliff!'

Alert readers may wonder whether Catherine's capacity to imagine the annihilation of Heathcliff, or of the world, *but not of herself,* suggests an egoism that is simultaneously titanic and infantile, or titanically infantile. And her incapacity to imagine how her proposed marriage to Linton will affect Heathcliff (or, as Nelly points out, to see that Linton might not take kindly to her plans to use his wealth for Heathcliff's benefit) is terrifying. Yet Nelly's response to the passionate speech just quoted disables her as a reader of the symbolic texture of the novel: she claims that she cannot 'make any sense of your nonsense, Miss' except that Catherine is either 'ignorant of the duties you undertake in marrying' or simply 'a wicked unprincipled girl' (1.9.82).

It is crucial to the novel's ironies that Nelly (as here) sometimes has the opacity of character, in this case the opacity of a character who has just lied telling another off for being unprincipled, and sometimes (when the author takes charge) the translucence of a lens. When Catherine lies dying in volume 2, chapter 1, Nelly's own narrative describes how the sound of the beck comes soothingly on the ear, 'a sweet substitute for the yet absent murmur of the summer foliage, which drowned that music about the Grange when the trees were in leaf' (2.1.156–7). Edgar Linton, while watching over her tenderly in chapter 13, has brought her crocuses, which remind her of the melting snows upon the heights. With surprising disinterestedness, he wishes that she were still on those heights where the air might revive her. Such imagery underlines the fact that Catherine's famous declaration in chapter 9 was couched in the symbolic language of the novel and Nelly's dismissal of it as nonsense is therefore fundamentally disabling: her moral discourse, and the author's symbolic discourse have nothing in common. Moreover, in chapter 12 Nelly has kept the news of Catherine's 'illness' from Edgar. Refusing, as she sees it, to be the instrument of Catherine's moral blackmail, Nelly fails to recognize the *reality* that Catherine – a being of air and fire, of an altogether more nervous constitution than herself – really *is* what she has threatened to be; she is seriously ill.

Thanks to the retrospective compression of the narrative, these scenes, in which Catherine asks Nelly's advice on marriage (1.9), Nelly brings Edgar and Heathcliff into confrontation (1.11), and Cathy is nursed by Linton (1.13), and lies dying (2.1), are telescoped into a few chapters. Between these events, in chapter 13, Isabella, who has eloped with Heathcliff (this relationship being the cause of the confrontation in chapter 11), writes an astonishing letter to Nelly in which she queries whether the culture of the Heights has anything to do with 'the common sympathies of human nature'. Having lived just four miles from Wuthering Heights all her life she cannot understand a word spoken by the 'ruffianly child' Hareton Earnshaw, or 'recognise any sentiment which those around share with me' (1.13.136). Four chapters later Isabella runs the four miles from the Heights to the Grange and gives Nelly a circumstantial account of the atmosphere at the Heights in the week following Catherine's death. Hindley has decided to murder Heathcliff (who has become the real master of Wuthering Heights) and stands sentinel with his fearsome weapon, a combination of gun and sprung blade. In Isabella's sensational four-page narrative (2.3.174–8), Heathcliff attempts entry through the window, having found the door locked against him, then tears Hindley's knife from him, ripping open the owner's wrist, smashes the division between two windows, and leaps in. He then kicks and tramples upon Hindley, dashing his head repeatedly against the flagstones, drags his lifeless body to the settle, binds his wound, has a lengthy argument with Joseph who wants to call in a magistrate, and finally departs for bed.

Not until volume 2, chapter 15, nearing the close of the novel, is this night revisited. By now, the young Cathy has grown up, and has been taken captive by Heathcliff, who acquires her father's property by forcing her into marriage with his own ailing son, Linton Heathcliff. Edgar Linton has just died, with his daughter at his side (to be at his deathbed Cathy has to escape from Wuthering Heights through the window of her mother's childhood room). Despite his recent cruelty to Cathy, Heathcliff is moved enough in this chapter to tell Nelly what Edgar's burial has meant to him. While Edgar's grave was being dug he opened Catherine's coffin to gaze upon her face (embalmed by eighteen years under the peat, as the attentive reader of Lockwood's second dream will know). Heathcliff reminisces about the day Catherine was first buried; and how he tried to open the coffin at that time but was prevented by a sigh, and the sense of Catherine's warm breath at his ear. In his narrative of the night Isabella describes so sensationally,

> 'Having reached the Heights I rushed eagerly to the door. It was fastened; and, I remember, that accursed Earnshaw and my wife opposed my entrance. I remember stopping to kick the breath out of him, and then hurrying upstairs, to my room, and hers—I looked around impatiently—I felt her by me—I could *almost* see her, and yet I *could not!*' (2.15.290)

Heathcliff's brief narrative replaces Isabella's Gothic narrative of the titanic contest between Hindley and Heathcliff by a narrative of romantic desire in which Isabella, Hindley, Joseph, weapons, windows, bleeding, and battering, barely feature as details: they are entirely removed from the centre of Heathcliff's reality. It also reveals for the first time the meaning of Heathcliff's behaviour in volume 1, chapter 3, when he bursts into the room where Lockwood has just screamed aloud in his dream, tears open the window and calls to Catherine 'Come in! come in! [. . .] Oh! My heart's darling, hear me *this* time—Catherine, at last!' (1.3.27). We understand, for the first time perhaps, that Lockwood in chapter 3 has appropriated unconsciously (quite literally unconsciously) a moment Heathcliff has awaited for sixteen embittered years. So chapters 3 and 15 of volume 2 offer not the usual narratorial variants upon events, in which it may make sense to ask of two accounts which is true, but two entirely different events. They may occupy the same space and chronological moment, but they belong to two different genres and orders of experience. Indeed they have so little in common that Isabella's opening question in her letter to Nelly – 'How did you contrive to preserve the common sympathies of human nature when you resided here?' – now seems to be based on a wholly false premise: that there are such things as 'the common sympathies of human nature'.

Heathcliff's belated narrative of his experience of Catherine's burial not only rewrites Isabella's gothic narrative and helps to explain Lockwood's equally gothic dream, but also underwrites in a wholly new key Heathcliff's blistering contempt, in chapter 14, for all that Nelly, on behalf of the Victorian reader, holds dear. In the final chapter of volume 1, Nelly makes her way to the Heights, depressed by Edgar Linton's coldness towards his newly eloped sister, and finds herself making surprising judgements. She is impressed by Heathcliff as a 'a born and bred gentleman' and disgusted by Isabella who has already degenerated into a thorough little 'slattern'. Brontë, while manipulating Nelly, so manipulates the reader into sharing Heathcliff's contempt for his new wife and her cold-blooded brother, that Heathcliff's declarations carry the endorsement of the narrator and of the novel. Heathcliff, for purposes of revenge, has already dispossessed Hindley, demonized Hareton, and reduced Isabella to 'a slattern'. Yet he now speaks of his love for Catherine in language that sounds 'the moral' of the novel. He describes Catherine's life at the Grange as one of 'frightful isolation' in which she feels 'in hell among you'. If we believe him (and most readers do) it is largely because Catherine herself told in chapter 9 how she dreamt of being thrown out of heaven and rejoicing to find herself back on the moors. Moreover, Heathcliff's passion, now that his words come to us without being mediated by Isabella or Nelly, seems shot through with a Blakean depth. His dismissal of Linton's tenderness towards Catherine as 'that insipid paltry creature attending her from *duty* and *humanity!* From *pity* and *charity!*' (1.14.153) reminds of Blake's assault on precisely these pallid virtues in *Songs of Experience* and *The Marriage of Heaven and Hell*. His speech not only persuades Nelly to arrange a love tryst for him with her master's wife – a clear transgression of her own master code – but seems to carry the author's stamp of approval.

The resulting tryst, which is in romantic terms the climax of the novel, opens the second volume. The long-awaited love scene between Heathcliff and Catherine, as narrated by a mesmerized Nelly, is – in symbolic terms – a *liebestod*, a union of sexual encounter and death: which (again symbolically) proves fructifying. Catherine's love throes and death throes are also, effectively, birth throes, in which there is born the *revised* heroine who will eventually, unlike her mother, and despite a more elegant upbringing, consent to give herself to a man with whom – one might think – marriage really would 'degrade her'. Cathy's progress, paradoxically, is that she can take the step the mother feared to take. She may appear the weaker of the two, being Edgar's child as well as Catherine's, but is arguably, in this sense, the stronger, as an alloy may be stronger than either of its constituent parts. It is the sort of trope Tennyson might have employed. Lockwood, whose dream in chapter 3 invites one to consider the reality status of the first Catherine (child? woman? child-woman? sprite?), invites one in the closing words of volume 1, to consider the meaning of her daughter. What if Cathy is indeed 'a second edition' of her mother?

3. Readings

The bibliographical trope invites one to compare Cathy's childhood character – her attitude to her father, the way she experiences his death, her truancies and her ways of escaping imprisonment, her snobbish rejection of Hareton, her manipulation of Nelly, her relations with her menfolk, her dreams and her aspirations, her explorations of nature, even (in a prominent and repeated strain of imagery) her knowledge of birds – with that of her mother. One might instance the contrast between Catherine's barren landscape imagery in chapter 9, and that in the young Cathy's account of her quarrel with Linton Heathcliff, with its 'larks, throstles, and blackbirds, and linnets, and cuckoos pouring out music on every side', its 'swells of long grass undulating in waves' and 'the whole world awake and wild with joy' (2.10.248). Catherine's landscape is bare; Cathy's is animated. One is death-oriented, the other full of vitality. One might see this as borrowing Mary Shelley's contrast between the ice-fields of Chamonix, to which the Shelleyan Victor Frankenstein is drawn, and the fertile banks of the Rhine which the Wordsworthian Henri Clerval prefers. A similar and often noted motif is the link between Cathy's recognition of live bird song and her mother's sorting out the feathers of dead ones in chapter 12. Throughout volume 2, Brontë engages in second-generation replays of first-generation situations and tropes, as if to emphasize genetic continuities and evolutionary difference.

Such biological progression is implicit in the question: what kind of 'second edition' is Cathy? Lockwood, as usual, is missing the point: his delusion that it would be 'romantic' for Cathy to espouse himself is one of the novel's genuinely comic moments. But he does pose the critical question that most divides those critics who have seriously attended to it. When Emily Brontë invites the reader to transfer one's interest from Catherine to Cathy (an invitation many readers simply refuse) are we invited to perceive the 'second edition' as a revised, improved and corrected, or simply expurgated version of her mother? In short does the bifurcation embody a myth of evolution or of diminution? Was Q. D. Leavis right to see the second Cathy as having overcome inherited destructive tendencies? Or is Patsy Stoneman right to see the first Catherine as representing Shelleyan free love, an ethic of care and 'a generous pragmatism', an ideal to which neither Edgar Linton nor Heathcliff is capable of responding?

Making a choice between the two Catherines, in terms of which heroine represents the author's ethical imperatives, ought to be a simple matter, answerable by painstaking character analysis of the two heroines. In *Wuthering Heights*, however, it is complicated by a further generic question: is this novel an exercise in social realism in which all characters are equally 'real'? Or does the generally perceived difference in status of the characters – the mythological status of Catherine and Heathcliff as against the everydayness of Cathy and Hareton – hint at a different kind of structure altogether, one in which the first volume deploys the archetypes which in some sense inhabit all of us? To see the novel as inviting us to 'choose' may be missing the point, as we do if we attempt to choose between Blake's 'clod' and his 'pebble'. Also, since in our reading experience Cathy does not entirely replace Catherine (partly because we meet Cathy first and Catherine last), we perhaps need to ask what is implied by the spectral presence of Catherine the Elder throughout a novel in which she is dead for *most* of the plot time, and *all* of the narrative time? There is, after all, a metaphysical dimension to this novel, or as we may prefer to see it, a psychological one. Catherine's insistence that 'there is, or should be, an existence of yours beyond you' (1.9.82), and Nelly's question to Lockwood – 'Do you believe such people *are* happy in the other world, sir?'(2.2.165) – and the haunting at the close of the narrative may, taken together, constitute a reading instruction of at least equivalent power to the 'second edition' one. It is Nelly who reports on hauntings; but it is Brontë who entwines the names of Hareton and Heathcliff in the novel's closing image.

Read simply for its Catherine-Heathcliff plot – the cinema plot – *Wuthering Heights* is already capable of generating numerous interpretations, or seizing upon the reader's imagination in innumerable ways. It is, in the popular imagination, a romantic novel about a love affair transcending the opposition of family and society, and proving (if one reads to the end) that love is stronger than death. Centred on Catherine, it may be seen as a feminist novel about a heroine who is destroyed by the marriage choice forced upon her by a patriarchal society; or as the story of a young woman who fails to rise to the liberating challenge of her Romantic lover and destroys herself by making a more conventional marriage choice; or (from a more Marxist perspective) the tale of a young woman who marries for class despite sympathizing with her proletarian lover; or, more sceptically, as a psychological study of a young woman who fails to grow up. Readings centred on Heathcliff may find a story of how the harmony between two houses is disrupted by the introduction of an alien element, the demonic Heathcliff, and restored only when he dies; or a sociologically realistic story of a young orphan whose behaviour is warped into cruelty and control by cruelty and rejection; or a revenge novel about an outcast who acquires all the property of the two houses who have despised him. Taking account of its narrative technique, and the role of Lockwood and Nelly in mediating a narrative of passions they cannot comprehend, it also becomes a sceptical novel about the inadequacy of moral codes to render the complexity of human experience.

All of these multiple and by no means mutually exclusive readings are available to the reader who attends almost wholly to volume 1, and views volume 2 merely as an appendage. Yet the novel is also, clearly, a saga: it treats the intensification and resolution of conflicts between two ancestral houses, over a period of three decades. Recognizing that the bifurcated structure, with its insistent patterning, challenges us to arrive at a reading that does equal justice to parents and children, might help us to choose between these readings: instead, it moves each of them onto a different plane, leaving the choice as difficult as it was before. In the twentieth century, several divergent readings have been offered, which take account of the novel's bifurcation. Brontë's two-volume structure has been read almost equally persuasively, for instance, as mythologizing the conflict and eventual uniting of class interests (Terry Eagleton); as a bildungsroman, treating the working out of inherited and educational defects (Q. D. Leavis); and as depicting Cathy's pitiful accommodation to a male world after her mother's spirited rebellion (Gilbert and Gubar).

The twentieth-century critical history of the novel is worth a fuller encapsulation: no English novel has fructified so diversely for modern readers, and one reason for this is the challenge represented by its different bifurcations. Lord David Cecil, in *Early Victorian Novelists* (1934), noted that the entire novel is divided between just two houses and two families, no other location being depicted: there is on the one hand, Wuthering Heights, home to the Earnshaws, the 'children of storm'; and on the other hand, Thrushcross Grange, home of 'the children of calm, the gentle, passive timid Lintons'.[3] Together they compose 'a cosmic harmony'. The novel concerns the disruption and re-establishment of this harmony. Cecil's reading involved a detailed argument about how Heathcliff, though also 'a child of storm', is extraneous and therefore disruptive, creating conflict between father and son; how Catherine dislocates the order further by an unnatural marriage with Linton, a child of calm; and how this betrayal turns Heathcliff into a destructive force. He is not naturally destructive, but 'a natural force which has been frustrated of its natural outlet' (138). He uses his son Linton, a child of hate, to make Cathy his daughter-in-law. Hareton and Catherine, however, are children of love and so combine the positive qualities of their respective parents (kindness and constancy, strength and courage) whereas Linton Heathcliff combines the weakness and cruelty of his parents. Eventually, the death of the 'double negative', Linton Heathcliff, allows Hareton and Catherine's affinity to assert itself. Heathcliff, unable to sustain antagonism towards these two, ceases to be destructive and is reunited to Catherine. Thrushcross Grange becomes home to Hareton and Cathy; Wuthering Heights remains haunted by Heathcliff and Catherine. Cosmic harmony is re-established. Miriam Allott in 'The Rejection of Heathcliff' (1958) points out that the symmetry is not in fact as David Cecil says. The second generation does not re-establish the opening situation but modifies it profoundly – the conflicting elements are eliminated or synthesized. The novel asks: what kind of storm and what kind of calm are acceptable? At the end 'Earnshaw energy is modified by Linton calm. Heathcliff obsessions are excluded'.[4] She notes also the social symbolism of the migration: one culture displaces another. Nevertheless, 'there is', Allott rightly concludes, 'no escape for Emily from her emotional commitment to Heathcliff: there can only be an intellectual judgement that for the purposes of ordinary life he will not do' (205).

In *Myths of Power: A Marxist Study of the Brontës* (1975) Eagleton points out that the Brontës lived through some of the fiercest class struggles in English society. He sees the characters both as symbolic entities and as triumphs of ambiguity – we are never allowed to be sure whether Catherine is 'tragic heroine or spoilt brat', Heathcliff 'hero or demon', Nelly 'shrewd or stupid'.[5] Crucially, however, Catherine's tragic choice is a social one: she makes it on class grounds. She turns away from a natural relationship – outside family, society and class – which offers a different model of human possibilities and which would be subversive of society. Eagleton's reading capitalizes on earlier Marxist readings by Arnold Kettle and David Wilson. Kettle argued that Catherine and Heathcliff are moral rebels against social oppression. Together they stand for something finer than either the Grange or the Heights: Heathcliff is made inhuman by his degradation – but his inhumanity is precipitated by those who wield power, his dehumanization is a matter of his abandoning the humanity he represents and adopting the standards of the oppressor class. What redeems him at the end is the recognition of the human values he has denied in himself, as they re-emerge in Cathy and Hareton.[6] David Wilson, too, saw the book as one on which Emily Brontë symbolized in Catherine and Heathcliff the sympathy of the liberal intelligentsia for the working men of the hungry forties – as a sort of symbolist *Mary Barton*.[7] Eagleton's fine reading simply develops these points. Heathcliff shows how freedom is deformed by oppression, and 'he changes from being natural in the sense of an anarchic outsider figure, to adopting the behaviour natural to an insider in a viciously competitive society' (Eagleton, 110). So, in Eagleton's memorable encapsulation: 'Subjectively he is a Heights figure opposing the Grange. Objectively he is a Grange figure undermining the Heights [...] His rise to power symbolises at once the triumph of the oppressed over capitalism and the triumph of capitalism over the oppressed' (112). More broadly, in Eagleton's analysis, Wuthering Heights embodies a yeoman culture, Thrushcross Grange that of the gentry or bourgeoisie, and the novel shows how the future lies with a fusion. In this respect, the reading is in accord with Miriam Allott's.

In feminist readings, there is a tendency to see Catherine Earnshaw as a heroine before her time, or as victim of patriarchal power. Given that she seems as assertive and as wilful as anyone else in the novel this may seem not easily tenable, yet when Nelly describes the attraction of Edgar Linton to Catherine, she uses a very odd metaphor (Nelly is not always attentive to the author's metaphors). Linton she says, had as much power to leave Catherine 'as a cat possesses the power to leave a mouse half killed or a bird half eaten' (1.8.72). Given Nelly's concern to project Catherine as imperious, temperamental and just plain vicious, we might expect her to see Linton as the mouse: the metaphor, as Gilbert and Gubar have argued, draws attention to the fact that in a patriarchal structure, Linton, however, weak, has all the weapons: like the patriarchal bulldog which wounds Catherine, he is the one red in tooth and claw, simply as a man.[8] In her introduction to the current World's Classics edition, Patsy Stoneman presents the novel as a sort of rewrite of Shelley's 'Epipsychidion', in which Brontë promotes an ethic of free love, but explores whether Shelley's desire for a harem of sexually liberated young women is capable of gender reversion.[9] Catherine, in this reading, is a female Shelley, destroyed because her men are incapable of sharing her; they are driven to combative behaviour by the masculinist values their society endorses. She is, Stoneman claims, 'a generous pragmatist, making the best of her situation' (xxxvi), whereas her men are characterized by the desire for possession. She represents 'an ethic of care', whereas Edgar maintains the language of ownership, and Heathcliff the language of revenge. 'Only if we also adopt one of these positions can we quarrel with Catherine's assertion [concerning the confrontation in chapter 11] "that I am in no way blameable in this matter"' (xxxvii). How well the notion of Catherine as either caring or a pragmatist is supported by chapters 8 and 11 is perhaps debatable. Of greater concern, however, is that what Stoneman seems to be introducing is a one-volume novel. The argument does not address in any degree what is signified by the replacement of one Catherine by another: unless it implies that what is signified is defeat.

Three major readings, however, have addressed the generational issue. Inga-Stina Ewbank (in *Their Proper Sphere*, 1966) sees the novel centred upon the union of Cathy and Hareton – and (like Miriam Allott) upon what is excluded and what is retained from the original combustible elements at the start. She calls attention to the frequency with which the past flashes back upon consciousness. In chapter 11, Nelly momentarily sees Hareton as if he were her own playmate, Hindley, twenty years before. In chapter 33, Heathcliff is about to assault the young Cathy when 'of a sudden his fingers relaxed … [he] gazed intently in her face' stilled by her eyes. The novel specializes in scenes which repeat the same scenarios in different contexts. Catherine lies dead with Edgar asleep beside her; Heathcliff dreams of himself and Catherine cheek by cheek in the grave. Edgar Linton lies dead with the young Cathy sitting beside him; and a few weeks later the same Cathy sits beside the dead Linton Heathcliff, but with very different emotions.[10] The organization of the book, in two locations and two volumes, allows for almost every passage from one house to the other to involve 'an echo or an anticipation or both' of another such passage. So Ewbank sees the novel based (structurally and thematically) upon 'the principle of repetition with difference' (332–3). Q. D. Leavis, moralizing this approach in *Lectures in America* (1969), reads the whole novel as a realistic exploration of a daughter learning to avoid her mother's mistakes. Cathy, the two-volume structure implies, is the focus of the book, and undergoes the painful process of unlearning the values of false gentility she has picked up at Thrushcross Grange.

Heather Glen (in her extensive commentary in the Routledge edition [1988]) is especially responsive to the generational structure of the novel. The narrative is concerned not with the trajectory of a single life (as is *Jane Eyre*) but with the replacement of one generation by the next; with pregnancy and death, seasonal decay and renewal. Appropriately, Catherine makes her great declaration to Nelly while both are nursing the child Hareton who will marry the next Cathy. Almost every death in the novel, however perfunctorily treated, is associated with either a birth or with a contrastive vitality. The novel, in this most insightful of modern appreciations,

> portrays human beings as frail separate creatures who will decay and die. Their powerful urge to feel that their existence has a meaning beyond this, that they are in some way at home in the universe, is doomed ... to collide with these facts. Yet the intimations of continuing life in the final paragraph [i.e. the famous echoes of human names in the heath and harebells of EB's last sentence] point not merely to the unmeaning renewals of nature, but towards a significance in the novel's shaping which counters the bleakness of tragic finality in a far more suggestive way. And thus those intense irrational illusions expressed in Catherine's declaration of love appear less as simple 'folly' than as 'necessary' and familiar: not as mere illusions, but also as vital illusions, informing and creating a distinctively human world.[11]

The passion of Catherine and Heathcliff, several readings agree, is larger than life, but unliveable. That of Cathy and Hareton is less dramatic – and may never seize readers in the same way – but it grows and changes through time, accommodating itself to reality. Nevertheless, the second generation is striving to bring to life, as it were, what is life-enhancing in the unreal and demonic energies represented undiluted in Catherine and in Heathcliff (and, of course not at all in Lockwood except when he is asleep, and then only in perverse and destructive form). One could perhaps summarize what the novel has said to generations of readers in the closing lines of Philip Larkin's 'An Arundel Tomb' – they 'prove / Our almost instinct almost true: / What will survive of us is love'.

4. Interrogations

Given that one major concern of the Victorian age is with progress, another with holding on to allegedly common values, and a third is with evolution, the three most striking aspects of this novel's technique may suggest that its author designed its experimental form precisely to probe such concerns. One inescapable aspect of the novel is that the action takes place in two clearly symbolic domains, which speak different languages, and obey utterly different social codes: in the passage from one house to the other three hundred years of cultural differentiation seem to be annulled; the past may be as close as the house next door. Another is that in passing from one narrator to another we experience equally 'vertiginous displacing of one reality by another' (the phrase is Heather Glen's, 355), rendering moral codes and commonplaces null and void. The third is its two-volume, three-generation structure, with its clear reading instruction at the end of volume one, inviting one to consider the second Catherine as 'a second edition' of her mother, a structure which can be read both as progress and as regress. This particular facet of the novel seems designed to combine the idea of natural progress – the Romantic sense of organic evolution epitomised in the speculations of Erasmus Darwin – with a deep scepticism about whether humanity can in fact evolve, or whether its animal roots are of its essence. After all, every character in the book is illuminated by a range of animal and elemental metaphors: the novel's analogical matrix – drawn from landscape, weather, flora and fauna – is simultaneously late Romantic and proto-naturalist, as befits a text contemporaneous with scientific embryology, and with the researches of Charles Darwin and of Gregor Mendel.

The entire novel, in this sense, may be properly regarded as a sceptical sibling of *In Memoriam*. *Wuthering Heights* seems designed to destabilize Victorian ideas of 'progress', by asking – indeed showing – what is lost in the kind of refining social 'progress' England has had. Just three years later, in his own evolution-pondering work, Tennyson urged his compatriots to 'ring out the old, ring in the new', and to 'let the ape and tiger die'. Brontë was perhaps the greater ecologist: can we really, Brontë and Blake both asked, do without tigers? Heathcliff, after all, is a Brontëan warning to an age in which not merely Linton, but Lockwood, is coming to represent the norm. That, presumably, is why Brontë chose Lockwood as her narrator. Such a narrative strategy may allude to Mary Shelley's in as much as Nelly's narrative is addressed to Lockwood, just as Frankenstein's tale is addressed to Walton. Both novels share with a third iconic Romantic tale – that of Coleridge's Ancient Mariner to his chosen Wedding Guest – the implication that the primary narratee stands in need of what the teller has to tell. Lockwoods's massively repressed and refined condition is, perhaps, what the novel addresses, much as Frankenstein addresses Richard Walton's scientific tunnel-vision, and the Mariner addresses the Wedding Guest's brusque deficiencies; but nothing as simple as scientific over-reaching, or a crime against the one life, occupies the centre of Brontë's novel.

The opening sentence of the novel, '1801—', betokens a preoccupation with cultural time, as well as an authorial identification with a cultural time other than her own. Lockwood returns to the Heights in September 1802 to hear the close of the story. The frame narrative of this bifurcated tale of revenge unfolds during the year 1801–2; the telling of this tale of Romantic love is therefore contemporaneous with such high Romantic narratives as 'The Ancient Mariner' and that notoriously elusive drama of sexual politics, *Christabel*. The novel's determining events, however, have to do with Heathcliff's rebellion against coercive social codes, and these events, from the time of old Mr Earnshaw's adoption of Heathcliff, to Heathcliff's death, span the last three decades of the eighteenth century. Since Heathcliff, in many readings, embodies rebellion, it may be pertinent to note that his disruptive arrival at Wuthering Heights (from Liverpool, the Victorian gateway to America) coincides with the first tremors of American Independence, while the closing courtship of Cathy and Hareton – at the time of Lockwood's second visit to the North – coincides with the peace of Amiens, an interlude in the Napoleonic Wars. (Was Byron really Heathcliff's father, as critics have suggested, or was it perhaps the Corsican general?). Throughout this epoch, England was engaged, as Wordsworth put it in *The Convention of Cintra*, in two successive wars against liberty.

On the second page of the novel, poised on the threshold of the nineteenth century, the narrator pauses also on a literal threshold:

> I paused to admire a quantity of grotesque carving lavished over the front, and especially about the principal door, above which, among a wilderness of crumbling griffins and shameless little boys, I detected the date '1500' and the name 'Hareton Earnshaw.'

A delayed function of this passage is to set up the irony of the scene in which Cathy and Linton Heathcliff enjoy the dispossessed Hareton Earnshaw's inability to read this text (2.7.220); the more immediate effect, however, is to evoke a further threshold, that between the 'dark ages' and the Renaissance. The date '1500' seems designed to evoke a watershed in English cultural history, in this case a moment at which virtually nothing pertaining to modern culture had yet happened. True, the Tudor dynasty had been established by the battle of Bosworth field just fifteen years before Wuthering Heights was built, but by 1500 neither perpendicular architecture, nor the English sonnet, nor Hillyard's miniatures, nor any trace of English Renaissance or Reformation or (perhaps more pertinently) imperial enterprise or a coercive modern state, yet existed. The Grange, on the other hand, embodies the values of the enlightenment at its most refined, most controlled and controlling, and most attenuated. Moving from one house to the other across four miles of moorland you bypass three hundred years of refinement and stratification, and enter a region where (among other cultural signposts) standard English gives way to uncompromising dialect. Because of this symbolic freight, passage from one house to another is always, in this novel, associated with difficulty – the kind of difficulty Lockwood experiences so instructively in its opening scenes. At the close of the novel, in a migration allegorical of cultural change, Wuthering Heights is to be left to Joseph and its ghosts. The Grange, Brontë admits with some reluctance, represents the future (the reluctance is shown in the fact that while the final narrative pages linger at the Heights, the Grange itself is shut up); but its vitality, the novel implies by way of compensation, will be drawn from the rude Earnshaw endowment, quintessentialized in the union of Cathy and Hareton, and looking out watchfully from both in Catherine Earnshaw's eyes (2.19.322). The novel's abiding concerns – a concern generative of its telling bifurcations between narrators, between houses, and between generations – is a sceptical interrogation of such dominant Victorian narratives as the idea of 'progress'.

Chapter 7

Negotiating *Mary Barton*

Richard Gravil

> Slaves, toil no more! Why delve, and moil, and pine,
> To glut the tyrant-forgers of your chain? ....
> Shout, as one man, — 'Toil we no more renew,
> Until the Many cease their slavery to the Few!'
> —Thomas Cooper, 'The Purgatory of Suicides', 1845

> Such gentlemen as Feargus O'Connor,...together with the terrific population of Manchester, require a sort of check in awe.... The present excellent military arrangements under the surveillance of Colonel Wemyss,...will frustrate any mad anti-peaceful idea the Chartists may be urged to embrace.
> —*A Few Days at Manchester*; by 'Whitewood', 1839

> Capital, ... is but an instrument in the hands of certain classes, by virtue of which, these classes contrive to appropriate to themselves the real capital of the country at the expense of those who produce it. The nominal capitalist is ... a purloiner of real capital. He is a self-licensed plunderer.
> —*Poor Man's Guardian*, 1835

> The higher classes, not being obliged to labour for a maintenance, have abundance of leisure time, which they employ in learning, and thus form a class of educated people whose faculties are more developed, and who understand better than the labouring classes, how to promote the welfare of mankind.
> —Jane Marcet, *Rich and Poor*, 1851

> We're their slaves as long as we can work; we pile up their fortunes with the sweat of our brows, and yet we are to live as separate as if we were in two worlds; ay, as separate as Dives and Lazarus, with a great gulf betwixt us...
> —John Barton, *Mary Barton*, 1848

The polarization of rich and poor, these epigraphs suggest, was at its maximum when Elizabeth Gaskell set out to depict the abyss of present misery in which the poor consoled themselves with thoughts of that future gulf between Dives and Lazarus. Her solution involved the creation of a dual narrative voice capable of addressing a deeply polarized audience, but at the cost of a highly unstable text, as famously exemplified in chapter 3. Here Gaskell gives a vivid and persuasive sketch of the process of capital accumulation, showing how the poor weaver sees 'his employer removing from house to house, each one grander than the last', while the weaver and his fellows struggle to feed their children, yet immediately enters the now infamous caveat: 'I know that this is not really the case ... I know what is the truth in such matters'.[1] In this textual crux, what requires negotiation, however, is less whether Gaskell is right to undermine her hero's views, than whether the first 'I' and the second 'I' are the same, and whether either is Elizabeth Gaskell.

Coral Lansbury made the point very clearly as long ago as 1975:

> Nothing could be more unwise than to regard the authorial 'I' of the novels as the voice of Elizabeth Gaskell, particularly in the Manchester novels. There the narrator has a tendency to engage in false pleading and specious argument, while the workers demonstrate honesty and commonsense.[2]

Despite this assertion, well supported in the argument of Lansbury's chapter, and despite the authority of no less a work than Wayne Booth's *The Rhetoric of Fiction* as regards the ineluctable nature of implied and undramatized narrators, Gaskell has regularly been adjudged guilty on two counts: her 'middle-class' limitations, and failures in narrative sophistication.[3] It is commonly supposed (especially by those critics who perceive the realist novel as part of the hegemonic armoury of the bourgeois state) that Elizabeth Gaskell is culpable for preferring brotherhood to blood-letting. She is blamed for failing to explain the crisis of capitalism, or to articulate a legislative programme pre-empting a century or so of Liberal and Labour administrations. Yet if, indeed, novelists are 'conditioned' by their societies, and act as enforcers of bourgeois norms, it is surprising how little space has been devoted to discovering what, if anything, Elizabeth Gaskell's milieu might have conditioned her to believe.

Elizabeth Gaskell belonged doubly (by birth and by marriage) to a dissenting culture, which by the 1840s was politically riven. Unitarianism originated in the Presbyterians of the English revolution, produced such proto-Chartist texts as John Cartwright's manifesto *Take Your Choice!* (1777), and nurtured such indicative figures of the Romantic age as Joseph Priestley and William Hazlitt. (Gaskell herself is rumoured to have attended school with two grand-daughters of Joseph Priestley, returned from America in infancy.)[4] John Chapple points out that one of her uncles drew up Bolton's petition against the American War, and that her father, William Stevenson, in a work of 1796, quoted approvingly from Tom Paine's then very recent *The Age of Reason*. Stevenson became one of the earliest contributors to *The Edinburgh Review* (along with Brougham, Sydney Smith, Sir James Mackintosh), wrote on 'The Political Economist' for *Blackwood's* in the 1820s, and was later a co-contributor to the *Westminster* with John Stuart Mill. James Kay-Shuttleworth, whose *Moral and Physical Condition of the Working Classes Employed in the Cotton Manufacture in Manchester* (1832) appeared in the year of Elizabeth Gaskell's marriage, and depicted the condition of Manchester as distinctly alarming, was a colleague of Samuel Gaskell, her brother-in-law.[5] Other somewhat conservative works of the 1830s, of obvious interest to the Gaskell household, include Harriet Martineau's popular *Illustrations of Political Economy* (1834), and Dr Peter Gaskell's *The Manufacturing Population of England*, 1833 (a source for Friedrich Engels's more famous study of *The Condition of the Working Class in England*, 1844). In 1830, Manchester hosted the meeting of the British and Foreign Unitarian Association, which demanded the establishment of Domestic Missions, and William Gaskell was on the committee to which the 'missionaries', John Ashworth, George Buckland and John Layhe (who began their work just about the time Elizabeth Stevenson became Mrs Gaskell), submitted their reports. Those reports fed directly, Monica Correa Fryckstedt has shown, into the most harrowing passages of *Mary Barton*.[6] When the newly married couple published their first literary collaboration, 'Sketches Among the Poor', 1837, they did so in *Blackwood's*, where her father had developed his critique of political economy in the previous decade.[7]

In short, whatever her political condition when she arrived in Manchester, by the time she wrote *Mary Barton* in 1848 Gaskell stood in little need of being educated about the region by either of its celebrated visitors – Friedrich Engels or Charles Dickens. Moreover, there is probably much diplomacy, some disingenuousness and not a little irony, in her famous remark in the novel's Preface, 'I know nothing of Political Economy; or the theories of trade. I have tried to write truthfully'. Both Adam Smith's *An Inquiry into the Nature and Causes of the Wealth of Nations* (1776) and David Ricardo's *On the Principles of Political Economy and Taxation* (1810), promulgated a labour theory of value as well as a vigorous defence of capital from legislative interference. But the tendency of such conservative primers as Jane Marcet's popular *Conversations on Political Economy* (1816) was to remember only the latter. 'Political Economy', as taught by Marcet and by Harriet Martineau, held that no interference or combination could help the workers because the laws of political economy were fixed and immutable. One could argue that William Stevenson's critique of this position, in 1824–25, though polite and theoretical, takes much the same position as did John Stuart Mill in the radical Unitarian *Monthly Repository* in 1833 and 1834. Mill wrote scathingly about the complacent supposition that wealth went with 'sagacity, ingenuity, and economy', and was 'meted out proportionally to the worthiest', and appealed for 'more rational' modes of distribution than individual competition (*Monthly Repository*, 7 [1833] 576). He lambasted such 'story books and nursery tales' as Martineau's for enunciating narrow notions 'with as little qualification as if they were universal and absolute truths' (*Monthly Repository* 8 [1834] 319).

So the Unitarianism to which Mrs Gaskell belonged was a broad enough church to encompass both establishment and subversive readings of 'political economy'. On the one hand, there were wealthy factory owners, and fully paid-up propagandists for their view of economics, such as Harriet Martineau; on the other, W. J. Fox of *The Monthly Repository*, and the Howitts of *Howitt's Journal* and *The Peoples's Journal*, whose predilections were for some form of co-operative socialism. Martineau and Fox might meet as Unitarians and feminists, but not in their ideas on capitalism. Somewhere along this spectrum sat the Gaskells. They had family and/or social connections to Martineau and Marcet; yet William Gaskell was present when Fox made his impassioned address to the Manchester meeting which established the Domestic Missions, and Elizabeth

Gaskell, personally closer to the Howitts, published in *Howitt's Journal*.[8] The signals are mixed. Her environment licensed considerable latitude. What use did she make of that licence?

This essay seeks to clarify the issues surrounding the problematic narrative voice in Gaskell's most famous, and flawed, industrial novel. I will look, later, at some celebrated cases of narrative intrusion, in chapters 3, 6 and 8, relating these to their narrative frame, assuming, with Coral Lansbury, that while one function of the intrusions is to keep the implied middle-class reader on board, despite continuous assaults on 'his' views, another is a purposive alienation of the reader from middle-class apologetics. From its framing idylls to its organizing central metaphor of class murder (a specifically Chartist metaphor), the first half of the novel *can* be read as an ongoing republican critique, fully aligned with radical Unitarianism, of the sufferings of a Saxon proletariat at the hands of an alien ruling class. But such a reading is constantly troubled by the introduction's representation of the author, and the novel's representation of the narrator.

The author's disavowal of any position on 'Political Economy' renders problematic the authorial construction of a narrator who claims, in chapter 3, to know 'what is the truth' about capital accumulation, while declining to tell us that truth. In chapter 15 this same voice tells us that John Barton became 'a chartist, a communist', as if the two were synonymous, and belatedly reveals the 'truth' of capitalism: it was clearly in the masters' interest 'to buy cotton as cheaply, and to beat down wages as low as possible'. 'In the long run', this voice assures us, 'the interests of the workmen would have thereby benefited. Distrust each other as they may, the employers and the employed must rise or fall together. There may be some difference as to chronology, none as to fact' (15.170, 171). This truculent tone is hard to take, especially from the daughter of William Stevenson, who argued against identifying the interests of employers with the nation's, or from the author who has given us ample reason to know that clemming workers may not have much stake in 'the long run'.

Rapid transition from persuasive reportage to unpersuasive and transparently prejudiced generalization is a characteristic of the novel, and since the intrusive narrative voice is, itself, radically unstable, negotiating *Mary Barton* is considerably more difficult than weighing up the competing perspectives of such dramatized narrators as are found in *Wuthering Heights*. In *Wuthering Heights*, a far more sophisticated narrative, we recognize certain signals as designed to alienate the reader from Nelly Dean's or Lockwood's judgements, but we may fail to read similar signals as similarly intentioned in *Mary Barton*, partly because of uncertainty over the status of the narrative voice. Is this a single voice, albeit as divided between rebellion and conformity as Catherine Earnshaw's? Or should we posit two somewhat polarized narrative voices? Using Wayne Booth's terms one might hear an 'implied author' who at times criticises Barton for being insufficiently alienated and an 'undramatized narrator' who finds him excessively so.[9] One of these distrusts 'political economy' as class-based; the other trusts its abstractions. One, when there is something to be seen (such as the death of Mrs Barton), merges with her characters to see through their eyes and feel through their fingers; the other pontificates, asks rhetorical questions, and, behaving like an univited guest, stages moralistic tableaux (like the death of John Barton). Both, confusingly, use the first person singular; the first less often. Neither, perhaps, 'is' Mrs Gaskell: in Blakean terms, one is her 'emanation', a wholly sympathetic imagination; the other is her distancing 'spectre', or superego. When 'Gaskell' says, in chapter 15, 'so much for generalities. Let us return to individuals' (173), one voice dismisses the other.

Contemporaries

It would help if there were any firm grounds for believing, with Macdonald Daly, that *Mary Barton* is a militantly antisocialist piece of fiction in which Elizabeth Gaskell's mission is 'to persuade her readers to steer clear of the siren voices of socialism and atheism; [and] to resign themselves to the capitalist order which the former threatens' (xxvii); or for preferring Coral Lansbury's view that it promotes 'Gaskellian socialism' (213). But beyond her abhorrence of 'combinations' as destructive of individual conscience (symbolized in Barton's acting as a tool when he commits murder), we know little of Elizabeth's Gaskell's politics, other than by association. We do know what her contemporaries, whose antennae may – after all – be more sensitive than ours, made of *Mary Barton*. It is clear what Charles Kingsley, for instance, thought of the novel's ideological tendencies. If people want to understand why people become Chartists and Communists, says Kingsley, in a much-quoted passage, let them read *Mary Barton*:

> Do they want to know why poor men, kind and sympathising as women to each other, learn to hate law and order, Queen, Lords and Commons, country-party, and corn-law leaguer, all alike – to hate the rich, in short? Then let them read *Mary Barton*. Do they want to know what can madden brave, honest, industrious North-country hearts, into self-imposed suicidal strikes, into conspiracy, vitriol throwing, and midnight murder? Then let them read *Mary Barton*. Do they want to know what drives men to gin and opium, that they may drink and forget their sorrow, though it be in madness? Let them read *Mary Barton*.... If they want to know why men learn to hate the Church and the Gospel, why they turn sceptics, Atheists, blasphemers, and cry out in the blackness of despair and doubt, 'Let us curse God and die', let them read *Mary Barton*. God knows it is a book, Christian and righteous as it is, to try one's faith in God to the uttermost; to tempt one to believe that this world is ... nothing but a huge pitiless machine, with the devil and misrule, tyranny and humbug, the only lords thereof ... [10]

Extreme though this response might seem, it derives legitimately from the novel's own acidic articulation of working-class scepticism: 'The indigence and sufferings of the operatives induced a suspicion in the minds of many of them, that their legislators, their magistrates, their employers, and even the ministers of religion, were, in general, their oppressors and enemies; and were in league for their prostration and enthralment'.[11]

Kingsley's own *Alton Locke*, incidentally, was reviewed by David Masson in the *North British Review*, as conducting the reader 'to one point – the pronunciation of the terrible phrase "Organisation of Labour"; and the contemplation of a possible exodus at no very distant period out of the Egypt of our present system of competition and Laissez-faire, into a comparative Canaan of some kind of Co-operative Socialism.'[12] This judgement, even if correct, does not apply thereby to *Mary Barton*, but Maria Edgeworth also found that the novel was so despairing about the present system that it conducted her to thoughts of revolution: 'The fault of this book is that it leaves such a melancholy I almost feel hopeless impression.... It is in fact difficult to say – for we cannot make a new division and equal distribution of wealth without *revolution* and even if we could do this without injustice to the present possessors, of what permanent avail cd it be?'[13] Phenomenologically, then, two alert readers found *Mary Barton* a revolutionary text; conducive to thoughts of revolution.

Others found it wanting in correctness. Reviews by people wedded to mainstream 'political economy' were quick to point out the author's shortcomings. W. R. Greg, in the *Edinburgh,* complained that the novel slighted the masters and their 'unresting diligence, their unflagging energy, their resolute and street economy' (cited, Gill 25). James Martineau's *Prospective Review* complained that a reader unacquainted with Manchester would receive 'an erroneous idea of the amount of benevolence ever in operation there' and argued that although 'Barton's early improvidence and that of his parents are clearly admitted.... It ought also to have been more distinctly noticed, that it was the possession of those very qualities of foresight and thought wanting in himself, which caused the disparities of wealth and comfort that he viewed with such alienation and hate.'[14] In the *Westminster Review*, William Ellis and Mary Turner Ellis took the narrator to task for saying this of Barton: 'he spent all he got, with the confidence (you may also call it improvidence) of one who was willing, and believed himself able, to supply all his wants by his own exertions'. They are *pained* by such equivocation:

> We have made this painful extract, for the purpose of noting why the spending of all that an individual earns, however *confidently* he does so, not only *may* but *must* be called improvidence; and that sufferings such as described above, can have no abatement, unless provision be made continuously, and especially in times of extra wages, for the alternations and casualties that life is subject to[15]

Pouncing on Gaskell's prefatory admission, 'I know nothing of Political Economy' the Ellises comment: 'She is evidently labouring under the mistaken notion that there is something very difficult, dark and mysterious in political economy' (40). (Her father had suggested that its real principles were darker and more mysterious than those who preached it realised.) A future John Barton, the *Westminster* hopes, will know that it is his social duty to save money: 'If I do not perform this duty, misery is my inevitable lot. If my neighbours neglect it equally with myself, general misery must be the consequence.... My duty to myself commands me to acquire, by saving, a capital for myself – a duty which every well informed and well conducted labourer can perform' (60–61).

Such lessons, which constitute the whole agenda of Martineau's and Marcet's propaganda fiction, play no part in *Mary Barton*. Whether or not Gaskell shared her father's scepticism, she distances her novel from such simplifications. In *Rich and Poor*, Marcet set out to persuade her readers of the proposition, very palatable to the masters, that 'Inequality of Wealth [is] better for both parties, their interests being the same'. Her schoolmaster teaches that 'Since capital is the purse which pays the wages of the labouring classes, it is highly beneficial to them that this purse should be large and well filled'. The pupil grasps that 'the rich can never injure the poor, for they must become poor themselves before they can do the poor any harm'.[16] Harriet Martineau, who later lambasted Dickens's *Household Words* for publishing Henry Morley's powerful attacks on the masters for mincing people up in their machines, devoted the nine volumes of her *Illustrations of Political Economy* (1832–34) to proving the identical proposition that 'The interests of the two classes of producers, labourers and capitalists, are therefore the same; the prosperity of both depending upon the accumulation of CAPITAL'. Whether in the spread of woollen or cotton manufactures, or any other instance of the introduction of machinery, 'the interests of masters and men are identical'.[17] Eventually, Martineau's liberalism allows, when the free market has led to a perfect state of society, working men of talent (the Jem Wilsons and Job Leghs, perhaps) will rise to 'an influential rank' (143) but there is no other way. In the meantime, the lessons of 'political economy', as Noel Thompson summarizes the matter, were that the working classes were poor because they bred faster than capital did; that they should disperse to places and occupations where labour was needed; and that moral education might help them to breed later and less prolifically.[18] The only trace in *Mary Barton* of this ubiquitous truism of 'political economy' is Wilson's fond exclamation, 'twins is a great trial to a poor man, bless em' (1:13), in which no reader is likely to find an endorsement of Martineau's moralism.

The reviewers were surely right: what is striking about *Mary Barton* is the way it ignores the capitalist presuppositions of classical political economy. Too much can be made of eloquent absences, but the absence from *Mary Barton* of the moral agenda of 'political economy' (except in occasional and conspicuously inept interventions by an undramatized narrator, who may well be modelled on Martineau), seems to me of remarkable eloquence in a text of 1848. *Mary Barton* does not tell us that the poor breed too much, that their sufferings are their own fault, or that they need to be kept in check by the military: only a policeman's 'livery' in the deftly thematic opening chapter reminds of how alien middle-class 'law and order' might be (1.11). There is a further and even more eloquent absence. John Seed's informative essay, 'Unitarianism, political economy and the antinomies of liberal culture in Manchester, 1830–50' explores the contrast between liberal ideology and working-class realities in Manchester in the 1830s and 1840s. Organised networks of voluntary visitors (not all as inept as Dickens's Mrs Pardiggle, but undoubtedly in his mind) undertook to improve the working class on a huge scale.[19] Joseph Adshead's *Distress in Manchester* (1842) estimated that some 30,000 families were being visited by what Seed calls 'the agents of virtue'. The investigations of the Domestic Missions may well have been motivated by a sense that vice was at the root of suffering and ought to be exterminated, but as Seed argues, by the mid 1840s it became clear to the reports' authors that poverty struck the frugal and industrious, as well as the improvident, and that whatever the committee might wish to believe, something other than vice caused such widespread destitution.[20] Given that *Mary Barton* is minutely informed by the reports of Ashworth, Buckland and Layhe it is all the more significant that, by excluding from its frame even a trace of those middle-class 'agents of virtue' – unless we construe the narrator herself in that guise – the novel portrays virtue as indigenous to the backstreets, and as vigorously fighting its own battles with destitution and disease. The poor may be victims, but they are also their own agents of virtue, and capable of making their own contribution to social evolution.

In this respect *Mary Barton* seems less patronising than even such radical Unitarians as W. J. Fox. When Fox spoke in Salford, in 1830, at a dinner attended by William Gaskell, he compared 'the lower classes (as they are called)' to new geological formations:

> Like the strata which have been forming in the bottom of the ocean, the waves of wealth and of rank have rolled over them for ages; but the principle knowledge in them, like the central fire of which the geologists tell us, will heave them up to the surface (loud cheers), and when this redeemed land appears, we claim our portion to build thereon the temple of truth, and to sow it with the seeds of righteousness and joy (great applause).[21]

In the following year this same charismatic speaker – he became the principal orator of the Anti-Corn Law League – preached a sermon on 'The Claims of the Poor on the Followers of Christ'. Depicting the wretchedness 'imposed' on the poor by society, he asks 'must these things be ... Are we only to hope, and to wait ... to *do* nothing?'

> The arrangements of society may surely be so modified, as that, though comparative poverty may remain, yet its pestiferous atmosphere shall, in a great degree, be purified. Such hopes are not now the mere day-dreams which they were when Sir Thomas More wrote his utopia. They are rapidly advancing towards that solid and practical consistency which every intelligent and benevolent man should endeavour to assist them to attain. Wallace's 'Prospects of Mankind', the Social Contract of Rousseau, the speculations of Godwin, the wild agrarianism of Spence, the paternal school of Pestalozzi, the prophecies of the Millenarians, the co-operative sytem of Owen, and, far above all in distinctness and rationality, the social anticipations of St. Simon, are so many manifestations of a spirit labouring with a mass of incumbent difficulties.[22]

To Fox, these visionaries merely adumbrate the Saint-Simonian forms which society will assume when 'under the full influence of Christian principles'. He concludes, 'I urge upon you the claims, the moral claims, of your injured, wretched and degraded brethren; and, as the followers of Christ, demand of you in the name of Christ, JUSTICE FOR THE POOR' (6). There is, he points out, 'an antagonist power to the miseries of poverty', implanted in the 'sympathies of humanity', and it is a Christian duty (as the Domestic Mission reports in Manchester also argued) to cherish those sympathies, which are 'guardians within us of our brethren's rights'.[23] When (as Daly and others complain)

Mrs Gaskell looks to Christian brotherhood for a solution, she may or may not have envisaged it taking Saint-Simonian forms, but she took it on herself in *Mary Barton* to articulate those 'antagonist' sympathies, and allowed those sympathies to suggest whatever 'social anticipations' they might. Moreover, in allowing for the people to generate their own wisdom, however much she might wish to see it better guided, she frees Fox's geological metaphor from his somewhat disabling desire to impose his own truth on the new 'land' emerging from the abyss.

Narrative strategies

The central strategy of *Mary Barton* is to subject the reader to what students of *Star Trek* would recognize as a Vulcan mind-meld with John Barton, a chartist, trade unionist and class warrior. The death of Mrs Barton, almost as soon as she has been established as a central character, evokes the novel's most sustained piece of psychological realism in its treatment of John Barton's grief: these two pages, without parallel in early Victorian fiction, establish an affective bond which seems *designed* to carry the reader through numerous subsequent expositions of John Barton's opinions. Yes, his daughter is wheeled in later on, as a safer receptacle for the reader's identification (safe except for her forwardness and self-reliance), but this transference takes place only when her father has carried out the act for which Gaskell's own 'antagonist sympathy' has so amply prepared. The point that this is a murder by proxy is strongly implied in a generally disregarded comment in Raymond Williams's brief but classic reading: 'Mrs Gaskell planned the murder herself, and chose, for the murderer, "my hero, *the* person with whom all my sympathies went".'[24] The case for seeing this novel as one in which actual murder and social neglect are symbolically equated is simply stated. In 1842, Thomas Cooper the Chartist was famous for, and imprisoned for, rhetoric in which he compared the neglect of employers to wilful murder. Reflecting on the effectiveness of his oratory in prison, Cooper frightened even himself.[25] The presence of this equation in Barton's motivation seems so transparent, that the onus is on those who argue that Mrs Gaskell declines to dramatize it to explain what they think she is doing when she allows us to experience vicarious grief, vicarious anger, vicarious murder and vicarious repentance. Friedrich Engels did not originate the equation; nor does his endorsement of it preclude Gaskell's doing so. We know that Barton's child and Davenport and the Wilson twins are killed by ideology and neglect, and every page of chapter 6 is designed to make us feel very, very angry about that fact.

Gaskell's first chapter reflects on contemporary debate (epitomized in the writings of Southey and Macaulay) between nostalgia for the past, in the form of a half-timbered farmhouse, and recognition of the progressive elements of the present, in the greater intelligence observable in the urban countenance. This prelude not only portrays the cottage garden as having once been 'the only druggists's shop in reach' (thus introducing the Alice Barton theme of a dying rural culture: her symbolic death will span fifteen chapters), but reflects on its 'republican and indiscriminate order'. A moment later the narrator wonders whether the workers relaxing in Green Heys Fields might have been 'granted' a holiday, or whether it might have been 'seized in right of Nature'. These quiet republican grace-notes reflect the continuity in political discourse from the days of Cartwright and Paine to those of the Chartists: a continuity signalled most powerfully in the footnotes which stud her pages. *Mary Barton* makes numerous points about the culture of Manchester's workers (its charity, its decency, its pride, its grasp of science and labour relations) but one of the most powerful is the constant points of reference to its language. To True Whig sympathizers with America in 1776, the Jacobins of the 1789, the orators at Peterloo, and the Chartists of the 1830s, Britain's Saxon freedoms had been sold out to William's imposed aristocracy and never recovered. What Gaskell's Mancunian workers speak, she repeatedly insists, most conspicuously when presenting the clemming family in chapter 6, is the well of English undefiled, a language of Anglo-Saxon roots, preserved in the vernacular classics – a language to which the ruling class has grown alien. The angrier the author gets, the more footnotes appear: Chaucer, Wycliffe, Spenser and Mandeville share and amplify Wilson's shock at Mrs Davenport's reduced condition in chapter 6.

Yet in chapter 3, according to Eagleton and Pierce, 'Mrs Gaskell explains working-class opinion and then dissociates herself from it'. Citing her 'I know this is not truly the case', they argue 'she unites with her reader against her character'.[26] Such misconstruction will not do. The passage in question, after its persuasive depiction of how capital accumulates while the poor suffer, runs:

> I know that this is not really the case, and I know what is the truth in such matters: but what I wish to impress is what the workman feels and thinks. True that with childlike improvidence good times will often dissipate his grumbling, and make him forget all prudence and foresight.
> But there are earnest men among these people, men who have endured wrongs without complaining, but without ever forgetting or forgiving those whom (they believe) have caused all this woe.

Isn't something rather elusive going on in this passage? Parentheses in the novel, as here, signal Mrs Gaskell's unease: often, they draw attention to a process of negotiation, as in '(you may call it improvidence)' two paragraphs later, which invites us not to, and therefore enters that reservation about liberal ideology which the *Westminster* found so suspect. The paragraph break, rupturing what would otherwise read as a 'true ... but' construction, makes the passage especially hard to negotiate. Surely, if 'improvidence' means forgetfulness of prudence and foresight, the force of that 'But' is to imply that there is another kind of improvidence. Some may be improvident in this subversive sense, but those like John Barton do not forget so easily the wrongs they have suffered, or who has caused them. Perhaps, an under-voice in the text appears to suggest, only the improvident forgive and forget so easily.

Such testing of the term 'improvidence' is characteristic. The strategy of this novel, repeatedly, is to establish a point of maximum identification with John Barton before broaching an issue which we are invited to rethink. The tale, we might say, is subjecting the implied reader's ideology to considerable stress. Barton's dumb grief for Mary leads directly into a flashback, recollecting his rage with Mrs Hunter's conspicuous consumption, at the time of his son's death. Both griefs command assent for his views, later in the same chapter, of domestic service as a species of tyranny: when the reader is invited to judge whether there was any truth 'in his strong exaggerated feelings' it is entirely clear what judgement we are expected to reach. Similarly, when Mary's barbarous apprenticeship terms are itemized at the end of this same chapter the ironic force of 'and Mary was satisfied' is unmistakeable (3. 26, 27). In Chapter 5 we may feel, momentarily, that John Barton's response to the fire in Carson's mill is cynical: being 'well insured', he growls, 'they'll not thank them as tries to put it out'. Jem's heroism contrasts pointedly, we may feel permitted to believe, with this sourness. But chapter 6 opens by corroborating Barton's judgement at some length. The Carsons are glad to be relieved of 'the weekly drain of wages given for labour'. They have leisure to enjoy themselves. Of course, she says again, there is another side to the picture. This 'other side' is not, however, some marginal downside for the employers, but the deep and terrible gloom endured by the workers.

Chapter 6 exemplifies Gaskell's cutting technique and its purpose. From the Carson's pleasant excursions we cut to the Davenport cellar and John Barton's glorious deed (pointedly compared to Sir Philip Sidney's). From Wilson's nursing of Mrs Davenport we pass to the Carson's breakfast preparations. Renoir's cuts in *La Grande Illusion* are not more savage. The purpose is to frame Barton in the most enabling manner possible (he is after all '*the* person with whom all my sympathies went') when he enunciates his version of the labour theory of value:

> You'll say, (at least many a one does) that they'n getten capital an' we'n getten none. I say, our labour's our capital, and we ought to draw interest on that. They get interest on their capital somehow a' this time, while ourn is lying idle, else how could they all live as they do? (6.66)

To Wilson's designedly feeble objection that the masters suffer too, he replies 'Han they ever seen a child o' their'n die for want of food?'

Robert Owen's place in Manchester sympathies was such that whatever Gaskell knew about 'political economy' she would know about him, and as Trygve Tholfsen points out in *Working Class Radicalism in Victorian England*, Owen's labour theory of value was 'a sort of ideological truncheon' for the working-class movement. 'With one heavy blow it could demolish the moral and economic pretensions of the propertied classes. Owen stated the first of his premises with the starkness of an axiom in geometry: "Manual labour, properly directed, is the source of all wealth, and of national prosperity".'[27] Gaskell is not likely to have agreed with Thomas Hodgskin that capital has 'no just claim to any share of the labourer's produce, and that what it actually receives is the cause of the poverty of the labourer',[28] but what Mrs Gaskell thought is beside the point. This novel eschews argument: it works not through the Martineau method of using parables to endorse propositions in 'political economy' but by dramatic sequencing which ensure that Barton's is its dominant voice.

Suppose we start reading chapter 8 on the reasonable assumption that Gaskell is unsympathetic to Barton's Chartism. We might anticipate at some point that the narrator will overtly dissociate herself from his opinions. We are told that he is reading Feargus O'Connor's notorious *Northern Star*, but the narrator does nothing to challenge his views about the connection between long hours and industrial accidents. Instead, we move into a summarizing passage on working-class distress, almost directly transcribed from the Domestic Mission reports. As Monica Fryckstedt's transcriptions show, all that Gaskell has done in enumerating 'the sufferings and privations' of the poor at this date is to ensure that the authentic documentary details are not muffled by official language: John Layhe's 'sustenance and warmth' become 'food or fuel', for instance, but his data are unchanged (8.85). This contextualization in documented sufferings introduces the novel's merge with history, John Bartons's engagement with the Chartist petition of 1839, and his pride in being chosen as a delegate.

The closest thing to an overt negation of Barton's and the Chartists' ideas is a vague reference to those who 'spoke and acted with ferocious precipitation' (after a paragraph explaining through minute particulars how they have been driven to do so). But the only precipitation *shown* is an act of faith. The Chartists, says the narrator, in a curiously angled passage, 'could not believe that the Government knew of their misery':

> they rather chose to think it possible that men could voluntarily assume the office of legislators for a nation who were ignorant of its real state; as who should make domestic rules for the pretty behaviour of children without caring to know that those children had been kept for days without food. Besides, the starving multitudes had heard, that the very existence of their distress had been denied in Parliament; and though they felt this very strange and inexplicable, yet the idea that their misery had still to be revealed in all its depths, and that then some remedy would be found, soothed their aching hearts, and kept down their rising fury. (8.85–6)

It isn't Gaskell's writing at its best, or as clear as it might be, which is perhaps just as well for the novel's reception. The reference to 'children' links the novel's perspective with Mill's insistence that 'the poor have come out of leading-strings, and cannot any longer be governed or treated like children. To their own qualities must now be commended the care of their destiny' and whatever advice is offered must be 'tendered to them as equals, and accepted by them with their eyes open'.[29] Once noted, the irony in the passage is both savage and doubly directed. Chartism was at fault, one of Mrs Gaskell's dissonant voices is saying, for its naive faith in the integrity of Parliament. Even Barton is implicitly criticized for his willingness to trust a paternalist system. At the end of a superbly compacted scene in which he receives his neighbours' advice on what to tell 'the parliament men' (the dialogue here is written with nothing less than love), he replies: 'when they hear o' all this plague, pestilence and famine, they'll surely do something wiser for us than we can guess at now'. Such faith in one's betters, a jaundiced narrator seems to imply, can lead only to disillusion.

Other 'condition of England' novels, Disraeli's *Sybil* (1845) and Charlotte Bronte's *Shirley* (1849) reserve the central action for middle-class persons. Gaskell's novel gives a uniquely working-class perspective on such middle-class figures as appear. Mr

Carson is indifferent or vengeful, until humbled by suffering; his arrogant son plans to ruin Mary Barton; the women of the household, unreal and ineffectual, corroborate Barton's sneer at a typical 'do-nothing lady, worrying shopmen all morning, and screeching at her pianny all afternoon, and going to bed without having done a good turn to any of God's creatures but herself' (1.10). In chapter 15, in a much discussed passage, the narrator's tactical confusion about who is the creature and who the creator in *Frankenstein*, credits the middle class with authorship of working class ignorance and violence. Contrariwise, it speaks of Barton as 'actuated by no selfish motives; ... his class, his order was what he stood by, not the rights of his own paltry self' (15.170). Moreover, the novel comes very close to condoning the murder. In chapter 16, Carson and his fellow masters, waiting for Barton and his fellow unionists to present their demands, are compared to 'the Roman Senators who awaited the irruption of Brennus and his Gauls' (16.182): not for the first time, the masters are compared to an alien occupying power. Harry Carson, junior, as cynical about workers as he is about their daughters, invites his own death by cruelly cartooning the raggedness of the workers' spokesmen. Leading up to John Barton's fatal action, the narrator tells us of his distress at the injuries of 'a knobstick' (16.189), and his compassion for a child (17.198). After the murder the focus is not on Mr Carson's grief but on his desire for vengeance, and the narrator's sharp judgement on his morality – 'Oh! Orestes, you would have made a very tolerable Christian of the nineteenth century' (18.213) – may call for, but does not elicit, any similar judgement upon Barton.

But after the murder, as everybody knows, John Barton disappears; the heart goes out of the novel; and the novel slips (almost) out of the canon. In short, being no Dostoevsky, Mrs Gaskell changes genre. The insoluble conundrum of labour/capital relations gives way to an easier one: how Mary is to exculpate her lover without implicating her father. The very look of the pages in chapter 22 shows how sober realism gives way to staccato romance and never really returns: 'The paper! "O father!"' (243) occupies a paragraph, as does 'It struck two; deep, mirk, night' (245). The change of genre does most damage in the dire handling of the death of John Barton. In chapter 3, while three long paragraphs explore John Barton's numbness and grief, the narrative voice is silent. In chapter 35, Mary – the one character with a right to focalize this scene – is supplanted entirely by a fussily intrusive narrator, a sort of benign Mrs Pardiggle, whose interjections break up the page into a collage of forced gestures, phoney dialogue and trite comment. It is all (but as writing, rather than as death scene) intensely sad. Mrs Gaskell never again allowed what she called 'London thought coming through the publisher' to lobotomize her novel at mid-point.

Politically, as well as generically, we seem to be in a different novel. Up to this point in the novel the articulated judgements of the undramatized narrator tend to be riddled with contradictions, or undermined by the imaginative truths of the implied author: paradoxically, the novel itself ceases to make sense when it ceases to be dialogic. After the murder, the voices coalesce; radical dissonance gives way to a commercially guided liberalism. A half-hearted attempt is made to resolve the novel's primary theme in chapter 37, the first scene in which a spokesman for the working class meets a spokesman for the masters without standing cap in hand. We might wish that someone other than Job Legh were chosen to explain Barton's way of thinking to Mr Carson at this point; even Stephen Blackpool, confronting Josiah Bounderby in *Hard Times*, makes a much better fist of it. Job Legh's primary role has been to symbolize the path of self-improvement and worker's self-education (again, significantly, without any suggestion of such processes depending on middle class agents). But the novel's final phrase, and reading instruction – '"Dear Job Legh!" said Mary, softly and seriously' – seems to endorse not only this authentic role, but also his caricature of Barton's more radical views, views which neither Jem nor Mary has ever grasped.

The emigration of Mary and Jem also leaves us ambiguously positioned. To abandon England is to condemn a class-ridden system which seems beyond cure; to go to Canada rather than the United States seems to draw back from embracing republican solutions. In fact the portrayal of Jem as inventor and emigrant comes surprisingly close to endorsing two of Harriet Martineau's three solutions for the condition of the working class. Martineau's didactic novella, *A Manchester Strike*, preaches, inter alia, that reduced wages involve no real hardship, as in time they must lead to lower prices. It concludes that 'the conditions of labourers may best be improved by three means'. These are: 'By inventions and discoveries which create capital'; 'By husbanding instead of wasting capital: for instance by making savings instead of supporting strikes; and BY ADJUSTING THE PROPORTION OF POPULATION TO CAPITAL'.[30] This last point combines two of Martineau's favourite themes: if only the workers could be induced to breed later and less, or to emigrate, the grand desideratum of adjusting the proportion of capital to labour could be achieved. Gaskell, in adopting emigration, chooses the least offensive of these two propositions, but also the one that opens the prospect of building a new society in a new world. Given her own extensive American associations, and the political traffic between Manchester and Boston (Manchester's Domestic Missions were inspired by a Boston philanthropist, and Emerson lectured in Manchester), the choice of Canada rather than the United States is a little odd. Did Gaskell feel that a republican gesture would be one challenge too many for the liberal reader? In any case, the motif is already sufficiently barbed: it symbolizes the costly haemorrhage of talent to the new world. Benjamin Franklin, Richard Price, John Cartwright and even Adam Smith had all seen America as the future. In 1780 Thomas Pownall prophesied that unless 'a Cherub with a flaming sword' could be stationed in mid-Atlantic, there would be 'an almost general emigration to that New World', and that 'the most useful enterprising Spirits, and much of the active property will go there also.'[31] After Waterloo, and Peterloo, this prophecy seemed to be materializing quite alarmingly and the wave of emigration – intrinsically a levelling process – provoked acrimonious argument in the British press. One sub-text of *Mary Barton* is the debate about the cultural meaning of this latest exodus; did England, or its class system, have a future at all?

Chapter 8

Nell, Alice and Lizzie: Three Sisters amidst the Grotesque

Alan Shelston

Victorian fiction, the dominant literary form of its period, retains its popularity for the modern reader, whether in the academy or the living room. For university courses it is packaged in annotated single-volume texts; it is transmitted into the home in televised adaptations that to a greater or lesser degree capture the spirit, if not the substance, of their originals. But rarely do we receive Victorian novels as their first readers received them. Those bulky paperbacks that intimidate even the most assiduous students do little justice to the processes of serialization and instalment that allowed the original readers to engage with the narrative over an extended period of time; their covers, designed by the marketing men, reflect a huge culture shift from either the paper covers designed for the original numbers of Thackeray or Dickens, or the often beautifully gilded and embossed bindings of Victorian volumes. And while we are aware of the contribution made by the illustrators to Victorian fiction their work is rarely produced with the quality of the originals, or with regard to the importance of its placement within the text. All of these features were important matters for the Victorian publishing industry: for them, as for us, fiction was a cultural product in a very competitive market-place. But they were also part of the total reading experience, and that is something that we tend to neglect. In this essay I shall examine three well-known Victorian fictional texts, trying to keep in mind that original reading experience. In particular I want to consider the conjunction of illustration and text as it reflects one of the more potent cultural motifs of the period, the inter-relationship of femininity and menace. I begin with the most famous projection of all of this theme, Little Nell in *The Old Curiosity Shop*, since I believe it to have set a pattern which can be traced through English fiction at least until the end of her creator's career, and to some extent beyond it.

Amongst Dickens's novels *The Old Curiosity Shop* probably remains one of the least read today. It has perhaps never recovered from Oscar Wilde's famous dismissal to the effect that 'no-one without a heart of stone could read it without bursting into immediate laughter', an observation that has helped many a lecturer in search of signs of life in the audience, but which has done little for the reputation of Dickens's novel.

It is worth remembering that Wilde could respond in that way precisely because the book had been such a success for previous readers. His joke is a direct echo of a comment by the Victorian poet Edward Heavysides in an essay of 1850, when he wrote that 'it must be a hard heart indeed that can read with indifference the history of the life and death of this promising child.'[1] George Ford cites Heavyside's comment as evidence of the enthusiasm for *The Old Curiosity Shop* that was sustained throughout Dickens's lifetime: Wilde's is the view of a later and more cynical generation. Contemporary with it though was the much more sympathetic response of George Gissing:

> As for the heroine of *The Old Curiosity Shop*, distaste for her as a pathetic figure seems to me unintelligent. She is a child of romance; her death is purely symbolical, signifying the premature close of any sweet, innocent and delicate life.[2]

This is clearly written in a context where the death of Little Nell has become a current joke: indeed it might well have been written as a rebuke to the author of the most famous joke of all about her. Gissing was arguably a better judge of these matters than Wilde. *The Old Curiosity Shop* is arguably the most ambitious, as well as the most complex, of Dickens's early fictions. In terms of its narrative energies, its comic and imaginative invention and its overall organization it is a very fine novel indeed, and in its presentation of its heroine within an environment typified by the grotesque it sets a pattern that is central in the development of Victorian fiction. Writing of the 'frail vessels' who typify the Victorian heroine, Henry James noted 'how absolutely, how inordinately, the Isabel Archers, and even much smaller female fry, insist on mattering'.[3] James, who was severe about Dickensian methods, had rather different heroines in mind of course, but it was Dickens's heroines, Nell and Little Dorrit, who were actually defined in terms of their diminutive stature. It is worth reminding ourselves that James's Maisie and his Nanda Brookenham, like Dickens's Nell, find themselves unprotected in alien and sinister worlds in which the reader's response to the drama of threatened innocence is paramount. Maisie, sitting on Beale Farange's knee while his clubland friends blow smoke in her face, is threatened just as Nell is threatened by the cigar-smoking Quilp; Nell, like Nanda, is of an increasingly awkward age. If we can free ourselves from the mythology that has accreted around Dickens's text we can see that Nell alive, as much as Nell dead, was a figure of central significance to Victorian literary culture.

The Old Curiosity Shop, more than any other of the early novels, consolidated Dickens's reputation. As Forster tells us, 'the published book was an extraordinary success'.[4] The implied distinction between the 'the published book' and the serial publication of the work is an important one: the novel was born out of the failure of *Master Humphrey's Clock*. But Forster's admiration of the work is unqualified and his analysis of its qualities is worth quoting at some length. Noting the accidental circumstances of its inception – 'It began with a plan for but a short half-dozen chapters' – he emphasizes its formal coherence, a coherence that depends upon the sustained contrast between the heroine and her surroundings:

> Yet, from the opening of the tale to that undesigned ending; from the image of Little Nell asleep amid the quaint grotesque figures of the old curiosity warehouse, to that other final sleep she takes among the grim forms and

carvings of the old church aisle; the main purpose always seems to be present. The characters and incidents that at first appear most foreign to it, are found to have with it a close relation. The hideous lumber and rottenness that surround the child in her grandfather's home, take shape again in Quilp and his filthy gang. In the first still picture of Nell's innocence in the midst of strange and alien forms, we have the forecast of her after-wanderings, her patient miseries, her sad maturity of experience before its time. Without the show-people and their blended fiction and realities, their wax-works, dwarfs, giants, and performing dogs, the picture would have wanted some part of its significance ... And when, at last, Nell sits within the quiet old church where all her wanderings end, and gazes upon those silent monumental groups of warriors, with helmets, swords, and gauntlets wasting away around them; the associations among which her life had opened seems to have come crowding on the scene again, to be present at its close.
(Forster, I: 87)

Forster's biography is not normally noted for its critical insights, but here he surpasses himself, identifying the central conception upon which *The Old Curiosity Shop* is constructed. Nell is a product of the post-Romantic sensibility, an early Dickensian version of the child who 'dwelt among th'untrodden ways', and whom there were 'none to praise / And very few to love.' She dwells not beside the springs of Dove however, but in the heart of the city, and when she leaves London it is to expose herself to the threats of a world in which the grotesque, animate and inanimate – the theatre-people, the waxworks, the gamblers, the bargemen and the industrial workers (to say nothing of Quilp and his 'filthy gang'), the statuary and the effigies of the graveyards and churches – is always the normal. Dickens had been around this course before, of course, in *Oliver Twist*, where Oliver's pilgrimage similarly exposes him to a cast of adults who are intimidatingly larger than life. Male and female created he them. A strong dimension of this theme is obviously sexual. Oliver's innocence, typified by the cleanness of the sheets between which he sleeps at Mr Brownlow's and threatened by the filth of Fagin, as well as Nell's has powerfully sexual implications. In *The Old Curiosity Shop* Dickens makes the situation explicit by imposing all the weight of the menace upon a pubertal girl. At the same time to read the threat to innocence in exclusively sexual terms is to over-simplify. What we have here is a larger drama of innocence and experience represented by the child's exposure to the outside world.

Returning to Forster's comments, it is clear that he has in mind as much the illustrations to the novel as its text. These were an essential part of the reading experience, particularly so in that for his *Master Humphrey* project Dickens went to great trouble with them, arranging for them to be set, not separately as in the earlier novels and as was to become the convention, but within the text itself. This was a more costly process but, as Joan Stevens has shown in detail, it was a deliberate strategy, providing for the appearance of the illustration at the exact key moment.[5] Furthermore for *Master Humphrey's Clock*, including *Barnaby Rudge* as well as *The Old Curiosity Shop*, Dickens commissioned two illustrators, supplementing the work of Hablot Browne with that of George Cattermole, an illustrator of historical subjects who specialized in antiquarian architecture, both interior and exterior. Forster's sequence of references to Nell asleep in the shop, to her sitting in the church amidst the monumental statuary, and to her final sleep are all to scenes of this kind (figures 1, 2, 3) and we can see from them just how much this contrast of feminine and grotesque was integral to Dickens's overall design. The first of them, with Nell's innocence reflected in the light that illuminates her bed contrasting with the darkness enshrining the antique furniture, concludes the opening chapter: mysterious faces – masks and ornaments – peer from the gloom. In the two later illustrations this contrast is replicated: it is often said that in *The Old Curiosity Shop* England is an extended cemetery; one might equally argue that all of England seems to have become an antique shop. The narrative opens in the curiosity shop itself: no illustration places the feminine within the grotesque more effectively than the one which initiates the reader into the text (figure 4).

More terrifying than the inanimate grotesque, however are the living grotesques that surround Nell. Mostly famously Quilp, of course, and in his case much of the illustration was allotted to Browne, exploiting his talent for comedy and caricature (figure 5). Perhaps because of the separation of responsibilities between Cattermole and Browne, Quilp and Nell rarely appear in the same illustration, as indeed they rarely appear together in the novel, once Nell and the grandfather have fled from London. Rather do they pursue parallel and contrasting courses through the narrative, Quilp's frustration increasing as Nell draws nearer to her sanctuary. The separation is of course essential to the sense of menace. One of Browne's finest illustrations is of Quilp's death by drowning (figure 6). As we know, 'Virtuous men pass mildly away,' and Dickens exploits the traditional contrast between good and bad deaths in the cases of Quilp who dies disregarded and in agony, and Nell who passes away so mildly that, as with the death of Cordelia, it is impossible to detect the moment. As with Fagin, however, Quilp's menace is compromised to a degree by the comedy which surrounds him: a far more disturbing figure is the old sexton who welcomes Nell to her final resting place as the novel approaches its conclusion. His passage with Nell into the old church provides for the most powerful illustration in the novel, a single illustration incidentally supplied not by either of the commissioned illustrators but by Dickens's personal friend, the artist Daniel Maclise (figure 7).

Maclise's illustration comes at a key point in the build-up to the novel's climax. Nell and her grandfather have come to the old church in the countryside where it is becoming increasingly clear that their journey will end. Dickens is already intimating to his readers that Nell will not outlive the final pages, but at this point she is to take some form of employment as a guide to visitors to the church. With the sexton, she inspects an old well that lies inside the church, and the illustration here is a perfect example of the effect of illustration set within the text. As Stevens points out, the dialogue above the illustration ('"Look in" said the old man, pointing downwards with his finger / The child complied, and gazed down into the pit')[6] leads the eye directly into the illustration whose verticals – the crutch, the pointing finger, the rope and the beams – then take not only Nell's eyes, but those of the reader into the black depths, moving them on to the words beneath the

THREE SISTERS AMID THE GROTESQUE 105

1 Nell in bed. S. Williams

2 Nell among the tombs. George Cattermole.

106 ALAN SHELSTON

3   Nell dead. George Cattermole.

MASTER HUMPHREY'S CLOCK.

4   The shop. George Cattermole.

THREE SISTERS AMID THE GROTESQUE 107

5   Mrs Quilp's tea-party. Hablot Knight Browne.

6   Quilp's corpse. Hablot Knight Browne.

"A black and dreadful place!" exclaimed the child.

"Look in," said the old man, pointing downward with his finger.

The child complied, and gazed down into the pit.

"It looks like a grave, itself," said the old man.

"It does," replied the child.

"I have often had the fancy," said the sexton, "that it might have been dug at first to make the old place more gloomy, and the old monks more religious. It's to be closed up, and built over."

The child still stood, looking thoughtfully into the vault.

"We shall see," said the sexton, "on what gay heads other earth will have closed, when the light is shut out from here. God knows! They'll close it up, next spring."

"The birds sing again in spring," thought the child, as she leant at her casement window, and gazed at the declining sun. "Spring! a beautiful and happy time!"

7 Nell and the sexton. Daniel Maclise.

text that confirm the significance of what has been seen. As Alice will memorably ask, "'what is the use of a book ... without pictures or conversations?'"[7] And to this wonderful visual strategy, we can add the basic contrasts between darkness and light, age and youth, innocence and impending death, all of them thematically central to *The Old Curiosity Shop* itself.

Illustration, I suspect, leaves a greater impact on the mind than text, and certainly the graphic rendering of Little Nell imposed itself on the Victorian consciousness. We are never told how old she is, although it is a fair assumption that, like her Wordsworthian forerunner, she is exterminated just at the point of awakening sexual consciousness. The echoes of Wordsworth are so resonant that Dickens surely must have had the Lucy poems in his mind. If Lucy 'seem'd a thing that could not feel/The touch of earthly years,' Nell 'seemed a creature fresh from the hand of God' (*OCS* 539). Nell is dead by now of course, as Lucy soon was to be. The consequence – 'O the difference to me' – is felt by the old grandfather, just as it is by the speaker of Wordsworth's poem. But whereas Lucy has no obvious successors in the Wordsworthian corpus, Nell established the iconography of pre-sexual – but of course potentially sexual – innocence for generations to come. That pre-pubertal body, in its high waisted and long-skirted dress, with the falling hair, the slender exposed arms and the delicate ankles, became the model for the type.

Exactly the same terms, of course, can be applied to Carroll's – or rather John Tenniel's – Alice. Tenniel illustrated Dickens's *The Haunted Man*, and both he and Carroll must have been amongst the early readers of *The Old Curiosity Shop*. We have no direct evidence that Carroll had read this novel in particular, but he was a regular reader of Dickens, and he certainly shared Dickens's imaginative sense of the comically grotesque that found expression, for both them, in character creation and in narrative. But *Alice in Wonderland* is most famously a work of literary parody, most obviously so in its songs and nonsense rhymes, but equally, *pace* William Empson in *Some Versions of Pastoral*, in its controlling ideas. Furthermore the remorselessness of its logic, in itself reinforced by self-reflexive parody, provides a frame of reference that subverts the sentimentalism of the romantic love convention. As Alice discovers, both the world underground and the world through the looking-glass are lonely and heartless places in which the individual has to trust to her own wits to survive. But its simplest and central parody lies in the figure of the heroine herself, who in her determination to overcome the obstacles put in her way rejects outright the Victorian convention of the submissive heroine, and explicitly the model provided by Nell. Rather does she imitate the Jane Eyre who, having survived the terrors of the red room, tells Mr Brocklehurst that the best way to avoid perdition is to 'keep in good health and not die'. Like Nell, Alice finds herself suddenly and inexplicably embarked upon a voyage of discovery. But whereas Nell is lowered into the ground at the end of her journey, never to return, Alice's descent at the beginning of her narrative via the rabbit-hole into 'what seemed to be a very deep well' (10) initiates a test of her resourcefulness that will conclude with her triumphant return to life. As she says when she 'opens out like the largest telescope that ever was' at the beginning of chapter 2, '"curiouser and curiouser"' (16). The word 'curious', in itself something of a curiosity, given its ambiguities, recurs through Carroll's text in what one might argue is a subliminal echo of Dickens's title. Alice is surrounded by 'a Duck and a Dodo, a Lory and an Eaglet, and several other curious creatures' (23); when she tells her own story to the Gryphon and the Mock Turtle, 'the Mock Turtle drew a long breath, and said "That's very curious"' and the Gryphon replies '"It's all about as curious as can be"' (92). Like Nell, Alice has to pluck up her courage and ask her way of the various strangers that she meets; she too has to hold off the approaches of a gallery of grotesques who threaten her every move. Both *The Old Curiosity Shop* and the Alice books can legitimately be seen as sublimations of their author's affection for pre-pubescent girls – or rather of girls who were even then at the point of crossing that boundary in their sexual development that their patrons(?) admirers(?) lovers(?) could not cross. Dickens's solution was imposed upon him by the death of his Beatrice, Mary Hogarth; Carroll, perhaps more self-aware, knew the distinction between the Alice of the story and the Alice to whom it was told. His reward to them both was the gift of the life to which Alice, in both volumes, returns.

Tenniel's representations of Alice reflect her parodic role in both narratives – perhaps inadvertently since he is far less successful with Alice herself than with the figures that surround her. His Alice has the body, the clothes, the shoes and the slender bare arms of her predecessor; she has too the hair flowing below her shoulders, if exaggerated now to pre-Raphaelite proportions. The difference lies in her sturdy and altogether more purposive physical frame, and particularly in her sometimes disproportionately large head and dome-like forehead, which nevertheless allows her to face her adversaries on at least equal terms (figure 8). But Tenniel, one feels, like so many of his fellow-illustrators of the period, took far more pleasure in the illustration of fantasy than of reality. Carroll's own drawings of Alice, if artistically inferior to the familiar Tenniel drawings which replaced them, are arguably more interesting.[8] But the grotesque creatures of the Alice books, who crowd in upon Alice exactly as do the grotesques of *The Old Curiosity Shop* upon Nell, provided Tenniel with opportunities of the kind to which Cattermole and Hablot Browne similarly responded in Dickens's novel. Tenniel's work is more regular in its formal design, as in the illustrations of the Duchess holding the baby (figure 9) or of Alice confronting the Queen of Hearts (figure 10), but the facial distortions in the former are close to Browne's Quilp while his ability to fill the frame, again typical of many of the *Old Curiosity Shop* illustrations, achieves a claustrophobic effect that is obviously appropriate to the adventures underground.

The illustration of fantasy, and in particular the presentation of fantasy-literature in carefully designed and crafted books, had been a growth industry in the years between *The Old Curiosity Shop* and *Alice in Wonderland*. These books, in their decorated bindings and with their illustrations carefully integrated with the text, proliferated in the 1850s and 60s and were products of a consumerist culture. In particular the illustrated fairy story, invariably adopting as its central motif the innocent child confronting the

THREE SISTERS AMID THE GROTESQUE 111

8   Alice with the creatures. John Tenniel.

9   The Duchess with the baby. John Tenniel.

10   Alice and the Queen of Hearts. John Tenniel.

world of fairy, became a feature of the literary culture in the form of a gift-book for middle-class children: Dante Gabriel Rossetti's illustrations for his sister's *Goblin Market* first appeared in 1862, pre-dating *Alice in Wonderland*, by just three years. Dickens's five *Christmas Books*, all published between 1843 and 1848, remind us of how close he was to the spirit of the genre. The care with which these volumes were prepared is reflected in Dickens's selection of the most prominent illustrators and engravers of his day; these included Leech, Stansfield, Doyle and Maclise, and for the last of them, *The Haunted Man*, Tenniel himself. The result at its best, as in the decorated title-page of *The Chimes* or the textual layout of *The Battle of Life*, was a quite remarkable blending of fantasy and sentiment. Like Dickens, Carroll took great care of the production quality of his works right up until the end of his life, as is shown both by his recorded instructions to Tenniel and by his Prefaces to late reprints of both of the Alice books and, as Rodney Engen records, he 'would test all his potential illustrators by their ability to combine what he called "the pretty" with the grotesque.'[9] Carroll and Tenniel, like Dickens, were thus working very much within both the artistic and the commercial conventions of their time. But the link from Alice back to Nell reminds us – if we needed reminding – that these were re-formulations of a more deeply-rooted myth about the significance of the feminine, and of the threat to it, for the post-Romantic literary sensibility.

11   Alice and the White Knight. John Tenniel.

    There is one further analogy to be drawn between the Alice books and *The Old Curiosity Shop* and one that is again highlighted by illustration. In Dickens's novel his heroine is accompanied throughout by her grandfather, a helpless figure whom, in a reversal of their roles, she increasingly has to protect: the final full-scale illustration of the novel shows him bewailing her loss. The parallel figure in the Alice books, in the sense that he provides the same comparison between youth and age, is the White Knight in *Through the Looking-Glass*, with his 'mild blue eyes and kindly smile' (119) and if he is a more lovable figure than Nell's grandfather, again it is the old man who is vulnerable and the young girl who assists him when he keeps falling from his horse. Donald Rackin persuasively argues that the chapter devoted to this episode is an expression both of the love felt by Carroll for Alice Liddell, and of his willingness to release her from it, facing the truth that the passage of the years will bring her to maturity and him to his death. Rackin cites in particular the gravitas of the penultimate chapter, (Chapter 8t: 'It's my own invention'), and especially the Knight's farewell to Alice, which effectively brings the chapter to its conclusion.[10] His case is supported by the positioning as the frontispiece to *Through the Looking Glass* of one of Tenniel's finest illustrations, that of the White Knight and Alice (figure 11). Death is itself the subject of parody in the Alice stories in which, as the Gryphon says, '"they never executes nobody you know"' (83), and in which not only the heroine but everyone else survives and the worst fate to be endured is to be stuffed into a teapot. But whereas *Alice in Wonderland* is headed by a lyric recalling 'a golden afternoon' in which 'Full leisurely we glide', Carroll's prefatory poem to *Through the Looking Glass* anticipates a parting from his child-listener that is couched in ambiguous and sombre terms: 'Come, hearken then, ere voice of dread / With bitter tidings laden, / Shall summon to unwelcome bed / A melancholy maiden! / We are but older children, dear, / Who fret to find our bedtime near' (115). Alice takes her parting from the White Knight in the penultimate chapter of *Through the Looking Glass* and turns away 'to be a Queen!', but she does so just as finally as Nell takes her parting from the Grandfather in the concluding pages of *The Old Curiosity Shop*. As the narrator observes as the White Knight sings his farewell song, 'of all the strange things that Alice saw in her journey Through The Looking-Glass, this was the one that she always remembered most clearly. Years after she could bring the whole scene back again, as if it had been only yesterday' (218–19). A world without death, of course, is both the privilege of childhood and the ultimate fantasy. While the child Alice lives free of the knowledge of death it is precisely this knowledge that lies at the end of Nell's quest. It is one of the paradoxes of the reputation bestowed upon *The Old Curiosity Shop* that what we have come to see as the ultimate example of Victorian sentimentality is in fact its moment of greatest truth: when a young girl dies she has gone forever, and all that those who remember her can do is mourn their loss.

To return, finally, to Dickens. The icon of the child-woman set amongst the grotesque, variously adapted, features in a number of his major novels. In *Dombey and Son* Flo Dombey moves from the forbidding interior space of her father's house to the benevolent curiosities – 'chronometers, barometers, telescopes, compasses, charts, maps, sextants, quadrants' – of the Wooden Midshipman's shop. Esther Summerson's situation in *Bleak House*, as a heroine with a role as the adult narrator of her own story, is rather different, but her visit to Krook's grandly titled 'Rag and Bottle Warehouse' provides the opportunity for another Browne illustration of this recurrent scene. For Carroll/ Tenniel also, shops had their curiosity value (figure 12). In *Little Dorrit* the heroine lives out her child-life under the shadow of the Marshalsea and here the conventionally grotesque has been replaced by a more sinister environment of menace, illustrated by one of the most beautifully designed of all of Browne's plates for Dickens (figure13). And in Dickens's last full-length novel, *Our Mutual Friend*, completed or, if we follow Henry James, 'dug out as with a spade and pickaxe', in the same year as the publication of *Alice in Wonderland*, we see the final development of the pattern.[11]

12   Alice in the shop. John Tenniel.

Like *The Old Curiosity Shop*, *Our Mutual Friend* is replete with the grotesque, but whereas in the earlier novel this is embodied in both its positive and its negative forces – in Mrs Jarley as well as in her waxworks, and in Dick Swiveller and the Marchioness as well as in Daniel Quilp – in *Our Mutual Friend* it is almost exclusively threatening in its implications. The shop in question this time is a taxidermist's. Its stock in trade consists of 'human warious' and its proprietor, Mr Venus – 'Preserver of Animals and Birds [and] Articulator of human bones' (*OMF* 83) – is a specialist in reconstructing skeletons and restoring stuffed animals. A somewhat similar trade, in that it depends upon the adornment of substitute human bodies, is the dolls' dressmaking of the crippled Jenny Wren, another child-adult who has to look after her drunken father. Rather more sordid is the trade in the detritus of the dust-mounds owned apparently by Mr Boffin, and lusted after by the one-legged Silas Wegg, while the most sinister business dealing of all arises from the scavenging from drowned bodies undertaken by Gaffer Hexam and his rival in trade Rogue Riderhood. The world of *Our Mutual Friend* is the world of the perversely grotesque just as, on another level, its multi-plot structures seem to represent a deliberate perversity on the part of an author

13   Little Dorrit's Party. Hablot Knight Browne (original title).

determined to confuse his readers. In the late Dickens novels plot itself becomes a metaphor for the constrictions of the fictional world: the characters not only exist in a grotesque world, a world in which the grotesque *is* the reality, they are caught up in stories so curious that only the curiosity of the reader can release them. And in *Our Mutual Friend* the ultimate curiosity is death itself, never more powerfully represented than in the opening pages when Lizzie Hexham cannot bear to look at what her father is searching for as she rows their boat on the murky waters of the Thames. Far from being a world without death, the world of *Our Mutual Friend* is a world in which there is no escape from it.

Lizzie, of course, is the heroine of the story, her self-sacrifice in the cause of her ungrateful brother preparing us for her love for Jenny and for her final scene in which she nurses Eugene Wrayburn back to life. But unlike the earlier heroines she is rarely confronted with the more obvious examples of the grotesque: she never for example crosses the door of Mr Venus's shop. Most obviously that is because she never needs

14 The Bird of Prey. Marcus Stone (original title).

to: from that opening chapter the grotesque is all around her. In this novel the ubiquity of the grotesque means that Dickens can effectively isolate what might be called the mechanically grotesque, making it even here the subject of a rather bleak comedy. Lizzie's situation is most powerfully impressed upon us when she is with her own father and in her home, and here Dickens achieves a reality of oppression that surpasses the formulaic. And just as the menace becomes more real, so does the heroine. Early in his writing of *Our Mutual Friend* Dickens referred to it as 'a combination of drollery and romance': it is an interesting reflection both of his sense of his novel's chemistry and of the distance that modern criticism of the novel has travelled from it.[12] But the romance was to be darkened as the novel progressed, and for all the grotesquerie ('drollery') that characterizes *Our Mutual Friend*, it is a novel in which Dickens strove for a greater truth both of internal and external character. For this novel Dickens chose a new illustrator, Marcus Stone, himself a product of a new realism in illustration. Initially Dickens seems to have exercised the same control over Stone that he had done with Browne: for the cover design he insisted that 'the dustman's face should be droll and not horrible', and that he wanted 'Boffin's oddity ... to be an oddity of a very honest kind, that people will like.'[13] Stone's frontispiece for the novel, 'The Bird of Prey', shows Gaffer Hexham and his daughter trawling the river (figure 14), and his single drawing of Lizzie alone, 'Waiting for Father' (figure 15), shows her looking into the fire in the hovel where she lives, awaiting Hexham's return from his gruesome business.

In both drawings Lizzie retains the flowing hair and the slender arms of her predecessors but she is now unmistakably a sexual figure dressed in, given her circumstances, a somewhat improbably high busted and full-length gown. Both hair and bodily form were key indicators of emergent sexuality for the Victorian novelists – one thinks for example of George Eliot's careful correlation of Maggie Tulliver's physical to her emotional development as she charts her progress in *The Mill on the Floss*. The 'slight youthful' figure who takes Tom from school has a 'broad-chested figure [with] the mould of early womanhood' when, in 'her seventeenth year' she sets out to meet Philip Wakem in the Red Deeps. Finally it is the physical appearance of 'this tall dark-eyed nymph with her jet-black coronet of hair' that captivates Stephen Guest (*The Mill on the Floss*, bk 1, ch. 7; bk 5, ch. 1; bk 6, ch. 2). George Eliot's novels were never illustrated in the first instance but the effect in these instances is distinctly pictorial. It suggests indeed how much Eliot, who expressed herself as being superior to illustration, owed to its conventions.

In *Our Mutual Friend* at the point where 'Waiting for Father' is inserted, the text projects Lizzie through the eyes of Eugene Wrayburn who is peering in through her

15 Waiting for Father. Marcus Stone (original title).

window. He sees, we are told, 'a deep rich piece of colour, with the brown flush of her cheeks and the shining lustre of her hair, though sad and solitary, weeping by the rising and the falling of the fire' (*OMF* 163). Earlier in the novel the same fire has been the focus of a conversation between Lizzie and her brother Charlie, where Lizzie sees in its flames images of both past and future while Charlie sees nothing. The pattern is one Dickens had used before, and to similar ends. Lizzie's care for Charlie echoes Florence's love for Paul and Lousia Gradgrind's protective concern for her younger brother, Tom, in *Hard Times*. The acquisition of these vulnerable brothers for the solitary heroine certainly provides for a greater psychological realism on Dickens's part. Tom Gradgrind observes that to be able to find things in the fire is 'another of the advantages, I suppose, of being a girl' (*HT* 53). But like Lizzie, Louisa is not just a girl but a child on the edge of womanhood – 'a child now, of fifteen or sixteen, but at no distant day [she] would seem to become a woman all at once' (*HT* 12) – and what these child-women see in the pictures in the fire are intimations of the inexpressible, pictures of what has irretrievably gone or of what lies, if only indistinctly, in the future. At this moment in *Our Mutual Friend*, Lizzie, surrounded by the trappings of death, knows only her unhappy past and her sordid present, and she can have no notion of the future which in the form of Wrayburn is gazing in upon her. Stone's drawing represents precisely the combination of physical and psychological realism to which Dickens's text aspires.

For the most part Stone's other drawings for *Our Mutual Friend* are uninspired, and it would seem that Dickens himself came to take less interest in this aspect of his novel. Where Stone's interiors do identify the element of the grotesque they do so in a way that is much more subdued: in the illustration of Mr Venus's shop, for example, we note the skeleton and the stuffed monkey in the bottom corner of the drawing, but this is domesticated grotesque, oddity as ornament, falling far short of the macabre humour of Dickens's text (figure 16). What this signifies however is not so much the limitations of the artist as the development of the form. The great age of the illustrated novel had passed. The small female fry would continue to matter, and artists would continue to draw them, but as the adult novel internalized its characterization so illustration inevitably became repetitive, mechanical and finally redundant. There is after all a limit to the variations that can be played on the theme of a young woman gazing into the fire, or a couple staring obliquely past each other, as Stone shows us in the case of John Harmon and Bella Wilfer. In this respect it is interesting to compare Stone's representation of Lizzie with Tenniel's drawing of Alice in the drawing-room in the first chapter of *Through the Looking Glass* (figure 17). Alice's circumstances are rather more comfortable than Lizzie's, but both of them are projected as domesticated young women in interior situations waiting for something happen in the world of the inner life.

Dickens's death in 1870 effectively marked the end of the kind of collaboration between novelist and illustrator that he had done so much to promote. From now on such illustration of realist fiction as survived would be confined to the kind of dramatization of character and incident that figured in magazine serializations – for example in *The Cornhill*, and later, where Hardy was concerned in *The Graphic* – while the fantastic

16 Mr Venus surrounded by the trophies of his art. Marcus Stone (original title).

17 Alice in the drawing room. John Tenniel.

became exclusively the province of illustrators of children's literature like Walter Crane, Laurence Houseman and ultimately Arthur Rackham. The division is a significant one: in one sense the novel can be said to have come of age. 'Anything that relieves responsible prose of the duty of being ... good enough, interesting enough and, if the question be of picture, pictorial enough ... does it the worst of services,' Henry James observed magisterially in his dismissal of illustration as an adjunct of fiction.[14] But for that short period, equivalent effectively to the passage of Dickens's career, prose and illustration combined to provide the Victorian reader with a cultural artefact that was both meaningful and accessible, and us with one of the most potent images of Victorian fiction.

Acknowledgement

The editor and the author wish to acknowledge the contribution of the School of English and Linguistics, the University of Manchester, towards the illustrations for this chapter.

Chapter 9

The Androgyny of *Bleak House*

Richard Gravil

> It was for Dickens a fundamental belief, as it was for the great majority of his contemporaries, that man's nature, his psychological and emotional make-up, differed, fundamentally and inherently, from woman's. —Michael Slater
>
> A woman who is too gifted, too intellectual, to find scope for her mind and heart in the education of her child, who pants for a more important work than the training of an immortal soul ... is simply not a woman. She is a natural blunder, a mere unfinished sketch. —Eliza Lynn
>
> [Women] are, in fact, from their own constitution, and from the station they occupy in the world, strictly speaking, relative creatures. —Mrs Ellis
>
> 'Now, I tell you, miss', said Mrs Bagnet; 'and when I say miss, I mean all!' —*Bleak House*[1]

When Dickens characterizes the legal world in the virtuoso first chapter of *Bleak House*, and the world of fashion in his second, he chooses as their representative figureheads the Lord Chancellor in his foggy Court of Chancery and Lady Dedlock in her freezing mode. What connection, as the novel keeps asking, can there be? The connection is Honoria Dedlock's illegitimate daughter, who in chapter 3, leads us into the Lord Chancellor's office before her narrative is sixteen pages old, radiating sunlight into the chill and foggy lives of the law's wards and victims. In the symbolic logic of the novel, the cure for legal deadlock and dereliction is the extra-legal relict of Lady Dedlock's passional summer. What could be more polarized, at mid-century, than a fallen woman and her child, on the one hand, and the constitutional majesty of the law? If it is a calculated insult to the polite reader, to select a fallen woman as the focus in one narrative, it seems an equally calculated one to have her bastard child given sole narratorial rights (and virtually exclusive rights to correct judgement in matters of morality) in the other. What possessed Dickens to do it?

Bleak House belongs to a period in which 'The Condition of England' (or of America) and 'The Condition of Women' seemed to many of Dickens's associates inseparable. Margaret Fuller's *Woman in the Nineteenth Century* (1850) is part of the context, as is America's Seneca Falls Convention of 1848. Miss Wisk, whose views on woman 'and her Tyrant, Man' are given short shrift in chapter 30, seems an emissary for the Convention's radical position, and one not at all welcome to Dickens or to many of his female associates. 'The history of Mankind,' wrote Lucretia Mott and Elizabeth Stady Canton in their 'Declaration of Sentiments', adopted by the Convention, 'is a history of repeated injuries and usurpations on the part of man toward woman, having in direct object the establishment of an absolute tyranny over her. To prove this, let facts be submitted to a candid world....'[2] They were, of course, parodying the Declaration of Independence. Five years later, Thomas Wentworth Higginson took up the question of what was signified by woman's constitutional non-existence in Jeffersonian democracy. To argue that in America's free states 'there is no class of persons who do not exercise the elective franchise' suggests that 'women are not even a "class of persons;" they are fairly dropped from the human race.'[3] Dickens was aghast at speechifying women during his American odyssey in 1842, and well aware of the rising chorus of dissent from that quarter since his visit. The alarm he expressed in *Martin Chuzzlewit* is echoed in the abrasive list of organizations in chapter 8 of *Bleak House*: 'the *Women* of England, the *Daughters* of Britain ... the *Females* of America' (my italics). His essay 'Sucking Pigs' (*Household Words*, November 1851), confirms that at this date, Dickens's conscious sympathies were by no means with the woman's movement: he ridicules women for 'agitating, agitating, agitating', and attacks an imaginary Julia Bellows for holding forth to the public, while there are nine little Bellowses 'to mend, or mar, at home'. In creating Esther as an anti-Bellows, he might be expected, therefore, to model her on the stereotypical 'angel in the house'. But that, in any exact sense of that term, Esther decidedly is not. Her own position often seems contemporaneous with the liberal feminism of, say, Maria Grey and Emily Shirreff, whose influential *Thoughts on Self-Culture Addressed to Women* was first published in 1850, two years before Esther's narrative began serialization in March 1852.

Bleak House precedes John Stuart Mill's and Harriet Taylor Mill's *The Subjection of Women* by sixteen years, but their arguments appeared much earlier, in an essay on 'Enfranchisement of Women', *Westminster Review*, July 1851. In any case, feminist arguments were, and had been, part of the culture in which Dickens's readers grew up. His friend John Forster, supported women's suffrage as early as 1846.[4] The arguments of Mary Wollstonecraft and William Godwin were kept alive in Unitarian circles, and *Bleak House* comes from a culture familiar with such texts as William Thompson's Saint-Simonian *Appeal of One Half of the Human Race, Woman, Against the Pretensions of the Other One Half, Man, to Retain Them in Political and Thence in Civil and Domestic Slavery* (1825), and W. J. Fox's Unitarian 'A Political and Social Anomaly', *Monthly Repository* 6 (1832). The latter propounds the anomaly, made famous by Mill, of a land in which a woman's constitutional options are to be Queen, or nothing. Dickens, along with John Stuart Mill, was part of Fox's circle. His links with Fox, Douglas Jerrold, and William and Mary Howitt and their journals – that is, with the leading journals of radical, and radical feminist, Unitarianism – are well attested.[5] In a sense, *Bleak House*, like Thompson's *Appeal* (co-authored by Anna Wheeler), the journalism of the Howitts, and the joint essays of the Mills, belongs to a minor genre of androgynous texts, though here the co-author is imagined.

Its very form suggests that *Bleak House* is Dickens's conscious response to an outbreak of unprecedented agitation on the woman question, and that whatever the novel's message, the medium critiques the insufficiency of a gendered perspective. It suggests that the condition of women is, to Dickens, not only a huge chunk of the condition of England, 'One Half' of it at least, but one that requires of him far more imaginative investment than his satire on the law. This is not the first essay to address that question: Ellen Moers, for one, has seen *Bleak House* as a novel consciously exploring, but more dialogically, what Dickens had already tackled journalistically, the matter of what makes women 'agitate, agitate, agitate'.[6] But there is a further question, more often implied than addressed in the numerous fascinating discussions of Esther's preoccupation with mirrors and with names: does Esther herself, if we read what she says, and see what she sees, when not looking in her mirror, vocalize a critique of the position of women? Here I shall suggest that, to a surprising degree, the novel vocalizes – albeit through an innocent and inoffensive eye – that part of the feminist case which Dickens could not but endorse. As it happens, that part constituted almost the only common ground of nineteenth-century feminisms.

Of the following mid-century voices, which, if they were not identified, would be thought female, and which male?

> America, France and Germany, in doleful chorus, lament the slavery of woman, and the tyranny of man. [But] the great majority of our readers are sober Christians.... We know that the entire psychical contrast of man, and his sweet coheiress of immortal life, is nowhere so emphatically declared as in the Book of Absolute Verity. (Coventry Patmore)[7]

> [If] the reader of these pages has ... acknowledged her inferiority to man, [and] has examined her own nature, and found there a capability of feeling, a quickness of perception, and a facility of adaptation, beyond what he possesses, and which, consequently, fit her for a distinct and separate sphere; ... I would also gladly persuade myself, that the same individual, as a Christian woman, has made her decision not to live for herself, so much as for others; but above all, not to live for this world, so much as for eternity. (Mrs Ellis)[8]

> To make one half of the human race consume all their energies in the functions of housekeeper, wife and mother is a monstrous waste of the most precious material that God ever made. (Theodore Parker)[9]

> It is undeniably a sad sight to see women ... come pouring out of workrooms into the street, at meal-time... It is a dreary thought—how few of them can make bread or boil a potato properly; how few can mend a gown; how few can carry an intelligent and informed mind to their own firesides, and amuse their children with knowledge, and satisfy their husbands with sympathy. (Harriet Martineau)[10]

> I for one (with millions more) believe in the natural superiority of man, as I do in the existence of a God. (Caroline Norton)[11]

> [I]f warmth of feeling, quickness of sympathy, ardour and generous devotion, are qualities we prize and love in the other sex, how painfully must their absence be felt in her whose mission on earth is to live for others. (Maria Grey and Emily Shirreff)[12]

> Homes deserted, children – the most solemn responsibility of all – given to a stranger's hand, modesty, unselfishness, patience, obedience, endurance, all that has made angels of humanity ... trampled under foot, while the Emancipated Woman walks proudly forward to the goal of the glittering honours of public life, her true honours lying crushed beneath her, unnoticed. (Eliza Lynn)[13]

> Lawmakers have perceived and acted upon the plain and unalterable fact, that [woman's] interests can never be sufficiently distinguished from the interests of men to warrant any extensive separate consideration. (Coventry Patmore 524)

Coventry Patmore's discourse upon woman's constitutional nonentity – blending complacency, offensiveness, tortured logic and patriarchy red in tooth and claw – would undoubtedly be identified as male. He continues: 'Men must be legislators, from their greater strength and courage, and from their superior vigour of mental and bodily constitution; but if by reason of this women are sufferers from the caprice and tyranny of men, it must be remembered that they themselves have taught and trained the tyrants. *Their very sufferings are their own work*; for by exerting their full influence as mothers in a right direction, they might have trained a race of men with truer feelings, and a keener apprehension of justice' (531). So there we have it: men's virtues are their own, their faults entailed upon them by the daughters of Eve; if Tulkinghorn pursues Lady Dedlock to destruction, blame his mother.

The remaining voices in my collage would be harder to 'sex'. As Sheila R. Herstein points out, in her study of Barbara Bodichon, it was possible for women to campaign for particular rights, or at least the redress of specified wrongs, while repudiating, with surprising vigour, the concept of female equality.[14] Eliza Lynn is a case in point. When she summarized 'The Rights and Wrongs of Women' in these terms in *Household Words*, she undoubtedly had Dickens's full support:

> The laws which deny the individuality of a wife, under the shallow pretence of a legal lie; which award different punishments for the same vice; the laws which class women with infants and idiots, and which recognise principles they neither extend nor act on; these are the real and substantial Wrongs of Women, which will not, however, be amended by making them commanders in the navy or judges on the bench. To fling them into the thick of the strife would be but to teach them the egotism and hardness, the grasping selfishness, and the vain glory of men, which it has been their mission, since the world began, to repress, to elevate, to soften, and to purify.[15]

Essentialism of this kind, according to Olive Banks, was a major strand of nineteenth-century feminism. Catherine Beecher (educational reformer and author of a *Treatise on Domestic Economy*, 1841) not only 'stressed the differences between men and women, in terms of their natural abilities and their social roles', but saw woman's great mission as 'self-denial ... if not for her own children, then for the neglected children of her father in heaven'; she is 'necessarily the guardian of the nursery, the companion of childhood'.[16] In the professional world, Beecher thought, women's proper role was as teachers. The Grey and Shirreff position, cited above, that woman's mission on earth is to live for others – a position powerfully contested by Mill – is not far from George Eliot's refusal to part with 'that exquisite type of gentleness, tenderness, possible maternity suffusing a woman's being with affectionateness, which makes what we call the feminine character' (Banks 89). Feminists, Banks argues, did not contest the ideal of female moral superiority, but transformed it, and the doctrine of separate spheres, into an 'invasion of the masculine world ... by womanly values' (90). If so, it could be argued that Esther Summerson is ahead of them. Such essentialism remains an element in social thinking throughout the century. It was present in Beatrice Webb, and in such gender-revolutionary figures as Havelock Ellis and Edward Carpenter, while a bona fide feminist such as Ellen Key could believe that 'feminism ... had everything to do with the social recognition of motherhood' (Banks, 102).

Victorian feminism, as depicted by Philippa Levine and by Olive Banks, took as its primary issues the control of male lust, drink and violence, the woman's right to custody of her children, and an ongoing campaign against denial of property rights to women.[17] Dickens, though generally perceived as belonging with Coventry Patmore and the 'angel-in-the-house' school rather than with even the most liberal campaigners for women's rights, was in practice sound enough on these issues, and of course his notoriously sexless heroes conform very much to the model required by the later brand of social purity feminists. In the years during which *Bleak House* germinated, his most regular correspondents were the Gaskells and Angela Burdett Coutts, and one of his most regular themes, the prospects for the reclamation (preferably in Australia!) of fallen women. He campaigned against physical abuse of women as early as 1849; he supported bills to enable women to possess their own earnings; and during the nation-wide controversy stirred by the case of Caroline Norton, *Household Words* carried eloquent articles on the wrongs of women, particularly in 1854, 1855 and 1856, that is, throughout the three years following the serialization of *Bleak House*. Did he, one wonders, write *Bleak House* because he was exercised just enough by the feminist cause to attempt an exploration of the world from a woman's point of view? Or did the experience of being Esther Summerson, for eighteen creative months, teach him to feel the constraints of 'patriarchy'?

Esther's indictment

Esther's character is undoubtedly composed in part upon the best authorities. 'In order to ascertain what kind of education is most effective in making woman what she ought to be,' said the best-selling Sarah Stickney Ellis, one must enquire 'for what she is most valued, admired, and beloved', namely 'For her disinterested kindness.'[18] Moreover, in her particular position, vis-à-vis John Jarnydyce as her guardian and future husband, she knows what she ought to feel, however much restlessness she guiltily experiences. There may be spiritual equality between men and women, says Ellis, 'yet, in the character of a noble, enlightened, and truly good man, there is a power and a sublimity, so nearly approaching what we believe to be the nature and capacity of angels, that as no feeling can exceed, so no language can describe, the degree of admiration and respect which the contemplation of such a character must excite.' The beatification of Jarndyce in Esther's narrative rarely approaches quite this elevated sense of the devotion owing to 'a truly good man'. Dimly conscious that marriage to him is not what her inmost self is calling for, Esther reminds herself constantly, and with a transparent struggle that has exercised a number of critics, that 'To be permitted to dwell within the influence of such a man, *must* be a privilege of the highest order; to listen to his conversation, *must* be a perpetual feast; but to be admitted into his heart – to share his counsels, and to be the chosen companion of his joys and sorrows! – it is difficult to say whether humility or gratitude *should* preponderate in the feelings of the woman thus distinguished and thus blest.' This is not Esther, as it happens, but Mrs Ellis (*The Wives of England*, 65; italics mine).

Esther herself, unlike Mrs Ellis, develops a curiously insistent critique of what might be called 'patriarchy'. Yes, she does ingratiate herself with her co-author, and with the middle-class reader Dickens aimed to reach, by presenting as her first satiric victims Mrs Jellyby and Mrs Pardiggle (monstrosities deprecated by J. S. Mill as jeering at the non-domestic female, yet praised by the equally feminist George Gissing as truthful depictions of human monstrosity).[19] It is only later in the novel that we grasp how these figures fit into a cross-gendered system of abuse and neglect. Alongside Chadband, Smallweed, Turveydrop and Tulkinghorn, after all, Mrs Pardiggle and Mrs Jellyby appear both well-intentioned, within their lights, and relatively harmless. In any case, Mrs Pardiggle is not criticized for visiting, but for doing so without understanding, and for martyring her children (as Skimpole martyrs his) to her own ego. Mrs Jellyby is criticized not for charitable zeal, or devotion to high ideals, but for being part of the imperial complacency that thinks it can export civilization from what Dickens sees as the heart of darkness in this 'boastful island'.

Moreover, Esther loses no opportunity (and makes many) to draw attention to the victimized woman as a staple of her society. She may see her own life as a 'progress', rather than a process of victimization, but she resents being stalked by the artful and sensual Guppy (chapter 13). She suffers, as she tells us pointedly, from the 'disagreeable gallantry' of Mr Turveydrop (14.229) and is relieved when her disfigurement causes this to cease. While Skimpole rhapsodizes on how the slaves on American plantations give the landscape a kind of poetry, Esther wonders 'whether he ever thought of Mrs Skimpole and the children, and in what point of view they presented themselves to his cosmopolitan mind' (18.295). The Mills would associate American slavery and the subjection of women, but Esther is there before them. In her narrative, too, we see Miss Flite, caged and spellbound cager of songbirds, as an abused abuser, once capable of economic flight, now a supplicant at court. When Dickens requires Esther to dismiss Miss Wisk in a sentence or two on her *idée fixe* about 'her tyrant Man' she does so; but she has already, by that point, defined male-female relations not exclusively, but preponderantly, in terms which support Miss Wisk's view of the question.

No, Esther does not endorse Miss Wisk, whom she meets at Caddy's wedding, or Mrs Jellyby's later enrolment in the cause, though she does persist in calling Caddy by her maiden name. Moreover, her sharpest comment on Turveydrop's exploitative household (she observes many preparations 'for enhancing the comforts of old Mr Turveydrop, and a few for putting the newly married couple away cheaply at the top of the house' [30.477]) occurs just five pages before Miss Wisk's demand for 'the emancipation of Woman from the thraldom of her Tyrant, Man' (483). Having thus underlined Miss Wisk's analysis, if not her solution, Esther turns to Skimpole. She tries valiantly to get Jarndyce to address the matter of Skimpole's continued exploitation of Richard – 'I thought it was to be regretted that he had ever introduced Richard to Mr Vholes for a present of five pounds' (43.671) – and has regrets that Skimpole should 'have anything to do with anyone for whom I cared' (676). She reaches the nub of the problem, however, when she reveals how Skimpole, too, consigns his fledglings, and their partners, and *their* offspring, to 'nests up-stairs'. Worse, he has given his daughters just enough education 'to be their father's playthings in his idlest hours'; he neglects his invalid wife; and in his domestic seraglio 'his own apartment was a palace to the rest of the house' (677, 679).

How much of Esher's focus upon these matters constitutes a response to Jarndyce's unconscious appropriations (and how much these dramatize or diagnose Dickens's own), it is hard to say. It is at Mr Jarndyce's wish that Esther is conveyed to London. From Mr Jarndyce she receives Charley ('If you please, miss, I am a present to you, with Mr Jarndyce's love', 385). She becomes, by fiat of Mr Jarndyce, Mrs Woodcourt. The same Mr Jarndyce – who cannot bring himself to act upon Skimpole's material acquisitiveness and his abuse of Richard – adopts Richard's widow Ada, and her child, to adorn his own widowed state. I am not sniping at Jarndyce here: it is part of the novel's force to depict some of its most compassionate characters – Miss Flite, Mr Jarndyce – as ineluctably contaminated by the grasping nature of society. It is the case, however, that Esther who conceives herself as bound by laws of gratitude to Mr Jarndyce struggles conspicuously, and repeatedly, and unsuccessfully, to persuade herself that marriage to him is all that she desires.

So Esther's role in *Bleak House*, far from dramatizing an unalloyed 'angel in the house' ideology, might be thought to express the assumptions of Maria Grey and Emily Shirreff in their *Thoughts on Self-Culture*. 'The complete dependence in which a young woman spends her youth', they argue, 'is naturally unfavourable to the acquisition of judgement and decision' (Grey and Shirreff 205). It is nonsense that 'decision of character in women' is 'opposed to feminine gentleness and modesty of deportment. Nothing can be more mistaken'; in any case, 'Women ... may be fully equal to men in moral courage' (206, 211). Esther might well agree with Grey and Shirreff that, in politics, 'removed from the actual strife ... of public life ...[women] might become the peacemakers in men's divisions, instead of adding to the clamour of party' (296). She certainly knows, in diagnosing Mrs Pardiggle's incapacities, that as Grey and Shirreff put it, 'Imagination alone enables us to enter situations wholly unknown to us, [so that we can] read at a glance what may be utterly foreign to our personal experience, and acquire that quick perception of feeling which, in a kind heart, produces equally rapid sympathy' (324–5). Women, however, according to Grey and Shirreff, 'are rarely very deficient in imagination' (327): if we agree, it must follow that Mrs Pardiggle, Aunt Barbary, Mrs Rachel, Mrs Snagsby, Judy, are all freaks of nature and that Nature is astonishingly careless in disbursing those traits which, theoretically, belong naturally to men and women. That is, while Dickens dramatizes the development of judgement in Esther, very much according to Grey and Shirreff, he also questions (despite an ingrained desire to see women as naturally good, naturally sympathetic, naturally caring) the essentialism of their, and Eliza Lynn's, position.

There is also the much discussed matter of Esther's sexual identity. Esther repeatedly assures us of the benevolence of Jarndyce, yet her transparent unease in her engagement confirms most readers' sense that she is sacrificing too much to gratitude. She is walking, as it were, straight into marriage with a more genial Sir Leicester, rather than seeking her own Captain Hawdon. Yet she is, after all, her mother's daughter.[20] Repeated doubling of Esther, via veils and mirrors, with both Lady Dedlock and with Hortense, merely confirms what we need to know in order to understand one of Esther's first 'big scenes', Guppy's first proposal of marriage. Esther herself (in a revealing slippage of tense) says of Lady Dedlock, when meeting her for the first time, that after a few moments '*I knew* the face quite well'. As Jo, George and Guppy constantly remind us, Esther is in appearance wholly her mother's daughter: but when we see Lady Dedlock managing Guppy in their much later interviews, we might well feel that *we know* this behaviour quite well. Startled by Guppy's proposal, in chapter 9, the mild-mannered and ever-grateful Esther suddenly collects herself: she is haughty, imperious, disdainful, imperative, and quite untouched by sympathy for the hapless Guppy. In short, she becomes her mother. Frostily handled by Lady Dedlock when he has the temerity to hint that she has a daughter (chapter 29), Guppy must feel he has been here before. Moreover, the response of mother and daughter to these interviews with Guppy, is the same. Lady Dedlock melts; Esther finds herself weeping. She feels 'as if an old chord had been more coarsely touched than it had ever been since the days of the dear old doll, long buried in the garden'. The doll, we perhaps intuit, symbolizes Esther's prospects of motherhood; its burial a voluntary infibulation. Esther, curiously, never articulates her choice of sexual fulfilment – Jarndyce does so for her – but for many hundred pages the reader is manipulated into requiring that somebody does.

Essentialism

But why always Esther? What of the other narrator's views? If we are unsure why Esther is uneasy at being stalked by Guppy, the other narrator helps. He shows us Guppy as a Tulkinghorn in embryo: most sinister when in pursuit of women's secrets ('a lady started up; a disguised lady, your ladyship' who hired a crossing boy to find the grave of her deceased lover, and 'I can lay my hands on him at any time'; 29.467). Much male activity in *Bleak House* seems designed to play out this hunting theme: 'Man is the hunter, woman is his game', Tennyson's King Hildebrand explains, in a contemporaneous politicization of Krook's obsession with skins, 'We hunt them for the beauty of their skins.' By and large, because they are treated in Esther's narrative, Turveydrop and Skimpole are seen less quickly than are Smallweed and Tulkinghorn as vampires, whose ultimate prey is the female. If the novel has a plot, and many early commentators were not sure that it had, it is the ruthless pursuit of Lady Dedlock by Tulkinghorn, for having enjoyed a passional summer before her marriage to Sir Leicester. One of the oddest, yet perennial, misconceptions about Tulkinghorn is that his malignancy is motiveless. On the contrary, it is specified, unambiguously, in the one and only insight we are given into the contents of that otherwise hidden mind: the root of his belief system is that there are too many women in the world and 'they are the bottom of all that goes wrong in it' (259). He is the enforcer: the malevolent essence of patriarchy. He will use women, of course, as do the ambiguous Mr Bucket, and the hapless Guppy, but he will not advance them. Hortense, expecting some reward for her collaboration in Mr Tulkinghorn's pursuit of her mistress, is threatened instead with 'houses of correction (where the treadmills are, for women)' (42.667). This treadmill image in one narrative occurs just a few pages before the other shows us Mrs Skimpole's treadmill.

The novel depicts, repeatedly, in the brickyards and Tom-All-Alone's, as in relations between patriarch and matriarch in Grandfather Smallweed's bleak house, chronic domestic violence. Jenny, with her black eye, and Liz, with her bruised breast, are matched in the Turveydrop and Skimpole households by subtler forms of exploitation. And, for once, the never wholly convincing argument that violence against women in Dickens's novels is an expression of his own aggression towards the species, is wholly inapplicable. If, as is sometimes argued, the battery of Estella, the burning of Miss Havisham, the bludgeoning of Mrs Joe (in *Great Expectations*), the murder of Nancy (in *Oliver Twist*), and the freezing of Lady Dedlock, remind women not to challenge the boundaries set for them by patriarchy, might one not equally argue that the fates of Krook and of Tulkinghorn serve to remind patriarchy what the price might be – on, or before, the day of judgement – for the collection of women's hair in sacks, or the slow torturing of women who do overstep such marks?[21] Nor do any of the instances of suffering in this novel have anything about them suggestive of ennoblement through suffering, the other perennial cliché of Dickens criticism. They just suffer.[22]

Nor is domestic violence his only area of sensitivity. He scores rather well on essentialism. In virtually successive scenes of 'his' part of the novel, we pass from the Bagnet household to Chesney Wold. Matthew Bagnet would have no opinion on anything were it not for the incisive and decisive Mrs Bagnet (442). To her, all men, including Jarndyce and Woodcourt, are (as my fourth epigraph suggests) 'relative creatures'. In Chesney Wold, likewise, the titled numbskull is much in need of my Lady's opinion and is very wise to defer to it, and to her ways of handling situations (452). For a marriage to amount to the union of mind and matter (the phrase used to describe Mrs and Mr

Jellyby) may be undesirable, but it seems, in this novel, ubiquitous. The Patmore model of manliness and womanliness as being a union of polarities – male mind united to female heart, strength to sweetness – is inverted too often for the technique to be dismissed as coincidental. The paradigm established by Esther's Jellybys and Pardiggles is taken for granted in the third-person narrator's Bagnets and Dedlocks. It is also addressed, with variations, in Mr Badger's subordination to Captain Swosser and Professor Dingo (in Esther's narrative), in Mrs Snagsby's superior if mistaken powers of penetration (in the third-person narrative), and in the especially curious case of Mrs Bucket. Dickens was not often sympathetic to a widening sphere of female activity: only nursing, primary education, schools of decorative design, met with overt approval in *Household Words*. Yet he published a wondering account of muscular Frenchwomen towing barges, humping pyramids of faggots along country lanes, and insisting on being the companions not the playthings of their partners.[23] In the case of Mrs Bucket he addresses specifically the professional potential implied in Mrs Bagnet. Both women (like Mrs Snagsby) are natural detectives (as, of course, is everyone in this novel, including the reader: we sniff clues to survive). But whereas Bucket's professional success rate is ambiguously presented, Mrs Bucket achieves with considerable despatch the evidence which will convict the murderess Hortense. So that he and Mrs Bucket can operate as a pair of connubial pincers, it is necessary for Bucket to absent himself from felicity awhile, though, in general, we are told, 'he highly appreciates the society of Mrs Bucket – a lady of natural detective genius, which if it had been improved by professional exercise, might have done great things, but which has paused at the level of a clever amateur – '. Whose parenthetical, and regretful, comment is this? Mr Bucket's, in free indirect discourse? The third-person narrator's? Dickens's?

One effect of the third-person narrative is that while less overtly dialogic than Esther's, it does allow for a cultural pluralism regarding the proper sphere of women. In general 'the novel comes into contact with the spontaneity of the inconclusive present', says Bakhtin, 'the novelist is drawn towards everything that is not yet completed'.[24] Throughout this novel, cultural stereotypes are thus routinely investigated. Curiously, the major moments in which women wrest control of events in this novel, whether for good or for ill, arise from their venturing outside the domestic sphere. Mrs Jellyby and Mrs Pardiggle had undoubtedly better stayed at home (in one case) or attended to it (in the other). Yet, had Esther, or Mrs Bagnet, or Mrs Rouncewell, or Mrs Bucket, or Lady Dedlock, stayed at home, the novel's few conclusive events – providing a tincture of decisive actions in an otherwise corrosive or entropic male world – would not have occurred. Moreover, Mrs Bucket, potentially professional, is not the novel's only or most concrete instance of widening spheres, of the kind regularly argued for in radical Unitarian journals. The neglect of Caddy Jellyby's domestic education may require an extensive re-education for her (moral: home-makers are made, not born?), but with no assistance at all, she ends up running the Turveydrop business and fully enjoying the rewards of her enterprise. Mrs Bagnet, Ellen Moers has pointed out, is not merely a homemaker but an entrepreneur, the successful proprietress of a musical instruments shop, and Mrs Rouncewell a prototype of the professional housekeeper, to whom all those anonymous Mercuries answer. Even the notoriously passive Ada, as several critics have observed, sets up house with Richard on her own initiative, in defiance of Jarndyce's prohibition. If we have no woman's movement in *Bleak House*, we have, Ellen Moers has suggested, masterful women on the move; and in most cases, with both narrators' evident approval and the author's bemused assent.

The Bagnets, the Jellybys, the Carstones, the Dedlocks and the Buckets, with their very different social configurations, exist in order to refute one of Mrs Ellis's first rules of engagement. 'As women, then, the first thing of importance is to be content to be inferior to men – inferior in mental power, in the same proportion that you are inferior in bodily strength' (*Daughters* 11). Dickens might have agreed with her that a young woman should indulge her intellectual yearnings only 'provided she has nothing better to do; by which I would be understood to mean, provided she does not consequently leave undone what would render her more useful or more amiable as a woman' (Ellis, *Daughters* 75). But he specializes, from *Bleak House* on, in couples or siblings whose role is to demonstrate the superiority of women, not merely in a moral sense but as intellectual and imaginative beings: Louisa Gradgrind in *Hard Times* is morally, intellectually and imaginatively her brother's superior; as Lizzie Hexham is her brother's and her suitor's in *Our Mutual Friend*. Not only does Dickens, in the caring figures of Jarndyce, Snagsby, George, Woodcourt, subscribe to (and, as much as anyone, create) the (dominant) fictional ideology that men need to be more like women, but he demonstrates conclusively that Mrs Pardiggle and Mrs Jellyby and Mrs Snagsby are by nature under-endowed with precisely those qualities which are *supposed* to be their special endowment. They are simply not equipped, as are Trooper George and John Jarndyce, for the tender and domestic (George's manly bosom has room for Jo, Gridley and Sir Leicester).

Essentialism was under attack at this date, but to attack it was to be in the minority. It was possible in the middle of the nineteenth century to believe, with Mrs Ellis and Patmore, that women were naturally constituted differently from men and should therefore content themselves with the minor morals of life; or with Grey and Shirreff, and Catherine Beecher, that although women should have more scope, they were naturally designed to specialize in the affections; or with Harriet and J. S. Mill that nothing whatever can be known of woman's 'nature' until society stops constraining it. If these three positions constitute a three-point scale of feminism, *Bleak House* – taking both Esther's resentment of patriarchy and the male narrator's critique of essentialism into account – scores about 2.5. The contrast in the narrative voices *may suggest* polarisation of masculine and feminine, initially, but it works to reduce that polarity. Enacting an assimilation of masculine judgement and initiative by the feminine principle, and of feminine compassion by the male principle, the form itself corroborates, thereby, the novel's repeated demonstration, comic in the main, that essentialism will not do.

The androgynous form

I have left the matter of the dual narrative to the end, or almost the end, in the hope that I can now appraise its androgyny fairly briefly. Famously, one half of this richly experimental novel is focalized through an omnipresent eye, covering an immense social and geographic range, capable of microscopic close-up in which even the animal tissues of legal parchments become vividly present, or of panoramic vistas in which the entire constitutional fabric is reduced to absurdity and entire classes of people reduced to interchangeable ciphers. It is, at the outset, characteristically denunciatory. It is capable of levelling itself at the sovereign herself on equal terms, hectoring her and all her right reverends and wrong reverends for taking too little heed of those, like Jo, who are in need 'and dying thus around us everyday'. It is also, without a doubt, male: public, confident, analytical, not to be taken in by appearances, knowing, experienced, worldly. The other half of the novel is narrated artlessly by (we come to understand) a happily married woman whose narrative, constantly making way for perspectives other than her own, renders the diffidence of an inexperienced, unworldly, repressed, illegitimate young woman thoroughly dependent on others for her 'progress' from stigma to acceptance. Esther is unable to see herself as the centre of her own story until its closing paragraph. This narrative is, inescapably, female: as female as Dickens could make it, after (it sometimes seems) prolonged study of the best authorities in womanliness at mid-century.

Where 'his' is a narrative of suspicion, pursuit, hunting and destroying, hers specializes in errands of mercy, reclamation, salvage, healing. One narrator wishes to torch the whole corrupt pile (like Blake's prophet in 'London', or like the sardonic Carlyle who invites the reader of *Sartor Resartus* to welcome a thousand years of conflagration as the price of finding ourselves again in a living society). The other picks her way patiently through the fog with a moral lantern, finding goodness all around her, and content (like the other side of Carlyle) to do the duty that lies nearest her. While the voice of Experience excoriates the system, the other voice proclaims the values of Innocence: they exhibit, that is to say, the two contrary states of the human soul. Nonetheless, both voices identify with the hunted, the victimized, the exploited, the weak, while the very structure of the book proposes, if it does not articulate, synthesis, a synthesis of Swift's *saeva indignatio* with Blake's visionary innocence. As the entropic arch in Chesney Wold is 'sapped and sopped away' (2.20) until all that is left is a metaphorical one falling in chapter 55 (855), a psychic one takes its place, created by the impersonal narrative leaning towards sympathetic identification, and the personal one learning the necessity of judgement.

'The truth is', Coleridge observed, 'a great mind must be androgynous'. And although Dickens is held by many (including Carolyn Heilbrun, from whom I cite Coleridge's remark)[25] to be as male as writers come, *Bleak House* illustrates by a form of concentration of the supposedly 'masculine' how far his own usual voice is from that condition. At first, the third-person narrative entertains no point of view other than its own controlling perception: the world has gone into mourning for the death of the sun, and its institutions and constructions are in an irreversibly entropic state. Its people appear first only as types, or classes, or instances. Lawyers illustrate Carlyle's verdict on the 'mechanical age': 'eighteen of Mr Tangle's learned friends, each armed with a little summary of eighteen hundred sheets, bob up like eighteen hammers in a pianoforte, make eighteen bows, and drop into their eighteen places of obscurity' (1.18). Miss Flite and Mr Gridley, on their first appearances, are simply 'a mad little old woman in a bonnet' and 'the man from Shropshire'; they acquire identities in Esther's identity-centred narrative. Even in the case of Jo, Dickens makes some (wildly unconvincing) efforts to suppress his sympathies far enough to treat him as an it, a disgusting spectacle, indistinguishable from the brutes. *Bleak House* dramatizes, that is, the male function of seeing 'the big picture', while indicating the untenability of the reification involved.

Esther, on the other hand, comes to each character without preconceptions. When she sees Grandfather Smallweed, in chapter 62 she sees only 'an old man in a black skull-cap, unable to walk' (lame patriarchs, including Sir Leicester and Mr Turveydrop, are a motif of *Bleak House*); she does not 'see' him at all as the cardboard epitome of rapacious malevolence we have been shown up to that point; but we are never permitted to find out whether the redemptive powers of the domestic Esther could find a human centre even in him. Esther's own perceptions begin from the premise that people are human and kindly until proven otherwise. In character, her early mode is that of the innocent eye. Resisting Mrs Pardiggle's invitation to join her charitable rounds, she protests that she is unqualified:

> That I was inexperienced in the art of adapting my mind to minds very differently situated ... That I had not that delicate knowledge of the heart which must be essential to such a work. That I had much to learn, myself, before I could teach others ... For these reasons, I thought it best to be as useful as I could, and to render what kind services I could, to those immediately about me; and to try to let that circle of duty gradually and naturally expand itself. All this I said, with anything but confidence; because Mrs Pardiggle was much older than I, and had great experience, and was so very military in her manners. (8.128)

Clearly, Esther knows her Carlyle: '*Do the duty which lies nearest thee*, which thou knowest to be a duty, thy second duty will already have become clearer.' If she has not read this exemplary precept in *Sartor Resartus* itself, she may have come across it in Grey and Shirreff, where the counsel is offered to unmarried women, whose dependent position circumscribes their power of exertion within very narrow limits. Agreeing that such women may well be 'tempted to pine for a more enlarged, or a different sphere' Grey and Shirreff advise: 'no human being, endowed with moral and intellectual faculties, placed in relations to God and her fellow-creatures, can be without many and important duties to perform; and the ambitious wish for more often springs rather from a disregard of actual duties' (94). They might almost have Mrs Jellyby or Mrs Pardiggle in mind. This, of course, is the moral ground of Esther's satire; satire no less effective for its being, we have to believe, wholly innocent of satiric intent.

At the start of the novel, her sharper insights – diagnosing 'rapacious benevolence', for instance – are attributed to others. She begins, it is true, to rumble Skimpole very early, wondering why he is so unaccountably free of the responsibilities of life, yet she discounts that perception – almost denies having had it – since it would involve going against her guardian's pre-emptive judgement. Yet it is she, rather than her guardian, who, at the heart of the novel, rebukes Richard's failure to understand Jarndyce (591), and sees no proof of Skimpole's unworldliness in his 'having his expenses paid by Richard' (593). When she critiques Richard's education (in chapters 13 and 17, along with Mrs Badger's smattering of accomplishments) she does so in ways remarkably suggestive of George Eliot's in *Mill on the Floss*. In chapter 38 she cuts, sharply, through Guppy's equivocations. In chapter 61, though incapable (as who wouldn't be?) of arguing Harold Skimpole into a sense of obligation, she makes peremptorily clear her moral judgement on his treatment of Richard, of Jo, and of Jarndyce. In advising Richard and in worsting Skimpole she assumes, that is to say, the functions of guardianship. In fact, she takes the initiative surprisingly often in conversations where Jarndyce is silently present (almost as silent as Mr Jellyby) or incapable of judgement. It is she who, in chapter 24, takes it on herself to explain to Trooper George how 'we' are acquainted with Gridley, and who, in the same chapter, passes judgement on the 'case in progress – if I may use a phrase so ridiculous in such a connection'. She 'remonstrates' with Mrs Rachael, and pointedly uses the death of Gridley and the despairing cry of Miss Flite to shadow Richard's fate. She not only appropriates, that is to say, the perceptions of her guardian, but stiffens them with resolution.

Nor is Esther, for long, confined to narrative but denied the masculine prerogative of symbol. She both confirms aspects of the other narrator's symbolic method, and modifies them or or initiates her own. Although, in chapter 5, it is Richard who fancies that the bones in Krook's shop are the bones of clients, thus alerting the reader to the full apocalyptic horror of the place (Ada's hair, like Lady Jane's skin, are perceived as potential additions to the accumulating sacks of hair, heaped skin, piled bones in this processing plant), it is Esther who describes Krook himself as 'on fire within', yet cold without, and who reports his self-perception as a marine version of the grim reaper: 'I've a liking for rust and must and cobwebs. And all's fish that comes to my net'. Before the third-person narrator matches this stroke with Vholes 'making hay of the grass which is flesh' (chapter 39), Esther in chapter 37 has seen the red eruptions around his cold lips, and noted, also, how this man of impaired digestion conveys Richard 'to Jarndyce and Jarndyce' behind 'a gaunt pale horse'. The third-person narrator simply confirms Esther's insight, that both are avatars of the grim reaper, and plays his own macabre variations on her theme.

Refuting Coventry Patmore, by design, Esther and her co-narrator also challenge Barbara Gelpi. In theory, Gelpi writes, there are two possible sorts of androgyne, 'the masculine personality fulfilled and completed by the feminine and the feminine fulfilled and completed by the masculine'. But male theorists of androgyny find it easier to envision the first kind, rather than the second. 'They simply take for granted woman's inferiority: it is impossible for the female vessel to contain masculine intelligence and spirituality, while it is not only possible but natural for the masculine vessel to be filled and fulfilled by feminine emotion and physicality.[26] Not even Jung and Naumann look forward to 'woman's realisation that within her lie masculine qualities of intellect and aggression'. Rather, 'her recognition and integration of those qualities is considered a risky business, fraught with peril' (Gelpi 158).

Hortense, undoubtedly, reminds of that risk and peril, but is not the Dickens of *Bleak House*, veiled as Esther Summerson, and not merely imagining but imaginatively being her, an exception to this rule? Conceived on the Ellis model Esther may have been, but she matures on the Grey and Shirreff model, and in some respects transcends even that. Women characters who go further, and follow the radical Unitarian route of widening professional activities, may be presented as somewhat problematic in their femininity, but they are there. Dickens's ambivalence, on this, belongs to his culture; to Mrs Gaskell and Florence Nightingale, as well as Mrs Ellis and Queen Victoria, and even in a surprising degree George Eliot and Harriet Martineau (Martineau, like Dickens's impersonal narrator, sometimes seems to take the view that women may do what they like, as long as they also make the beds and wash the greens).[27]

Few people, at mid-century, seem to have been certain that this particular floodgate could be opened without obliterating (in Sir Leicester's terms) 'the landmarks of the framework of the cohesion by which things are held together!' (40.648). Dickens himself was undoubtedly drawn to Mrs Ellis's powerful formulation of domestic ideology. He can also, as did Victorian feminists, attribute moral superiority, a 'clear eye' as Mrs Ellis would have it, to his women characters, but without (it seems to me) her caveat that this superiority is applicable only to 'the minor morals of life'. If the world is to be made a better place, the reader of *Bleak House* is at liberty to conclude, it will be because the virtues and the strengths of the woman's sphere come to suffuse the man's. Consciously, no Dickens novel endorses a public role for women; unconsciously this one renders untenable its own resistance to such recognition.

When Esther's narrative ends in a (serendipitously prescient) Dickinsonian dash, leaving the future open, she has, ostensibly, only her own looks in mind. In her case, we may feel, such narrowing of focus is a triumph of self-esteem. Yet this 'his/her' narrative has consistently suggested a wider application of that coy ' – even supposing – '.

Chapter 10

Middlemarch and 'the Home Epic'

Nicola Trott

The year after George Eliot's death, W. M. W. Call named *Middlemarch* 'A provincial epic'. His label was intended to offer mixed praise at best;[1] but it brought together terms that George Eliot herself had used, at the very beginning, and end, of her novel. The first is found in the studiedly unassuming subtitle, announcing *Middlemarch* as 'A Study of Provincial Life'; the second in the unexpectedly ambitious, and open-ended, 'Finale' to the work as a whole:

> Marriage, which has been the bourne of so many narratives, is still a great beginning, as it was to Adam and Eve .... It is still the beginning of the home epic – the gradual conquest or irremediable loss of that complete union which makes the advancing years a climax, and age the harvest of sweet memories in common.[2]

Call's 'provincial epic' seems to have been suggested by George Eliot's own intriguing and oxymoronic expression:[3] 'home epic', the form that *Middlemarch* ascribes to the journey of marriage, itself seeks to marry opposing terms, the epic and the home – and, implicitly, man and wife, the male and female principles.[4] Rather like marriage in this respect, the oxymoron draws such apparently stable binaries into testing proximity with one another. At this juncture in the novel, the specific marriage in view is that between 'Fred Vincy and Mary Garth', who, sympathetic readers are assured, have 'achieved a solid mutual happiness'. They have also both become authors in a small way – he producing a treatise on farming, she 'a little book for her boys, called *Stories of Great Men, taken from Plutarch*'.[5] Their works are a source of social comment, for narrator and neighbours alike. Sensing an attempt to cross the sexual divide, Middlemarch is quick to impose more normative patterns of behaviour: Fred's writing is assumed to be by Mary, on account of the lowliness of its subject-matter ('turnips and mangel-wurzel'); hers is taken to be his, since 'he had been to the University, "where the ancients were studied"' (890). In this way, the narrator tartly observes, 'there was no need to praise anybody for writing a book, since it was always done by somebody else' (891).[6]

This question of authorship reveals something of the complexity of George Eliot's representation of gender relations. Much Victorian thinking on marriage, from Sarah Stickney Ellis to John Ruskin (whose writings appeared in the period between the novel's historical setting and the date of its composition), had been sustained by a theory of sexual difference which assigned men and women to opposite, but 'complementary', roles and worlds. Middlemarch's collective misattribution of Fred's and Mary's publications tacitly subjects the 'separate spheres' doctrine to ridicule. At the same time, though, the narrative quietly registers the fact that Mary's stories endorse the tradition of *Great Men* and in doing so adopt a format that is identifiably and limitedly 'feminine': her book is 'little', and is written 'for her boys', who are presumably expected to follow their father to the exclusively male University where the classical canon of 'greatness' is upheld.

Even so, Mary's book is a kind of 'home epic': it has taken on heroic subjects, and these ancient, and masculine, models have acquired a new lease of life through their domestic setting and function.[7] In fact, Plutarch has already been used to establish Mary's role in keeping Fred up to scratch: as 'the theatre of all [his] actions', and an 'audience' that 'demands [his] best', she is on a par with the friend of 'an antique personage' whose saying the narrator quotes (from Plutarch's 'Apophthegms of Kings') in chapter 24.[8] Fascinatingly, it is in this same chapter that the homely roots of Mary's adult writing lie buried. Her own childhood education can be deduced from the scene in which her mother is busy in her kitchen, making pies and 'giving lessons to her youngest boy and girl' (3.24.276). Mrs Garth's lessons are as much about the capabilities of 'woman' as about 'The Subjunctive Mood or the Torrid Zone' – 'She thought it good for them to see that she could make an excellent lather while she corrected their blunders "without looking"' (275) – but ironically they are tilted against the female sex. Her son being tired of grammar, Mrs Garth moves on to the household washing and to 'the story I told you on Wednesday, about Cincinnatus' (277). What ensues is a miniature, and mock-heroic, version of the battle of the sexes, with brother and sister competing over the telling of the story. Their sex-war is a lighter reminiscence of that between Tom and Maggie in *The Mill on the Floss*. While Letty has the tale pat, and wishes to tell it 'straight on, as mother told it us', Ben makes a hash of it, but proudly identifies Cincinnatus' virtues of wisdom and bravery with his father's (277). And, indeed, the reader may infer that the Roman countryman who was appointed dictator of Rome, defeated her enemy in a day, and returned once more to his farm, has a vernacular, English counterpart in Caleb Garth.

Here, apparently, is another sort of 'home epic'. The Garths' kitchen bears witness to the intimate integration of classical culture into everyday life, through both childhood learning and adult labour – including, in Mary's case, the work of writing. The ambitiousness of *Middlemarch* emerges partly in the form of these live connections with the ancient world, where 'home' becomes a context in which heroic structures and inheritances are domesticated, transmitted and revised. But George Eliot also injects a shot of satire into a scene that otherwise threatens to sentimentalize the Victorian artisan-hero; for Mrs Garth presents a comedy of self-contradiction. A strong female character, she preaches female subordination: though she put men's failings down as 'natural', 'She was ... – where is the blameless woman? – apt to be a little severe towards her own sex, which in her opinion was framed to be entirely subordinate' (275). Ben is granted a superior right to speak, and Letty's attempts to 'conquer' her brother by elbow-force draw the 'awful' reprimand from her mother, that '"Cincinnatus, I am sure, would have been sorry to see his daughter behave so'" (278).

The narrator's wry, if sympathetic, observation of the girl-child's predicament draws on the techniques of mock-heroic: 'Letty felt that between repressed volubility and general disesteem, that of the Romans inclusive, life was already a painful affair'. In putting this mock-epic tradition to work, the novel gains for it an unprecedented tonal range and flexibility. George Eliot's version of the idiom is able, for instance, to pass from the narrator to the private thoughts of one of her more satirical characters: in Book 4, Will Ladislaw relieves the tedium of helping Mr Brooke 'in arranging "documents" about hanging sheep-stealers' with 'a tickling vision of a sheep-stealing epic written with Homeric particularity' (39.422).[9] In the narrator's hands, mock-epic periodically broadens to an archly reflexive commentary on 'the means of elevating a low subject' so as to satisfy the class-conscious demands of the fashionable novel-reader: although 'Historical parallels are remarkably efficient in this way', they take up valuable space, and 'It seems an easier and shorter way to dignity, to observe that ... whatever has been or is to be narrated by me about low people, may be ennobled by being considered a parable .... Thus while I tell the truth about loobies, my reader's imagination need not be entirely excluded from an occupation with lords' (4.35.375). Not for the first, or last, time, it is the 'lords' whose dignity suffers by the comparison. Later in Book 4, an exchange of letters between Bulstrode and Rigg gives occasion for an extended simile on the 'effect of writing', which, even in 'our petty lifetime', has shown how an inscribed stone 'which has been kicked about by generations of clowns may come by curious little links of effect under the eyes of a scholar', and thereby offer a key, 'at last fix[ing] the date of invasions and unlock[ing] religions', or 'letting us into the secret of usurpations and other scandals gossiped about long empires ago' (41.448). All of which leads to the seemingly insignificant Joshua Rigg, inheritor of the Featherstone estate, and the still less prepossessing John Raffles, formerly 'the rather thickset Adonis of bar-rooms and back-parlours' (451),[10] now the blackmailing lush who happens, fatefully, to secure his brandy-flask with a scrap of paper signed by Nicholas Bulstrode. In considering these alternative textual paths, the narrator suddenly adopts an extra-terrestrial point of view, remarking that

> To Uriel watching the progress of planetary history from the Sun [in Milton, *Paradise Lost* 3.648–58], the one result would be just as much of a coincidence as the other.
> Having made this rather lofty comparison I am less uneasy in calling attention to the existence of low people by whose interference, however little we may like it, the course of the world is very much determined. (448)

Most striking here, perhaps, is the lightning-rapidity of the shifts in register and perspective. 'Home epic', in this case, suggests another refinement of mock-epic – and one in which the narrator means to be included, by virtue of a deceptively 'lofty comparison'. It is not just that two orders are brought into conjunction; the larger, and more radical, claim is that so-called minor elements are capable of generating epic effects. This being so, the direction of influence is instantly reversible: clowns rub shoulders with scholars, gossip with empires, Milton with Middlemarch, 'little links' and 'petty' lives with 'invasions' and 'religions'. Each component can react upon its neighbouring term as in a chemical exchange, the 'lofty' with the 'low'. And the medium through which that exchange occurs is writing itself.

Middlemarch, then, is a vast moveable feast in which there are no fixed correspondences between the heroic and the homely. Before indulging myself further in this 'home epic', however, I want to spend some time looking at the possible contexts for George Eliot's invention of the phrase. To apply such terminology to a *novel* may seem beside the point, or even fallacious. But, while the oxymoron is doubtless meant to sound a little strangely in the reader's ears, neither half of the equation is in itself an innovative label for prose fiction. Indeed, George Eliot seems to be drawing on a division in the theory of the novel that has developed over several decades.

Two nineteenth-century theories of the novel

Although the concept of 'home' appeals most obviously to an extra-literary domain, it can also be interpreted as a formal device and even as a full-blown narrative form. To take an extreme, but not unusual, example, Frederika Bremer, a Swedish writer whose *Home; or Family Cares and Family Joys* was translated by Mary Howitt in 1843, combines the three desiderata of Victorian domestic fiction – the middle class, a middle style, and a middling way of life. For W. E. Hickson,

> her tales appear rather as charming family biographies than novels. The story of 'Home' is simply the history of a family of the middle class, composed of husband and wife and children, to whom no events happened more extraordinary than those which to most of us are of everyday occurrence.[11]

In point of fact, Bremer's novel offsets the dressily feminine Louise against her awkward sister Petrea, who '"had an especially great inclination for great undertakings, and the misfortune to fail in them ..."' (quoted, Hickson 450). This sisterly contrast has a clear kinship with George Eliot's Dorothea and Celia. But the rigid corsetry of the 'domestic' criterion, among Victorian women's fiction and its critics, means that the issue of genre is also and inescapably one of gender. When Ebenezer Syme turns to the domestic novel in a survey of the 'Contemporary Literature of England', his judgement is that

> The quality of mind by which this sort of excellence is produced may not aspire to broad views, and cannot take a large grasp of character or passion; it is essentially a womanly faculty, and is most successful in those regions of observations over which the more philosophic inquirer passes in silence.[12]

This reductive gendering of 'the fiction feminine' (to cite Margaret Oliphant's name for the 'class')[13] suggests the kind of trap that George Eliot must have been keen to avoid, and which she herself used to anathematize various types of the genre in her less than sisterly essay on 'Silly Novels by Lady Novelists'.[14]

One way of avoiding such stultifyingly restrictive labels was to adopt the highbrow criterion of 'epic'. That sort of talking up of the novel was under way in the eighteenth century (Clara Reeve, for instance, identified the romance as 'an Epic in prose'),[15] but seems to have gathered pace after 1850: in successive years, W. C. Roscoe argues that the novel, in 'its present complex form ... fuses into a homogenous new mould the old distinctions of epic and dramatic'; Percy Greg, that 'The epics of the present time are called historical romances'; and David Masson, that 'The Novel, at its highest, is a prose Epic'.[16] History, whether in the shape of the historical novel (George Eliot's beloved Scott) or the historical epoch (Carlyle's *French Revolution*, 'that great prose poem, the single epic of modern days'),[17] provides something like the conventional definition of epic as a grand heroic or national narrative. In stating his case for the epic brand of fiction, Masson quotes both the dictum of Baron Bunsen – '"Every romance," he says in his preface to one of the English translations of the popular German novel *Debit and Credit*, "is intended or ought to be a new Iliad or Odyssey"'[18] – and an obvious local authority in Fielding, whose Preface to *The History of the Adventures of Joseph Andrews* (1742) expressly casts his fiction in the Homeric mould.[19] And it is Fielding as the 'great historian' of *Tom Jones*, against whom George Eliot measures her own achievement in *Middlemarch*:

> A great historian, as he insisted on calling himself, who had the happiness to be dead a hundred and twenty years ago, and so to take his place among the colossi whose huge legs our living pettiness is observed to walk under, glories in his copious remarks and digressions as the least imitable part of his work, and especially in those initial chapters to the successive books of his history, where he seems to bring his arm-chair to the proscenium and chat with us in all the lusty ease of his fine English. (2.15.170)

Fielding is homely in manner, but not in form: the wonderful condescension of his 'arm-chair ... chat' – his willing descent into the vernacular – is countered by the florid grandiosity of his narrative. This dispersal represents a 'spacious[ness]' available only to more lengthy and leisurely days. Fielding is not a modern, then; and this being so, he serves the same purpose as the classics or ancients, becoming a giant beside whom the living, in their comparative 'pettiness', are dwarfed (an allusion to *Julius Caesar* 1.2.133–5). What Masson enthusiastically advocates as a continuation of epic by other means, George Eliot appears to set up as a sub-epic aside on the art of sinking in prose; but, just as her narrator's self-denigration is suspiciously disproportionate, so her concessions are more apparent than real. (Blackwood for one was quick to see an opportunity for flattering his author, writing to George Eliot after reading Book 2, 'You are like a great giant walking about among us' [*Letters* 5: 167].) The summoning of Fielding heralds, not a simple failure to compete, but a conscious rejection of his kind of epic style: instead of being 'dispersed over that tempting range of relevancies called the universe', the narrative announces that it will pursue George Eliot's own interest, in 'this particular web', and 'in unravelling certain human lots' within it. The web is doubly 'particular': it stands for a specific field of observation (not some vague 'range of relevancies'); and for the specifics or particulars of its chosen set of relationships. As such, the web corresponds to the realities of local and provincial life. And yet the narrative has already established a relationship of its own which, however ambivalently, aspires beyond the confines of Middlemarch: the example of Fielding keeps an epic scale in view, even as it makes for an insistence upon the 'concentrated' scene. The result, apparently, is a type of mock-heroic that is animated by the ways in which a given hierarchy of values may be inverted. A similar inversion takes place when, meeting the Casaubons on their honeymoon, Will Ladislaw describes the Roman art studios as 'a form of life that grew like a small fresh vegetation with its population of insects on huge fossils'.[20] (His disarming self-deprecation conceals a more biting innuendo: in the context of his feeling for Dorothea and in a Book called 'Old and Young', the sting in the tail is that Casaubon, and not just ancient Rome, is the fossil [2.22.245].)

From my brief unravelling of a double strand in nineteenth-century criticism, it should at least be clear that both 'home' and 'epic' are recurrent expressions for the form of the novel; and that they are typically encountered separately, as though they represented opposing schools of fiction. George Eliot, remarkably, seeks to marry the two. In the rather diffuse sense that *Middlemarch* appears to recognize, 'epic' is not so much a formal category as a way of describing the novel's constantly shifting relations to the concept of 'greatness', whether that concept be attached (as by convention) to the ideal, the classics, the masculine, or to the less specific imaginative aspiration involved in all types of creative endeavour. Such endeavour would naturally seem to include George Eliot's own; and it is part of my contention here that the novel's story may be seen to include the story of its own formal aspirations. 'Home', meanwhile, designates not just domestic life and the traditional realm of women, but also the provincial, the local, and the indigenous, as well as the bonds and obligations of social life in a wider sense. It too has literary purposes, in that it represents the complex process by which the 'epic' may be brought 'home', to English culture, and to the readers of English fiction. Such homeliness also ensures that the various idealizations grouped under the umbrella-term of epic become a vital part of the novel's 'web' of relations – that is, they are always specific, contextualized, or, to use George Eliot's early realist watchword, 'concrete'.[21]

For all the boldness of the conception, this recasting of realism was not entirely unforeseen: way back in 1859 Masson had urged George Eliot, then a newcomer among other known women writers (C. Brontë, Gaskell, Mulock), to expand the horizon of the novel to include 'reproductions of the grand, the elemental, the ideal as well as ... of the socially minute, varying, and real' (302). In doing so, he suggested the provinciality of current practice:

> It is as if, proceeding on the theory that the British Novel, in its totality, should be a Natural History of British life, individual novelists were acting farther on the principle of the division of labour, and working out separately the natural histories of separate counties and parishes. ... and at this moment readers are hailing the advent of a new artist of the Real school, in the author of *Adam Bede*. (Masson 259–60)

Although George Eliot's incognito was already beginning to break down,[22] Masson was presumably unaware that the authors of *Adam Bede* and of an article on Riehl's work on 'The Natural History of German Life' (*WR* [July 1856]) were one and the same. Yet he uses the positivist-scientific terms adopted by George Eliot herself in order to ask that the novel move beyond its own realist limits; and it is almost as though, in the 'provincial epic' of *Middlemarch*, George Eliot has heard and responded to the call. That some such ambition was indeed intended is confirmed by an essay of George Henry Lewes's. Published just as *Middlemarch* was beginning to appear, the article described Dickens's achievement in ways that defined precisely the ground that George Eliot might be said to have occupied: what Dickens lacked was the historical, philosophic, and 'reflective tendency'; what is more, the name given to his inadequate type of genius was none other than 'bourgeois epic'.[23] Lewes's phrase was in turn quite possibly echoing one of Matthew Arnold's, who in the 'Preface' to his *Poems* (1853) had coined the category of 'domestic epic' to signal the failure of the literature of the present to live up to the literature of the past.[24] This version of the battle of the ancients and moderns has brought the two halves of our oxymoron together, but in the context of the nineteenth century's *failed* epic enterprise.

Two decades before *Middlemarch*, then, the opposing commitments of Victorian art – to the heroic and the homely – had already been joined in serious aesthetic dispute. Significantly, too, Arnold headed his list of modern, sub-classical works with *Hermann und Dorothea*, Goethe's attempt to shoulder the burdens of Homeric epic by adapting it to a contemporary and provincial setting. Mention of Goethe immediately brings the issues involved back home: for, two years after Arnold's 'Preface', Lewes published his celebrated biography of the great German writer; and, there, had taken the same Homeric endeavour to be the genuine article, '"an epic crucible to free from its dross the pure human existence of a small German town, and at the same time mirror in a small glass the great movements and changes of the world's stage."'[25] Reading *Middlemarch* with these connections in mind, the novel may be seen as encoding George Eliot's relation to a similarly high purpose, and one which exceeds her professed remit of 'A Study of Provincial Life'. Eventually, the Goethean example floats free of narrative limitation, to emerge as the basis of a new kind of heroism: the epigraph to chapter 81, taken from the second Part of Goethe's *Faust*, ends with the urgent and effortful exhortation – underlined typographically for good measure – '*Zum höchsten Dasein immerfort zu streben*' ('Constantly to strive for life's utmost worth').[26] At the same time, however, the Arnoldian shadow cast over the terms 'home epic' suggests George Eliot's awareness of the difficulty of the task – an awareness which might be thought to hover in the background of the novel's recourse to a mock-heroic register; and to be deflected into Dorothea's doubtful pursuit of an epic existence, whether in the shape of her own awkward idealism, or of the narrator's dampening comparisons with St Theresa in the 'Prelude'.

Home *versus* epic

The 'home epic' I take to be constitutive of George Eliot's fiction in its dual, often contradictory, commitments, for whose brokerage 'marriage' is at once a symbol and a sign of mutual tension or interrogation. This responsiveness to the effects of 'collision' or 'conflict' reflects a sensitivity that was associated with memories of her own Coventry home-life, and theorized in her reading of Greek tragedy.[27] The powerful implication is that there are no 'separate spheres', no tidy complementarities of the sort that Victorian culture tended to inculcate or reinforce: it is the ironies of history, rather than 'nature', which lead the narrator to observe that 'a certain greatness in' women makes men nervous, 'nature having intended greatness for men', yet having unaccountably 'sometimes made sad oversights in carrying out her intentions' (39.424–5).

Outside the pastoral atmosphere of the Garth household, both the ambition to grandeur and the experience of domesticity are very much more fraught. Dorothea, Casaubon, Lydgate, all fail in their hopes of greatness; and it seems no accident that their marriages are difficult affairs also (I shall come back to the significance of this marital plot in due course). More often than not, then, 'the home epic' reflects a division, and indecision, between the (narrowly) ordinary and the (disablingly) exceptional. Not only is the oxymoron split between its constituent terms; worse still, it may offer a merely forced, or unhappy, union.

This kind of antagonism is lodged most clearly in the Lydgate-Rosamond relationship, the reason being that they are explicitly identified – he with a genuine possibility of greatness and an ambition to make Middlemarch the home of world-changing medical research; she, on the contrary, with an unrelieved preoccupation with social status and material goods.[28] Together they lead to a tragic conflict for Lydgate: 'Only those who know the supremacy of the intellectual life – the life which has a seed of ennobling thought and purpose within it – can understand the grief of one who falls from that serene activity into the absorbing soul-wasting struggle with worldly annoyances' (8.73.793). For George Eliot's readers, who, unlike Lydgate, are kept well beyond the call of the 'sirens' (31.333; and cf. the epigraph), the signs were there from the start. A sly jest in Book 4 puts Rosamond's father, the mayor of Middlemarch, on a footing with the Duke of Wellington: 'Mr Vincy, blustering as he was, had as little of his own way as if he had been a prime minister: the force of circumstances was easily too much for him'. The reason for his not having his own way at this moment is that his daughter intends to have hers, in the matter of marriage; and so 'the force of circumstances' is synonymous with Rosamond: indeed, the appalling implication is that Lydgate is about to be *married* to 'circumstance' – exactly the trivial and contingent world he has naively and loftily pledged himself to steer clear of (36.379). In this he is like other young hopefuls who – aided by heroic rhetoric – are deluded into 'thinking that Mammon shall never put a bit in their mouths and get astride their backs, but rather that Mammon, if they have anything to do with him, shall draw their chariot' (2.15.171).

Touchingly, Lydgate thinks of Rosamond as a rare exception to her 'circumstances' (16.190); instead, she is 'circumstance' incarnate, in the sinister form of 'that mild persistence which, as we know, enables a white soft living substance to make its way in spite of opposing rock' (36.379). The home-life that she presides over as Mrs Lydgate is no domestic idyll, but a fearful concentration of the thwarting and inflexibility that her husband meets elsewhere in Middlemarch. She represents the small-town mentality that is instinctively hostile to higher activity – or, in short, 'home' of the kind that is at war with 'epic'.

Yet, Rosamond too is seen as having hopes of her own, however impoverished; and her terror at the thought of losing Lydgate is briefly dignified by being turned, through allusion to Aeschylus' *Agamemnon*, into the path of ancient suffering, 'into foreboding of that ready, fatal sponge which so cheaply wipes out the hopes of mortals' (3.31.333).[29] The satire of Rosamond as a product of her schooling – 'a sylph caught young and educated at Mrs Lemon's' (16.189) – also links her to those areas of the novel which acknowledge that 'the force of circumstances' is felt most implacably by women. '[T]he state of perturbation ... caused by not being sufficiently occupied with large interests' is not gender-specific (*Letters* 8: 465; 21 August 1869); but Dorothea's under-occupation is: hers is 'the gentlewoman's oppressive liberty', from which she has hoped to be rescued by, of all things, marriage (3.28.307). At the close of the novel, Dorothea has had various plans, but '"never carried out any"' of them (8.84.878); and the narrowness of her place in the home has been memorably objectified in the optical effects of Lowick Manor, with its washed-out wallpapers and 'shrunken furniture' (307).

If 'home' can be a death-trap for masculine genius, then, it can also be a prison for its talented female inmates. Either way, the marital and domestic militate against the aspirational and heroic. But it is part of the subtlety of *Middlemarch* that these antithetical demands do not invariably stand so neatly opposed. Lydgate, for instance, is not without a streak of the vulgar materialism which assumes that one's goods and chattels should be of the best (15.179–80); and the narrative is acutely attentive to how a scientific and reforming intelligence need not spill over into other areas of life, including, crucially, those relating to sexual attraction. Indeed, Lydgate's gender politics are shown to be his fatal flaw: he takes the absurd, if entirely conventional, view of marriage, that it is the role of the 'perfect' wife to 'venerat[e]' her husband's 'high musings and momentous labours', yet never to step beyond 'the true womanly limit' (4.36.387; cf. 29.313). At the back of such thinking lies a crudely biological assumption about 'the innate submissiveness of the goose as beautifully corresponding to the strength of the gander' (36.391). The narrative irony is both sharp and dramatic: in this case, as the reader has been made aware, no such correspondence exists.

Not only are there mixed signals among the characters; their 'epic' inclinations are themselves subject to critique. Mock-epic tips over into a mockery *of* epic, on several grounds. Most insistent, perhaps, is the charge of unreality: Rosamond's singing of popular songs is excused with the dry comment that 'mortals must share the fashions of their time, and none but the ancients can be always classical' (16.190); Farebrother points out that, though the 'choice of Hercules is a pretty fable', 'Prodicus makes it easy work for the hero, as if the first resolves were enough', adding that 'Another story says that he came to hold the distaff' (18.218).[30] Hercules' domestication and diminishment tallies, not just with Lydgate's future, but also with the comparative analysis of classical texts which is underway among the 'higher critics' of the nineteenth century. This interpretative gap, between heroic posture and hidden reality, is largely opened to view in the fruitless and un-Herculean labours of Casaubon, who lacks the higher critical perspective in relation as much to his own 'small currents of self-preoccupation' as to his 'small monumental records' of anachronistic research into 'the still unwritten Key to all Mythologies' (3.29.313–14). Having neither a philological nor historical ground – being, in fact, 'as free from interruption as a plan for threading the stars together' – this doomed epic project cannot even 'bruise itself unawares against discoveries' (48.520). Struck with pity at the preposterous gulf between ambition and achievement, the narrator remarks: 'Doubtless some ancient Greek has observed that behind the big mask and the speaking-trumpet, there must always be our poor little eyes peeping as usual and our timorous lips more or less under anxious control' (314). The meaning of this citation is clear enough – once again, the heroic gestures of the classical world (in this case magnified by the conventions of its tragic theatre) conceal the truth of the human condition – but the source is harder to pin down. However, since the attitude expressed is more nineteenth century AD than fifth century BC – that doubt-insinuating 'doubtless' gives the game away – this would seem to be a rare instance, in George Eliot, of an inside joke. As it happens, the discrepancy between heroic mask and human actor had long ago been used, by Lewes, to dispute the prevailing, idealist reading of Greek tragedy:

> Never was a grosser prejudice than that current about the rigid ideality of Greek art. ... the Greek drama, so often cited as an illustration of this prejudice, how will it bear examination? The mixture of the divine and human – of heroic persons in gigantic masks, buskin and cothurnus, is striking enough; and in the action of the drama other incongruities occur. ... the furies are as *grotesque* as anything in Shakespeare.[31]

The ironies of Casaubon's situation have a formal function, then: they reflect George Eliot's attempt to acknowledge heroic idealizations and self-idealizations within the context of her novel's realist and sceptical commitments.

In this, covertly reflexive, narrative line, the scrutiny of epic often takes on a political colouring. To some extent, the class assumptions shared by literate Victorians were naturalized in their cultural appropriations of the classics. The conventional distinction between 'high' and 'low', on which the heroic tradition rests – Masson, for instance, assigns 'the higher' and 'the lower exercises of the poetic faculty' to the ideal and real respectively (302) – had a correspondence in the distinctions of social class.[32] And it is this correspondence that *Middlemarch* can be seen to disrupt. A comic episode in the classical class-divide occurs in Book 6, when Fred Vincy comes across a minor skirmish between the rural Luddites and the railway agents. Aided by his mount, Fred routs the angry group of labourers 'in smock-frocks' who have laid Caleb Garth's assistant out cold and 'were driving the men in coats before them with their hay-forks' (56.601). Nothing daunted, the leader of the gang, Hiram Ford, observing himself at a safe challenging distance, turned back and shouted a defiance which he did not know to be Homeric.

'Yo're a coward, yo are. Yo git off your horse, young measter, and I'll have a round wi' ye, I wull. Yo daredn't come on wi'out your hoss an' whip. I'd soon knock the breath out on ye, I would.' (56.602)

The Homeric defiance is Odysseus', shouted at the Cyclops after he has blinded the monster and made good his escape by ship: 'How do you like the beating that we gave you, / you damned cannibal?' (trans. Robert Fitzgerald, *The Odyssey* 9.427–94). The correspondences are intentionally imprecise, perhaps: Fred is no man-eater; while Hiram lacks Odyssean cunning and, unlike his Homeric counterpart, has actually been worsted in the fight. All of which suggests the sub-heroic; and yet the peasants are genuinely 'in possession of ... a giant's club' of their own, the 'undeniable truth which they know through a hard process of feeling', even though they know nothing of either Homer or 'the Rights of Man', that the coming railroad is good only '"for the big folks to make money out on"' (604–5).

The social injustice which excludes the poor goes hand-in-hand with the educational disadvantages which exclude women; and the marginalization of both groups is symbolized by their exclusion from 'the classics'. The position of women within the novel's representation of highbrow culture is at best exiguous, at worst notable only for its absence; and in consequence it draws some of the narrator's wryest humour. Under attack from the redoubtable Mrs Cadwallader, Mr Brooke retreats to a masculine line of defence: '"Your sex are not thinkers, you know – *varium et mutabile semper* – that kind of thing. You don't know Virgil. I knew" – Mr Brooke reflected in time that he had not had the personal acquaintance of the Augustan poet ...' (1.6.77–8). In the following chapter, Dorothea is caught declaring to Casaubon her desire to emulate Milton's daughters by reading "Latin and Greek aloud" to him, "without understanding" (7.87–8). She does of course ardently wish to 'understand' – and is 'beginning' to do so, in Latin at least, by chapter 29, and in Greek by chapter 37.[33] Casaubon's cautious assent has been taken as 'a precious permission' to learn because 'Those provinces of masculine knowledge seemed to her a standing-ground from which all truth could be seen more truly.' In this expectation, as might be foreseen, she is sorely disappointed. Rather less predictable and submissive is her motive for learning in the first place: the 'truth' she seeks would tell her how it is that 'men who knew the classics appeared to conciliate indifference' to poverty 'with zeal for the glory [of God]' (88). It is at this point, as so often in Dorothea's characterization, that questions of gender yield to wider social concerns. She repeatedly expresses anxieties about aesthetic escapism in a world of sorrow – a conflict of life and art which was much in her author's mind at the time of writing,[34] and which emerges in a series of mock-epic disjunctions, between '"little Homeric bits"' and some '"great object in life"', between a '"piety"' of enjoyment and '"fanaticism of sympathy"' (22.251–2), or between '"simpering pictures in the drawing-room"' and '"coarse ugliness"' outside it (39.424).

'Home' may be a trap; but the 'epic' for its part has no place for the homely, if that is understood to include the female and humble classes. And, here, ironically enough, the concept of 'home' and its limits comes back in, not as a force for simple denial, but as a means of exposing and redefining the limits of the 'heroic' itself. This, the final ground of George Eliot's dissent from the conventions of 'epic', turns upon the need for inclusiveness. In the would-be heroic surroundings of ancient Rome, Dorothea's tears release 'That element of tragedy which lies in the very fact of frequency' (20.226). In itself, this is nothing new: it confirms George Eliot's longstanding refusal of the art of the exceptional sufferer in favour of the reality of a suffering which is so widely distributed as to be almost imperceptible. This de-heroizing and democratizing impulse goes all the way back to the challenging of the fashionable reader in *Scenes of Clerical Life*. More striking, in *Middlemarch*, is the integration of that impulse among the conditions governing the narrator's speech acts. The epigraph to chapter 27 reads:

> Let the high Muse chant loves Olympian:
> We are but mortals, and must sing of man. (3.27.297)[35]

The switch to the human (here confirmed by a jaunty couplet) revises the heroic in ways that have been going on much more widely in Victorian realist fiction.[36] As a narrative position and voice, however, it is George Eliot's sole discovery; for it is underwritten by convictions deriving from the author's own humanism.

The human position

Given the narrative stance adopted in Book 3, Lydgate's Olympian disdain for the 'petty medium of Middlemarch' cannot be sustained for long (2.18.217). In fact, it has already run into trouble in the election of a hospital chaplain, an event producing a tussle between Bulstrode and his opponents in which Lydgate has had to cast the deciding vote. The epigraph to the chapter in question – 'Oh, sir, the loftiest hopes on earth / Draw lots with meaner hopes: heroic breasts, / Breathing bad air, run risk of pestilence ...' (18.207) – uses nineteenth-century fears of infection to bring grandeur into proximity and conflict with pettiness. The medical metaphor suits Doctor Lydgate, but also predicts his future, since his hopes are to be thus lowered and contaminated, as he is drawn into the same money worries – and recourse to the 'lots' of gambling – as beset Farebrother, a man he initially sees pityingly as quite unlike himself in having wasted his scientific talent. More immediately, though, the epigraph relates to Farebrother, who loses the chaplaincy to Tyke, but whose fine conduct in reduced circumstances 'made his character resemble those southern landscapes which seem divided between natural grandeur and social slovenliness' (207). This analogy expands upon the awkward juxtapositions of the epigraph, yet suggests that Farebrother remains innately 'heroic', if only in a small way. His is the purely moral victory, of a man who 'wants a wider range than that of a poor clergyman' (5.50.537), but whose homely virtues are nevertheless extraordinary: 'Very few men could have been as filial and chivalrous as he was to the mother, aunt, and sister, whose dependence on him had in many ways shaped his life rather uneasily for himself' (207). His kind and cheerful fulfilment of these claims exemplifies the sort of achievable – as opposed to exceptional – greatness that George Eliot was keen to recommend: 'Few are born to do the great work of the world, but all are born to this.'[37]

'Home' may be positively valorized as the 'small ... circle' of a realizable heroism. All the same, Farebrother is only partly heroic; and his limitations extend beyond his self-mocking reference to Hercules in chapter 18: 'he had not escaped that low estimate of possibilities which we rather hastily arrive at as an inference from our own failure' (218).[38] If Farebrother's failure results in low expectations, Lydgate's is preceded by excessive hopes. And, here, the coherence of the humanist outlook is partly due to the novel having access to much wider intellectual resources. The doctor's neglect of his 'medium' is an indication that he has not understood the terms upon which, in the modern world, greatness is to be achieved. His is an anachronistic conception of genius based on hero-worship, which ignores the realistic element in which even genius must do its work; and which puts all labourers on a level with their times: as Lewes had pithily remarked, 'There never was a solitary great man! There never was a great artist standing alone amidst a race of pygmies.'[39] Modern historicism has produced a great man in its own image – that is, achievements are now contextual and social rather than, as in the past, singular and heroic. (This revaluation has its apotheosis in the industrial age, 'that myriad-headed, myriad-handed labour by which the social body is fed, clothed, and housed', and which lives in the consciousness of Caleb Garth [24.283].)

The context for Lewes's exclamation was the appearance of the first two volumes of George Grote's monumental *History of Greece* (published jointly by Murray in 1846); George Eliot was reading the second volume in August 1868 (*Journals*, 133) and was tackling all twelve (1846–56) in 1869–70 (*Letters* 5: 156n). Grote's was a key work in the development of English versions of the higher criticism, which sought to apply new, positivist methods to the study of ancient documents. In classical scholarship, such criticism presented a thorough-going challenge to heroic traditions and values. The persistent allure of the colossal, totemic figure was nowhere more apparent than in the case of Homer, whose role in the conception of the hero coincided with the heroic role he was himself assigned in culture. Homer, or the tradition in which he was read, made an obvious higher critical target. When the continuous heroic narrative of *The Iliad* was subjected to sceptical historical analysis, the unique figure of 'Homer' gave way to the 'Homeric controversy', and the unity of his 'epic' to theories about its origin in episodic or multiple authorship.[40] In Lewes's words, 'It is only by falsely arguing from later practices, that we can ever conceive an early poet planning a gigantic and multiform work merely to suit some critical fancy of epic grandeur' (415).

For Goethe, the deconstruction of Homer into his component ballads meant a temporary liberation from the anxiety of his epic example. For George Eliot, it meant that any appeal to 'epic' status was likely to be complicated by the fact that, in the period to which her fiction referred, the whole concept of epic was under hostile scrutiny. (It is interesting that her Diary for 2 December 1870 records her both 'experimenting' with the 'Miss Brooke' story and 'reading Wolf's Prolegomena to Homer', the work which invented the 'Homeric question' [*Journals*, 141]). But the importance of the higher criticism, for *Middlemarch*, is that it is taken up by, and absorbed into, a narrative disposition. The implications are usefully summarized by Will who, in speaking to Dorothea about her husband's deficiencies as a scholar of the old school, observes that 'new discoveries are constantly making new points of view' (2.22.254). Viewpoints, then, are necessarily both multiple and mutable. Just seven chapters later, the narrator makes this famous self-interrupting turn: 'One morning, some weeks after her arrival at Lowick, Dorothea – but why always Dorothea? Was her point of view the only possible one with regard to this marriage?' (29.312). The abrupt removal of the heroine from the focus of narrative and readerly attention, is a deliberate affront to expectations.[41] At a theoretical level, it is as though the narrator has pulled up short to question the assumptions of the story along higher critical lines. Removing Dorothea from view suggests a disconcerting application of the Homeric question to the nineteenth-century novel and its hero(ine)-centred narrative. The sudden and unsettling disappearance of the main character requires the kind of scepticism and re-orientation that had worked to dislodge Homer from *The Iliad*. In *Middlemarch*, the shock of this act of displacement makes it seem akin to a withdrawal of authorial love. At the same time, it has a profound ethical purpose – the assertion of the alternative 'point of view' – which involves the central moral plot of the novel, and which at length returns Dorothea to a central role.

The question posed by the narrator, 'why always Dorothea?', is the rhetorical equivalent of this ethical purpose. The demand that it places on the reader, at this crucial turning-point in the novel, is intentionally made as difficult as possible: 'all our interest' and 'effort at understanding' is to be transferred from attractive bride to dismal husband. George Eliot first acted out this sort of aesthetic and moral test in the character of Amos Barton, in *Scenes of Clerical Life*. In *Middlemarch*, the test has a philosophical dimension, in that its foundation lies in the recognition of another as 'an equivalent centre of self' (21.243); and is still more severe, in that there is no escaping the fact that Casaubon's own 'point of view' is limited by the narrowest egoism. It is highly significant that the epigraph to chapter 27, which announces the humanist position of the narrator (and is quoted at the end of my previous section), also introduces the famous 'parable' of 'egoism', in which a 'lighted candle' is described as giving the 'flattering illusion of a concentric arrangement' to a randomly scratched 'surface of polished steel' (297). The narrator, whose speech acts benefit from a higher critical knowledge of 'new points of view', has to admit, in Casaubon and Rosamond, the most restrictive of perspectives.

The questioning of Dorothea's centrality, in chapter 29, is a synecdoche for the novel's resistance to the exclusive concentration on self, and the self-centring view of the world it produces. Such questioning also arises indirectly out of the facts of the novel's writing, which joined a separate narrative about 'Miss Brooke' to an existing story about Middlemarch (*Journals* 96). On publication, it was 'Miss Brooke' who opened the novel; and both the singularity, and limitation, of this female starting-point, and its openness to much more diverse materials, seem to be alluded to, in chapter 11, by analogy with the Greek historian, Herodotus. Remarking the 'stealthy convergence of human lots' in the 'vicissitudes' of 'provincial society', the narrator comments that 'much the same sort of movement and mixture went on in old England as we find in the older Herodotus, who also, in telling what had been, thought it well to take a woman's lot for his starting-point' (1.11.122–3). George Eliot's narrative method acquires the authority of a classical precedent. In Herodotus' account, the conflict of Greece and Asia begins with the abduction of Io, daughter of the king of Argos, by the Phoenicians. The homely cause of heroic struggle is centre-stage; but is also ready to be displaced by what follows. In *Middlemarch*, Dorothea's is one narrative viewpoint among many – and, indeed, with an eye on the 'convergence of human lots', the narrator immediately shifts the attention, noting archly that 'Io, as a maiden apparently beguiled by attractive merchandise, was the reverse of Miss Brooke, and in this respect perhaps bore more resemblance to Rosamond Vincy'.

The comparativist technique which brings an ancient historian into the frame also exposes him to the controversies of contemporary life. (One such adaptation emerges in chapter 48, when Herodotus is among the authors Dorothea is 'learning to read with Mr Casaubon'; but whom – unlike her husband – she approaches in a newly sceptical frame of mind [515].) *Middlemarch*'s manifold relations to the heroic or epic or tragic narratives of the classical past are continuous with its sweeping panorama of Reform-period Britain, the sliding scale of its changing social scene, and the various points of view by which the individual experience is articulated. Paradoxically, it is here, in drawing the parochial limits of her fiction, that George Eliot's horizon seems most expansive. Paradoxically, too, such expansiveness involves pointing out the limitations of a single central character.

The homing of epic

That the 'Finale' defines *marriage* as 'the beginning of the home epic' suggests that the institution is crucial to the moral and formal concerns of the novel. It is noticeable, for instance, that Dorothea's acknowledgement of 'an equivalent centre of self' comes about only after her wedding. And in all sorts of other ways, too, the ethical activity of the novel is marriage-related: the expression of Farebrother's goodness is repeatedly gathered around the Mary-Fred courtship (chs 52, 66), just as Dorothea's is exercised by the Lydgate-Rosamond-Will triangle (chs 80–82). Lydgate's and Casaubon's failures are marriage-dependent, since it is only on losing the bachelor state that Lydgate's potential comes to grief (76.822–3) and Casaubon's would-be heroic work comes to be scrutinized (20.232–3). As the latter case amply confirms, marriage does not correct the incorrigible; but it does expose certain sorts of illusion, about the centrality of self in the world, and the 'concentric' or 'providential' narrative that is constructed around it (27.297). Prominent among such illusions are those about the married state itself: Lydgate's naive confidence in female inferiority, which meets its nemesis in Rosamond ('Neverthless she had mastered him' [65.719]); Dorothea's avowed marriage-ideal of blatant sexual inequality, which meets its nemesis in Casaubon. Dorothea's delusions about marriage are the first and in some ways saddest indication of the part that delusions of grandeur, aided by inexperience, will play. Lydgate rightly infers her 'heroic hallucinations' regarding Casaubon (76.826); but these have their origin in a dream of her own duty-laden importance: 'Marriage ... was to bring guidance into worthy and imperative occupation'. In reality, 'The clear heights where she had expected to walk in full communion ... become difficult to see even in her imagination' (28.307); while, on the other side, it is as a husband that Casaubon's egoism – that anti-epic of 'a small hungry shivering self' – becomes, first apparent, and finally all-absorbing (29.314; 42.455–6).

Marriage, then, seems to be the moral testing-ground of the novel, for better, for worse: chapter 74, which takes as its epigraph the *Marriage Prayer* from the Book of Tobit, 'Mercifully grant that we may grow aged together', tests the Bulstrode marriage to the very limit (798). As that prayer implies, the married state is one which requires, indeed institutionalizes, the recognition of another's presence – or, in George Eliot's terms, another's 'point of view'. In this respect, as Dorothea remarks, '"Marriage is so unlike everything else. There is something even awful in the nearness it brings"' (81.855). Again and again, *Middlemarch* crosses 'the door-sill of marriage' in order to place 'equivalent centre[s] of self' in the closest proximity (20.228). These crossings mark the places where 'home' and 'epic' come into conflict; but also where both the ethical and formal developments of the novel occur.

Interestingly, the essential precondition of development is failure. This necessity includes, but is not exhausted by, the reservations about epic which belong with George Eliot's corrective class-consciousness or her qualified attachment to realism. That Dorothea, Casaubon, Lydgate, fall short of greatness in the context of their marital difficulties makes clear that the two halves of the oxymoron – 'home' and 'epic', female and male, domesticity and aspiration, real and ideal, intractable 'medium' and heroic fantasy – pull against one another in divisive and destructive ways. Perversely almost, failure becomes in itself one of the novel's grand preoccupations: '"Failure after long perseverance is much grander than never to have a striving good enough to be called a failure."' '"There is no sorrow I have thought more about than that – to love what is great, and try to reach it, and yet to fail"' (22.254–5; 76.821). It seems vital that both these statements are made by Dorothea, since it is through her example above all that the novel embraces, not just a failed epicism, but also a revised sense of the 'epic life'. This revision is arrived at after failure has enforced an agonizing abandonment of old beliefs. Dorothea, who married Casaubon in the 'great faith' of her own 'illusion' about his still 'greater' work, becomes by degrees 'altogether unbelieving' in it ('Finale', 896; 48.519–20). Her scepticism goes beyond a violation of the wifely vow of obedience, daring though this suggestion of 'rebellious anger' is (42.463). It also involves a fully critical stance that is incompatible with her early Evangelical strictness. Dorothea grasps the higher critical point, that Casaubon's 'Key to all Mythologies' is doomed, not because he has failed to write it, but because it cannot be written at all. No such unique 'Key' exists. His outmodedly monologic exercise can have only an ironic fulfilment in his own self-centred doubts and jealousies, which project themselves in minute pedantry of the sort that Farebrother, with unconscious satire, ascribes to the pen-name 'Philomicron' (17.202).[42] Even so, it is the larger and magnanimous action of *Middlemarch* to temper insight with 'pity', and scepticism with 'tenderness' (20.232, 234). The conflict between Dorothea's critical understanding and her 'resolved submission' is shadowed in Rome, and produces both the climax of Book 4 (42.455, 463–5) and the crisis of conscience surrounding Casaubon's death (48.519–20).

After that kind of spiritual intimacy, it is given to the 'Finale' to distance the reader from the action of the novel. Rather like the palinode to *Troilus and Criseyde*, though without Chaucer's chilling remoteness, the end brings in a disconcertingly 'epic' standard of judgement: of Dorothea's remaining life we are told that 'Her full nature, like that river of which Cyrus broke the strength, spent itself in channels which had no great name on the earth' (896). The image of strength broken by the 'force of circumstances' – here given the fearsome embodiment of Cyrus the Great, founder of the Persian empire – is only partly softened by the fact that these wasted 'channels' give way to another metaphor of water, registering Dorothea's 'incalculably diffusive' effect 'on those around her'. At first, the 'Finale' appears disappointingly ready to reimpose the kind of rhetorical disjunction between the heroic and homely, between 'ardent deeds' and 'insignificant people', which the body of the novel has so patiently called into question. But, by now, readers may suspect that all history has been reconceived as taking place in a continuous and inescapable 'medium' of 'daily words and acts'. And, as it happens, both the river metaphor and the Persian ruler have already been assigned a place in the history of Dorothea. In chapter 48, it was *Cyrus* whose strength was broken, as Dorothea stood, like another Antigone, 'at the door of the tomb' of Casaubon's learning, having given up on the reading that sustains his epic delusions, including, in Herodotus, the spurious history of 'the portents before the birth of Cyrus' (515–16).[43] Meanwhile, the river whose waters are broken by imperial conquest reaches back to a scene in which Dorothea's influence has been of a quite different order:

> The Rubicon, we know, was a very insignificant stream to look at; its significance lay entirely in certain invisible conditions. Will felt as if he were forced to cross his small boundary ditch, and what he saw beyond was not empire but discontented subjection.
> But it is given to us sometimes even in our everyday life to witness the saving influence of a noble nature, the divine efficacy of rescue that may lie in a self-subduing act of fellowship. (82.861)

The momentous Rubicon is diminished in accordance with the geographical evidence, yet still provides a mock-epic comparison between Julius Caesar, about to embark on a civil war by marching on Rome, and Will Ladislaw, whose entanglement with Rosamond seems to have ruined his relationships with both her and Dorothea. But a revision of this classical precedent reformulates both the basis upon which heroic significance is attributed, and the occasions on which it is to be found. 'Invisible conditions', of which Will is unaware, have already turned the tables on his humiliating exchange of 'empire' for 'subjection'. Those conditions have been determined by Dorothea herself. Her sympathetic experience of failure has also made her the means of a new ethical purpose. And that purpose revises the mock-epic scale of judgement by instantaneously returning the possibilities of 'noble' behaviour to 'everyday life'. If only in rare instances, the conflict of 'home' and 'epic' can yield to an effective synthesis.

Surreptitiously, then, the 'Finale' is the setting for two of *Middlemarch*'s most remarkable inversions of an epic scale of value. The adverse criticism which the novel's overt claims for Dorothea have attracted has tended to obscure the ways in which the narrative pursues this sort of 'hidden heroism'. But the possibility of such inexplicit connections is essential to the 'diffusive' and 'incalculabl[e]' revaluation of 'epic' that George Eliot appears to be seeking. Both narrative modes, direct and indirect, can be seen coming together in the heroine's dealings with Rosamond. In chapter 29, Dorothea had been an object of the narrative irony whose changes of perspective removed her from view. Now she is herself the agent of such change, through the process by which she has come to recognize another's 'centre of self': 'Was she alone in that scene? Was it her event only? She forced herself to think of it as bound up with another woman's life' (80.845; see also the chapter epigraph, from Wordsworth's *Ode to Duty*, and 76.819). On reflection, this line of questioning is most notable for its unannounced correspondence to the narrator's earlier interruption, with one crucial difference – that the narrator's and character's points of view have finally coalesced. In chapter 29, the questions, 'why always Dorothea? ...', had imposed the rhetorical equivalent of the marriage-tie upon a narrative that threatened to become absorbed by a single character. By the end of the novel, that Wolfian dispersal of the heroic interest among multiple '*dramatis personae*' (11.122) has taken on more generous interpretative possibilities. It resurfaces, through Dorothea herself, as the 'incalculably diffusive' sources of interaction and influence in George Eliot's fiction.

That Dorothea's personal influence is restricted to the 'small home circle' is partly due to the narrator's perception of determining historical conditions. But it is also a continuation of the married state from which – starting with that trying wedding-journey to Rome – Dorothea first emerged from the 'moral stupidity' of egoism (21.243). And it is in relation to this development, as much as to her 'unhistoric acts' (896), that marriage is finally defined as 'the home epic'. While Farebrother has been a hero of a kind, his heroism has been kept within rather strict limits – limits that seem to be bound up with his single status. He corresponds more to an epic manqué than to 'the home epic'. Dorothea, on the other hand, as the rhetoric surrounding her actions suggests, finishes by becoming the highest embodiment of that limited ideal. That is, she becomes a heroine of the epic of alternative 'points of view'.[44] This re-definition is necessarily diminishing of the individual ego; but it also finds room for the very largest implications of George Eliot's intellectual life, in its shift from ancient to modern, from metaphysical to humanist, from the vanished 'medium' of the Christian past to a new belief in "widening the skirts of light" (39.427). Dorothea has often been seen as meanly deprived of the scope for achievement which her author enjoyed; but in allegorical outline at least her is the ideal development of the age. In the midst of her Roman and marital crisis, the reassurance is offered that 'Permanent rebellion, the disorder of a life without some loving reverent resolve, was not possible to her' (2.20.226–7): that the narrative both attributes to Dorothea the experience of 'rebellion', and forecasts an end to its 'disorder', binds up her history with George Eliot's own, and allows her to be representative of a loss of faith which does not disintegrate into faithlessness or lovelessness. If the movement from 'Prelude' to 'Finale' is a movement from impossible standards to achievable ends, from misplaced idealism to a clearer-eyed realism, it is also one which expands again in another direction, to encompass Dorothea's apotheosis among those whose 'love' is 'a sort of baptism and consecration', by virtue of her 'holding up an ideal for others in her believing conception of them' (77.828–9).

One of the more extraordinary achievements of *Middlemarch* is that it devises an institution, marriage, and a rhetorical structure, 'home epic', within which both its ethical and formal purposes can be worked out, by means the most subtle and varied. For *Middlemarch*'s concern is the nineteenth-century novel as well as nineteenth-century society. It takes the marriage-plot, 'which has been the bourne of so many narratives', and has been especially powerful in English fiction since Austen, and makes it 'a great beginning' ('Finale'), a tradition that is suddenly opened out to a far grander conception than had formerly seemed possible.[45] In this endeavour, as we have seen, George Eliot was drawing on an alternative, epic line in the theory of fiction. The 'epic' is perpetually in unstable and difficult negotiation with the often antithetical demands of 'home'; and 'marriage' is the ground, if not of their reconciliation, then of their new and improved relationship. It is also the ground on which form and ethics meet. For if marriage is the objective correlative of the generic forcing of the modern 'domestic epic', about which Arnold had complained, then it is equally the basis for a critique of traditional epic and a revision of its terms. And this revision is the foundation, not of a 'religious order', as in St Theresa's securely 'epic life' ('Prelude'), but of a new, richly uneasy, aesthetic and moral order.[46]

It is indicative that both despair and aspiration, the sense of failure and the will to greatness, or the 'work that makes a higher life for me', are the constant companions of George Eliot's Diary (see her entries for 22 November 1868 and 27 October 1870; *Journals* 133, 141). In a novel much preoccupied with ideas of greatness, and with noble and ignoble hopes and lapses, George Eliot seems to have included the status of her own writing. The novel's failed epic grandeurs encode the failure of the epic form, but also its redefinition – a redefinition that rewrites the thwarted ambition which lies at the heart of Victorian literary culture, and in the process announces George Eliot's own project of 'home epic'.

Chapter 11

The Ghost of Doubt: Writing, Speech and Language in *Lord Jim*

Gerard Barrett

> I had a greedy relish for a few volumes of Voyages and Travels – I forget what, now – that were on those shelves; and for days and days I can remember to have gone about my region of our house, armed with the centre-piece out of an old set of boot-trees – the perfect realisation of Captain Somebody, of the Royal British Navy, in danger of being beset by savages, and resolved to sell his life at a great price. The Captain never lost dignity, from having his ears boxed with the Latin Grammar. I did; but the Captain was a Captain and a hero, in spite of all the grammars of all the languages in the world, dead or alive.
> —Charles Dickens, *David Copperfield*.

In the fourth chapter of Charles Dickens's *David Copperfield* (1850), the young protagonist is confined to his room as a punishment for not knowing his Latin grammar.[1] A contrast emerges between a painful experience of language as an oppressive system of regulations and an escapist literary fantasy fixated on the figure of a ship's captain. This conjunction of themes anticipates the subject of Joseph Conrad's *Lord Jim* (1900). In *David Copperfield*, the linguistic failure ironically becomes the occasion of a literary reverie, one that restores the hero's dignity through his identification with a character that is above language and all its travails. Turning to Conrad's *Lord Jim*, we find a similar set of ambitions but a far less happy outcome. The story of Jim is that of a boy who grows up to live out his fantasies of heroism at sea, fantasies that had been nourished by 'the sea-life of light literature'.[2] However, when his ship seems destined to sink during a storm, he joins his less conscientious crewmembers and abandons her, leaving eight hundred people to die. Jim finds the subsequent loss of dignity impossible to bear and during the inquiry that follows he becomes painfully aware of the inadequacy of language to express the real horror of what he had felt that night. Although he fails in his efforts to rehabilitate himself through words in the eyes of others, he partially recovers his honour in heroic action on the Malayan island of Patusan. Finally, he pays the greatest price of all in order to keep a promise that he makes there. His self-imposed death at the novel's close attempts to bridge the gulf that his life has opened up between language and the world.

To turn to *Lord Jim* after reading *David Copperfield* is to mark a series of innovations in the art of fiction. If *David Copperfield* is paradigmatic of the English novel in the middle of the nineteenth century, *Lord Jim* points the way for a new kind of novel at the century's close. While the hero of *David Copperfield* has absolute control over the story he tells, the narration of *Lord Jim* is dispersed among a number of narrators, some of them of doubtful reliability.[3] Although a detached, omniscient, third-person narrator recounts the first four chapters, the sudden switch to an involved, partially-knowledged, first-person narrator in chapter five creates subtle complications, not the least being this narrator's initial lack of sympathy for Jim's plight. Conrad's novel also disorientates the reader with its chronological displacements. While *David Copperfield* follows a straight line from its hero's birth to his maturity, the linear sequence of events in *Lord Jim* is drastically reshuffled from the chronological order in which those events actually occurred. *Lord Jim* also unsettles with its generic heterogeneity. On one level, it is an adventure story, a love-story, a courtroom drama, an exotic romance and a drunken anecdote with elements of slapstick and farcical misunderstanding. On another, it is a bildungsroman, a tragedy, an existential inquiry, a religious allegory and a meditation on imperial decline in the face of a *fin de siècle* revaluation of empire. This blend of popular with serious modes suggests that the novel is less an example of early modernism than, as Fredric Jameson has suggested, 'an anticipation of that later and quite different thing we have come to call variously textuality, *écriture*, post-modernism, or schizophrenic writing.'[4] As Jameson points out, Conrad's work spills out of 'high literature into light reading and romance, reclaiming great areas of diversion and distraction, by the most demanding practice of style and *écriture* alike, floating uncertainly somewhere in between Proust and Robert Louis Stevenson' (206). We can take this further and say that this uncertainty is a submerged theme of the novel itself. The gap between the aestheticism of Proust and the commercialism of Stevenson is one which the writing of Conrad's novel seeks to close, though this gap is also symbolic of a more fundamental contrast in Conrad's work. This contrast is the space between a vision that sees language referring directly and simply to an ordered world and one that sees language as a ghostly construct with an arbitrary and flawed relationship to the world's 'dismal aspect of disorder' (*Lord Jim* 186). Conrad's incorporation of writing, speech and language itself into the novel's storyline lifts his tale above the tradition of sea-literature into the developing canon of modernist fiction. In *Lord Jim*, going to sea proves to be no defence against having your ears boxed by the grammar book and all that it represents.

One of the features of language that Conrad exploits in *Lord Jim* is its ineluctable ambiguity. The language of the novel is highly figurative, creating a separate order of knowledge from that of the literal. Yet the novel's tropes, metaphors and similes do not exist in isolation. They are not poetic doodles employed to give the text a 'literary' texture. Rather, they perform a structural function, creating a textual web where disparate elements are linked. An example that illustrates this aspect of Conrad's narrative technique is the moment when the German skipper of the *Patna* surveys the eight hundred pilgrims coming on board and remarks, 'Look at dese cattle' (14) to his new chief mate. As the skipper's remark occurs at the end of a poignant description that emphasizes the humanity of the pilgrims, its immediate impact is to make for the kind of abrupt switch of tone and register that is a hallmark of the modernist work. It further serves to emphasize the novel's impressionism, the callous remark conveying how an individual perspective can seem to alter the very nature of what is observed. But the denigration of these pilgrims as 'cattle', with its accompanying associations of property and rubbish, also carries particular resonance for Jim.

Jim, we remember, is compared in the novel's opening line to 'a charging bull' (7), a comparison that suggests an intense, uncompromising masculinity. The German skipper's remark, however, raises the possibility that the simile also serves a more abstract, formal function. Later in the third chapter we find Jim on board the *Patna* studying the ship's charts, a scene in which a sheet of paper portraying the depths of the sea 'presented a shiny surface under the light of a bull's eye lamp lashed to a stanchion' (17). Although the bull's eye lamp in question is a common nautical object and as such belongs to the novel's literal dimension, the text is spinning a thread of connection between Jim, the Patna and the pilgrims that excludes the other crew-members. Jim, then, is intimately (we could say 'textually') connected with both the ship and its inhabitants before the actual abandonment of the ship occurs.

All of these considerations have implications for the scene in which Jim, during his negotiations with the pirates in Patusan, offers 'Gentleman' Brown 'a bullock' (236). On a literal level, Jim is offering the pirates food in return for their peaceful departure. On a symbolic level, however, Jim's offer suggests that he is unconsciously presenting himself as a sacrificial offering, trading his own life for the safety of Patusan. This, in effect, is what happens. The pirates leave, but not before committing a violent act that will lead to Jim's death. Furthermore, the movement from charging bull to castrated bullock insinuates that Jim's jump from the *Patna* has had an emasculating effect. The first comparison of Jim to a bull is, therefore, not an isolated trope but merely the first part of a series. The series only reaches its conclusion when Doramin stands up to shoot Jim at the novel's end: the 'unwieldy old man, lowering his big forehead like an ox under a yoke, made an effort to rise, clutching at the flintlock pistols on his knees' (245). As this narrative line indicates, the imagery of bulls, cattle, oxen and bullocks is one that yokes heterogeneous elements, such as masculinity, dehumanization, emasculation, sacrifice and vengeance, together. It is also possible that Conrad had other meanings of 'bull' and 'ox' in mind. He may, for instance, have been setting off the kind of bull that tries, by speculation, to raise the price of stocks, against an old nuance of 'ox', that of an ancient coin. Bear in mind that Marlow's first impression of Jim was that he looked 'as genuine as a new sovereign, but there was some infernal alloy in his metal' (32) and that this tragic flaw casts doubt on 'the sovereign power enthroned in a fixed standard of conduct' (35). In this interpretation, the novel's movement from 'bull' to 'ox' would signify a desired turn from the 'unreal' fluctuations of market capitalism to a more solid gold standard rooted in traditional labour. Literal oxen, after all, have traditionally been used for the physical work of pulling the plough, the very opposite of figurative bulls. This would parallel other desired turns in the novel, from appearance to reality, from words to action and from writing to the tradition of oral storytelling. Jameson suggests that this last regression expresses Conrad's 'impatience with the objective yet ever intensifying alienation of the printed book' (219). This alienation, which actually applies equally to the spoken word in the novel, is central to the disturbing new note the novel strikes in English fiction.

In the first chapter of the novel, we learn that Jim's work as a ship-chandler's water-clerk involved 'cheerily' (7) forcing business cards on the captains of incoming ships. Jim is thereby established at the outset as a purveyor of text that is concise, clear, confident, commercial, one-dimensional and referential. The business card exemplifies an uncomplicated relationship between language and the world. It represents a world where words have fixed meanings and staidly serve the interests of commerce and trade. Jim's job also involves conducting the ships' captains to a cool parlour that contains 'easy-chairs, bottles, cigars, writing implements, a copy of harbour regulations, and a warmth of welcome that melts the salt of a three months' passage out of a seaman's heart' (7). The snug conditions depicted here slyly evoke those in which bourgeois readers consumed their novels at the end of the nineteenth century. Conrad suggests that serious literature is incompatible with these conditions, needing a backdrop of turbulence and storm. At a later point in the novel, Marlow will pause during the writing of some letters to make a remark that aligns writing with more difficult conditions far from shore.[5] At the beginning, however, the implements of writing lie among cigars and other agreeable objects, establishing writing as an aspect of bourgeois culture that exists to perpetuate capitalist values. The kind of novel that the fireside readers of Conrad's day wanted was a literary equivalent of the harbour regulations in the parlour, namely, one that represents ordered and predictable standards of moral and social conduct.

This parallel between business card and bourgeois novel is reinforced by a simile that appears later in the first chapter. In an image that encapsulates Conrad's narrative technique, Jim is depicted looking down on factory chimneys that 'rose perpendicular against a grimy sky, each slender like a pencil, and belching out smoke like a volcano' (4). As factory chimneys are universally associated with industry, the presence of the pencil in this simile implies an alignment of writing itself with capitalist production. If the writer's labour is ultimately bound for a commercial market, then it may have to reinforce the values of the market in order to flourish there. The writing of *Lord Jim* has to negotiate this difficulty. It has to appeal to the bourgeois reader while simultaneously unravelling all his comfortable, untested assumptions. It must deliver a good yarn while also making the reader face the depths of man's nihilism and capacity for moral failure. The ramifications of Conrad's simile do not stop here, however. The further comparison of the chimney to a volcano foreshadows the exotic location where Jim's life will end, linking the novel's Malayan ending with its British beginning in one deft stroke.

The volcano and the smoking chimney are both avatars of the cigars that await the ships' captains in the parlour and these are precursors of the fiery cigar-ends that illuminate the darkness in which Marlow's tale is told. Marlow himself initially presents Jim's story as a tale that will 'make time pass away after dinner', it being 'easy enough to talk of Master Jim, after a good spread, two hundred feet above sea-level, with a box of decent cigars handy' (25).[6] The salubrious setting in which Marlow's tale of moral confusion and imperial decline unfolds does not seem promising for the intricate tissue of complexities it involves. As Edward Said points out, 'the essential story itself seems opposite to the conditions of its telling.'[7] The cigar encapsulates this paradox. Marlow himself is aware that the after-dinner cigar is emblematic of laxity in literature as well as in life, representing, as it does, a life that is 'easy, pleasant, empty, perhaps enlivened by some fable of strife to be forgotten before the end is told' (25). The comfortable conditions of the telling stand in ironic counterpoint to the tale of failure and doubt that is told.

The theme of failure which suffuses the novel is perhaps best exemplified by a vision of writing that is the opposite of that represented by the business card. It involves a shift on Jim's part from purveyor to author of text. Moments before he sacrifices his life in atonement for the death of Dain Waris, Jim makes two attempts to write a letter that will explain the events that have led to his impending death. Both efforts, written on the same sheet of grey foolscap, fail miserably. As Marlow describes it, Jim's text, along with being incomplete, is fraught with uncertainty concerning its aim and its audience:

> No date, as you observe. What is a number and a name to a day of days? It is also impossible to say whom he had in his mind when he seized the pen: Stein – myself – the world at large – or was this only the aimless cry of a solitary man confronted by his fate? 'An awful thing has happened,' he wrote before he flung the pen down for the first time; look at the ink blot resembling the head of an arrow under those words. After a while he had tried again, scrawling heavily, as if with a hand of lead, another line. 'I must now at once . . .' The pen had spluttered, and that time he gave it up. There's nothing more; he had seen a broad gulf that neither eye nor voice could span. (202)

Jim's failure to express himself in writing at this point starkly dramatizes his inability to justify and redeem himself through a coherent story. Furthermore, it raises the possibility that all such endeavours, by Marlow and countless others will ultimately meet with a similar fate. It is a symbolic moment, one that reflects *in extremis* Conrad's doubts about and difficulties with narrative art generally. The movement from belching chimney to spluttering pen is one of the things Jim's fall is designed to bring about. The contrast between the cheerily brandished business card and the despairingly abandoned letter encapsulates two contradictory views of writing. The writing of the novel attempts to steer a course between the opposing extremes of shallow commercialism and despairing incompletion. The spectre that haunts the novel is the idea that Jim's abandoned, incomplete text has more philosophical validity than any story he or anyone else could compose. The ink blot that resembles the head of an arrow is a symbol of falsehood, Marlow having previously used the image of 'an enchanted and poisoned shaft dipped in a lie too subtle to be found on earth' (188) to characterize the kind of utterance that dispels despair.

The extent to which writing is a theme of *Lord Jim* is a key component of the novel's modernity, as is the novel's obsession with its own status as a textual entity. Towards the end of the second chapter, there is a description of the *Patna* that initiates a recurring pattern of black on white:

> The *Patna*, with a slight hiss, passed over that plain, luminous and smooth, unrolled a black ribbon of smoke across the sky, left behind her on the water a white ribbon of foam that vanished at once, like the phantom of a track drawn upon a lifeless sea by the phantom of a steamer (14–15).

J. Hillis Miller suggests that the meaning of the novel might be found in Conrad's manipulation of this binary pattern of black against white and light against dark but stops short of reading the above passage as an allegory of writing.[8] The black ribbon of smoke, in this passage, calls to mind the ribbon of a typewriter, the action of unrolling suggesting the turn of the ribbon as new paper is fed into it. The unsettling element of the image is the insubstantiality and transience of the 'writing' associated with the ship. This is writing which vanishes as it appears and is thereby rendered ghostly and unreal. The trope performs a double function, not only foreshadowing the reams of text that will be wrapped around this ship but also insinuating the ephemeral and futile nature of all textual production.

The transient nature of writing becomes imbued with irony as the narrative unfolds. Marlow's first impression of Brierly, for instance, is initially communicated in a trope that appears under the rubric of writing. 'The sting of life could do no more to his complacent soul,' Marlow remarks, 'than the scratch of a pin to the smooth face of a rock ... his self-satisfaction presented to me and to the world a surface as hard as granite' (39). Marlow's awareness of Brierly's impregnability becomes the occasion of a figure that emphasizes the impossibility of writing at all; it is as if Brierly is somehow above the futile scratching of the pen that would try to pin him down. The full irony of the moment, however, only emerges when we connect it to a further remark of Marlow's concerning Jim. When Marlow offers to help Jim in the aftermath of the inquiry, Jim gratefully remarks that this has given him 'a clean slate' (112). Marlow's internal reaction to this is to dismiss the idea that life has any clean slates to offer: 'a clean slate, did he say? As if the initial word of each our destiny were not graven in imperishable characters upon the face of a rock' (112). The reader is presented, then, with two tropes linking human destiny to writing on rock, the second of which is a complete reversal of the first. The first presents writing as ineffective and the individual as imperishable; the second undermines this, portraying the individual as the transient embodiment of words already written. Perhaps one reason why Conrad emphasizes the impeccable whiteness of Jim's clothes is to insinuate that he is a blank page on whom countless words and endless interpretations will appear.

The page is a space that hovers uneasily between falsehood and truth. After the inquiry, Jim complains to Marlow that the story the other crew-members told, while not being a lie, was not the truth either, that there was not 'the thickness of a sheet of paper between the right and the wrong of this affair' (81). Yet if there is one page that can embody truth, it would hopefully be that of a ship's chart. The ship's chart should symbolize an ordered and reliable connection between man's picture of the world and the world itself. This, however, is made doubtful by the ironic juxtaposition of Jim in reverie beside it. Initially, everything is in order, as 'the sheet of paper portraying the depths of the sea presented a shiny surface [...] a surface as level and smooth as the glimmering surface of the waters' (17). As the passage continues, Jim becomes more and more wrapped up in fantasies of heroic action. These fantasies will ultimately be exposed as delusions. When Jim finally glances from the sea to the chart, he observes a perfect compatibility between the two. This compatibility is no less illusory for being presented as a form of writing: 'when he happened to glance back he saw the white streak of the wake drawn as straight by the ship's keel upon the sea as the black line drawn by the pencil upon the chart' (17). The irony of the scene is that these alignments of world and representation are mere phantoms, as illusory as the fantasies they frame.[9]

A more oblique figuration of writing and its attendant difficulties can be observed in the novel's beetle and butterfly imagery. Said has pointed out that Conrad's letters portray him perpetually struggling with language (99). He claims that a letter Conrad wrote on 4 January 1900 to Cunningham Grahame is revealing and quotes: 'But difficulties are as it were closing round me; an irresistible march of blackbeetles I figure it to myself. What a fate to be so ingloriously devoured.'[10] Although Said does not say exactly how this letter is revealing, he is probably alluding to the beetle motif in the novel itself. The traditional interpretation of the novel's beetle and butterfly metaphors is that they symbolize evil and cynicism on the one hand and idealism on the other.[11] The vicious pirate, 'Gentleman' Brown, is a beetle, while Jim is a butterfly, as Brown himself seems to recognize when he points out that Jim talks as if he were 'one of those people that should have wings so as to go about without touching the dirty earth. Well – it is dirty. I haven't got any wings' (227). This alignment of the most evil character in the novel with the failure of writing is given further support by the fate of a letter that Jim *did* succeed in writing. This is the letter that Jim sends to Brown offering him a clear road out of Patusan, which ends with the words 'I don't believe you want bloodshed' (235). Brown's response is to tear it into pieces and subsequently kill Doramin's son.

Butterflies, in this scheme, symbolize a tentative and ephemeral victory over the difficulties that beset the writing and telling of stories. The wings that Brown despises are glimpsed, metaphorically, when Marlow begins to recount Jim's story: 'With the very first word Marlow's body, extended at rest in the seat, would become very still, as though his spirit had winged its way back into the lapse of time and were speaking through his lips from the past' (24). Yet, when confronted with Jewel's need for reassurance, Marlow himself admits that, in the face of fear, 'even the winged words of truth drop at your feet like lumps of lead' (188).

The failure that dogs Jim's attempts at writing also haunts his efforts at speech. Jim's abandoned letter has a parallel in his broken-off utterance to Marlow:

> 'Tell them ... ' he began. I signed to the men to cease rowing, and waited in wonder. Tell who? The half-submerged sun faced him. I could see its red gleam in his eyes that looked dumbly at me ... 'No – nothing,' he said, and with a slight wave of his hand motioned the boat away. (199)

We see here an example of Conrad's symmetrical patterning, Jim's two efforts at significant utterance paralleling his two attempts to write the letter. His attempt to write the letter had itself been accompanied by a gesture that cancels speech; as he sat down to write, Jim made a sign with his hand, 'a dumb appeal for silence' (242), to his Malayan lover, Jewel. When he dies from Doramin's shot, he falls forward 'with his hand over his lips' (246), as if determined not to lapse into speech even in death. The origins of Jim's contemptuous attitude to the spoken word can be traced back to the inquiry into the abandonment of the *Patna*:

> For days, for many days, he had spoken to no one, but had held silent, incoherent, and endless converse with himself, like a prisoner alone in his cell or like a wayfarer lost in a wilderness. At present he was answering questions that did not matter though they had a purpose, but he doubted whether he would ever again speak out as long as he lived. The sound of his own truthful statements confirmed his deliberate opinion that speech was of no use to him any longer (24).

With insights such as this lying at the core of his work, it is small wonder that an early English reviewer of Conrad's fiction wrote that 'he gives you the idea of muttering the story to himself.'[12] Ironically, these thoughts go through Jim's mind just before he has his first glimpse of Marlow, the man who will subsequently tell his story for him, in the courtroom. The malaise that Jim succumbs to here explains the several instances of stammering that characterize his attempts at speech thereafter. Marlow, for instance, recounts how 'at the moment of taking leave he treated me to a ghastly muddle of dubious stammers and movements, to an awful display of hesitations' (95). Later, however, Marlow enlarges Jim's faltering speech into a universal principle, asking his audience if our lives are not too short 'for that full utterance which through all our stammerings is of course our only and abiding intention?'(136). One form that 'full utterance' has traditionally taken is the closure we associate with the realist novel. The modernity of Conrad's novel lies partly in its denial of closure; even as he begins to recite what he knows of Jim's story, Marlow wonders 'if there happens to be any end to it' (25). The incompletion of the stammered utterance becomes an opposing principle to that of closure, to 'those last words, whose ring, if only they could be pronounced, would shake both heaven and earth' (136). Against a backdrop such as this, Jim's subsequent shooting of an enemy 'through the mouth' (179) during a skirmish in Patusan becomes less a realistic detail than a suggestively symbolic gesture.

Speech is not only a theme within the narrative but also the dominant mode in which the narrative unfolds, with a large portion of the novel being related by Marlow. Conrad took outrageous liberties to do this, putting thirty of the novel's forty-five chapters into the mouth of one man in an after-dinner yarn that he calculated would have taken three hours to deliver.[13] Although nine hours would have been a more accurate calculation, Said suggests that we take seriously Conrad's protest that Marlow's narration could have been spoken during an evening. 'It is a surprising line to take, but Conrad was addressing what was to him always an important point, the dramatized telling of the story, how and when it was told, for which evidence was an integral part of the novel as a whole' (92). This, while being perceptive, does not explain why Conrad did not stretch Marlow's narrative out over several nights, as Albert Camus did in his much shorter and more plausible *La Chute* (1956).[14] However, if we must have recourse to Conrad's preface in defending the novel's flouting of realistic conventions, we might find Conrad's opposition of his three-hour tale to 'some speeches in Parliament [that] have taken nearer six than three hours in delivery' (5) more suggestive. This deliberate conjunction of Conrad's novelistic speech with the political rhetoric that emanated from the centre of the British Empire craftily insinuates that the broader, political implications of the story make it a tale worth staying up for.[15]

With both writing and speech occupying a privileged place in the novel's metaphorical scheme, it is inevitable that language itself should feature thematically. Language is a theme that had particular resonance for Conrad personally. As Owen Knowles has pointed out, 'Polish, English *and* French influences upon him made up a genuinely trilingual and tri-cultural identity.'[16] Yet if this multi-cultural background was ultimately enriching for Conrad's art, it does not seem to have been felt to be so by the man himself as he struggled to write. And although it does initially appear liberating within the text of *Lord Jim*, this liberation is subsequently undermined by irony. A multiplicity of languages, in *Lord Jim*, finally entails the kind of failures associated with writing and speech.

When we see Jim on board the training-ship in the first chapter, the narrator informs us that 'in the babel of two hundred voices he would forget himself, and beforehand live in his mind the sea-life of light literature' (9). This 'babel' of voices evokes a biblical myth that has gained increasing currency in modernist and postmodernist writing.[17] The myth denotes an era of linguistic confusion, when the proliferation of languages compromised men's ability to communicate. For Jim, the babel of voices that surrounds him in sound without meaning is a comforting phenomenon, one that paradoxically allows his imagination to soar in the realm of literature. This, however, is of a different order from the literature that Conrad himself was striving to produce. Conrad, in this passage, was placing himself at a distance from the kind of books David Copperfield consumed. That tradition will be exposed as insidious by the story that follows. Jim's story is a tragic version of Don Quixote's. His uncritical acceptance of the conventions of heroic literature and his childish identification with the heroes of these tales bring about his decision to go to sea, which in turn leads to his capitulation to fear on the *Patna* and ultimately to his death in Patusan.

The *Patna* is itself presented as a ship of babel, being 'owned by a Chinaman, chartered by an Arab, and commanded by a sort of renegade New South Wales German, very anxious to curse publicly his native country' (13). The implications of this state of affairs can be gauged from the previous paragraph, where lazy ships' officers are castigated for serving Chinamen, Arabs, half-casts or even 'the Devil himself had he made it easy enough' (13). This easy transition from Chinamen to the Devil is evidence of more than racism, of which Conrad has been accused.[18] It also suggests a vision of linguistic multiplicity that is diabolical. Although all of these men would have communicated through English, the narrator seems sceptical, to say the least, about their ability to run their ship effectively. At several points in the novel attention is brought to bear on the way foreigners speak English. Irony underlies the thick accent, twisted syntax, and mispronunciations of the 'patriotic Flensborg or Stettin Australian' who yells 'I vill an Amerrican citizen begome' (29). Gentle satire characterizes the portrayal of the French captain who rescues the *Patna*, with Marlow peppering his account with the captain's French phrases (84–7). Horror attends the portrayal of 'the dapper little half-caste' whose 'flowing English seemed to be derived from a dictionary compiled by a lunatic' (144). As this last example indicates, linguistic multiplicity in Conrad can seem less liberation than a frightening descent into meaninglessness. J. Hillis Miller may have been thinking of this moment when he suggested that *Lord Jim* itself is like 'a dictionary in which the entry under one word refers the reader to another word which refers him to another and then back to the first word again, in an endless circling' (39). Yet even this prospect of endless circling is less terrifying than a world where words have no meaning at all. For the young David Copperfield, the pain of being clobbered with a grammar book was at least comprehensible. The lunatic's dictionary Marlow imagines plumbs psychological depths of a distinctly modern character. With this kind of 'schizophrenic' writing, which looks forward to the textual nightmares of Borges, we are no longer in the Victorian Age.[19]

Few great novels are as haunted by the spectre of their own failure as is Conrad's *Lord Jim*. The paradox that emerges from this is that the novel uses language dynamically and poetically to express its profound lack of confidence about the very possibility of successful communication through narrative, be it written or spoken. The disquiet about language that permeates *Lord Jim* acts as a counterpoint to its technical innovations. While *Lord Jim* is densely structured, using repetition and ambiguity to create complex patterns and meanings, it simultaneously dramatizes the failure of writing and the inadequacy of speech to convey the texture of experience. As Said has pointed out, 'what Conrad discovered was that the chasm between words saying and words meaning was widened, not lessened, by a talent for words written. To have chosen to write, then, is to have chosen in a particular way neither to say directly nor to mean exactly in the way he had hoped to say or to mean' (90). *Lord Jim* is Conrad's finest dramatization of this problematic concern. Although all of Marlow's investigations hope to find some final 'exorcism against the ghost of doubt' (35), it is the novel's refusal to perform such exorcisms that make it less a nineteenth-century classic than the prototype of a more sceptical and modern fiction.

Chapter 12

Liking or Disliking: Woolf, Conrad, Lawrence

Michael O'Neill

To the Lighthouse and *Women in Love* are remarkable for avoiding adverse judgements of figures who might seem, and have been seen as, the villains of their respective pieces. The figures I have in mind – Mr Ramsay and Gerald Crich – are the beneficiaries of fictional visions and devices that preclude final verdicts: the presentation of these two figures constitutes the first and third sections of the current piece. *Heart of Darkness* also gives us, in Kurtz, a figure whose apparent glimpse into 'all the hearts that beat in the darkness'[1] ambiguously offsets that 'surrender' to corrupt 'desire' and 'temptation' (3.68) which invites unambiguous condemnation. In this work, a – to my mind – more fascinating inability to arrive at a final verdict concerns Marlow, narrator of and possible participant in Kurtz's moral degradation, and the subject of a brief discussion in this essay's second section. Certainly, for all their reaction against the Victorian novel, Woolf, Lawrence and Conrad share George Eliot's dislike for work that lapses from the picture to the diagram. In Lawrence's words from 'The Novel', 'the novel contains no didactic absolute. All that is quick, and all that is said and done by the quick is, in some way, godly'.[2]

    Analysis of all three works reveals a capacity – showing itself differently in each – to create an artistic illusion of the 'quick', especially in relation to human thoughts, feelings, and relationships. Traditional notions of characterization may seem to be banished by Modernist fiction: 'You mustn't look in my novel for the old stable ego of the character', Lawrence famously tells a perplexed Edward Garnett: 'There is', he continues, 'another ego, according to whose action the individual is unrecognizable, and passes through, as it were, allotropic states which ... are states of the same radically-unchanged element.'[3] But, as this account makes clear, Lawrence's quarrel is more with the 'old stable ego' than with 'character', which might be identified with the 'radically-unchanged element'. In all three works under discussion, there is a sense both that the 'old stable ego' has gone – we must not look for the kinds of summaries of motive and behaviour found, say, in George Eliot's *Middlemarch* – and that something centrally human still abides, eluding description and fixity, but commanding our legitimate interest.

I

That something can seem, especially in Woolf, mercurial and evanescent. In a fine passage in section 4 of the first part of *To the Lighthouse*, Lily Briscoe is shown considering the relative merits and demerits of Mr Ramsay and Mr Bankes. To put it this way, however, is to retreat from the challenge of Woolf's writing. For the passage couples an agile responsiveness to the movements of consciousness (implying Woolf's ultimate artistic control) with awareness that the process of 'considering' feels more like being overwhelmed:

> Suddenly, as if the movement of his hand had released it, the load of her accumulated impressions of [Mr Bankes] tilted up, and down poured in a ponderous avalanche all she felt about him. That was one sensation. Then rose up in a fume the essence of his being. That was another.[4]

If the point of view here is not exactly objective or fixed, Woolf eschews stream of consciousness. Asserting the adequacy of her language to do justice to what Lily experiences, she interests the reader in the process of rendition as much as the experience rendered; it is as if, in Conrad Aitken's words, 'she never for a moment wished us to forget the *frame* of the picture, and the fact that the picture *was* a picture'.[5] Yet the impact is not merely to aestheticize, even as we may admire the playfully overstated simile of the 'ponderous avalanche'. Woolf demands, too, that we experience a quicksilver movement of perspective that has us, in one sentence, identifying with Lily's 'accumulated impressions', and in the next, recognizing her recoil against her own subjectivity as she senses Mr Bankes's otherness, 'the essence of his being'. Such a recoil only confirms that subjectivity, and, before we consolidate 'the essence of his being' into some absolute, a further sentence tells us that this sense of otherness was 'another' 'sensation'. Continually, the deck of the novel, so to speaks, tilts, sending us sliding and sprawling, and yet admiring the writerly skill that keeps the ship afloat.

It is in the following paragraph that Woolf shows her virtuosic yet humane ability to capture the contradictoriness of feeling:

> How then did it work out, all this? How did one judge people, think of them? How did one add up this and that and conclude that it was liking one felt, or disliking? And to those words, what meaning attached, after all? Standing now, apparently transfixed, by the pear tree, impressions poured in upon her of those two men, and to follow her thought was like following a voice which speaks too quickly to be taken down by one's pencil, and the voice was her own voice saying without prompting undeniable, everlasting, contradictory things, so that even the fissures and humps on the bark of the pear tree were irrevocably fixed there for eternity. (29)

The passage mixes precision and indeterminacy. The precision belongs to Woolf's verbal rendering of Lily Briscoe's questioning of the meaning of her 'impressions', or, rather, of the whole business of having 'impressions' at all. The indeterminacy belongs to the possible meanings to be attached to processes of evaluation and judgement, and, indeed, to the language used to convey the sum of these processes. The run of four questions implicitly mocks the notion of cut-and-dried answers to the dilemmas they propose. To the first question, which might be taken to apply to the novel itself, the answer seems to be that nothing ever 'works out'. Only the work itself – as in Lily's painting – creates a sense of provisional shape. To the second question, the answer, given the novel's evidence, is that we judge in all kinds of inappropriate, rash, and inevitably subjective ways. The third question makes explicit the protest against simplification that has hovered round the first two questions: the very phrasing of 'add up this and that' indicates something mechanical and routine about the operations commonly referred to as 'liking' or 'disliking', where the similarity between the sounds shapes a deconstruction of their supposed difference. In so doing, it indicates that the fourth question is likely to warrant the answer, 'not as precise or uncomplicated a meaning as we might commonly suppose'.

As the passage continues, we have enacted for us the dithering in Lily's mind between the two men:

> You have greatness, she continued, but Mr. Ramsay has none of it. He is petty, selfish, vain, egotistical; he is spoilt: he is a tyrant; he wears Mrs. Ramsay to death; but he has what you (she addressed Mr. Bankes) have not; a fiery unworldliness ... (29)

Lily's ruminations make a touch laboured the kind of critical assertion that solemnly informs us that Mr Ramsay 'is heroic, but he is also a tyrant' (Hermione Lee, Penguin edn, xxvi). Yes, one wants to say, in response to that comment, but Lily has already said as much, and realized its insufficiency. It is not that Lily is exactly a Jamesian central consciousness; more that, like most feeling minds in Woolf, she quickly recognizes that the mobile flux of responses to others outstrips what turn out merely to be labels. 'For nothing was simply one thing' (202), as James Ramsay will belatedly see in section 8 of the novel's final part. In the earlier passage Lily's two 'buts' move in different directions; the first denies Mr Ramsay 'greatness', the second allows him 'fiery unworldliness'. The desire to find words for her sense of the two men is one of the things dramatized here; so, too, the twists and turns of the writing indicate, is the fact that she will find herself 'saying without prompting undeniable, everlasting, contradictory things'. Partly because of the high good humour of the passage, this endless compulsion on Lily's part to rephrase and change tack seems to us at once a kind of helplessness before the contents of her own mind and a form of freedom. Certainly, one takes from the passage less a conviction that one has found out something about either of the men than that one has been made privy to the novelist's own delight in the workings of consciousness: a delight that surfaces in the long sentence beginning 'All of this danced up and down, like a company of gnats' and ending with the readmission of something other than impressions and metaphors: those 'frightened, effusive, tumultuous' representatives of a world outside the mind, 'a flock of starlings' (30).

Erich Auerbach discovered in Virginia Woolf 'The design of a close approach to objective reality by means of numerous subjective impressions received by various individuals (and at various times)' (Goldman 42). What intrigues here is the idea that 'objective reality' can be approached by means of 'numerous subjective impressions'. In fact, the characterization of Mr Ramsay shows how Woolf implies the elusiveness of such a notion as 'objective reality'; even when we are told he 'was incapable of truth', in the aftermath of his deflating insistence that the weather would not allow James to visit the lighthouse, the writing suggests the difficulty of offering the view as 'objective'. After all, the preceding sentence seems less the product of an 'objective' narrator than of a voice shading, at least in part, into the consciousness of the children, especially James, and, perhaps, in the final words, into that of Mr Ramsay himself. Mr Ramsay is depicted

> standing, as now, lean as a knife, narrow as the blade of one, grinning sarcastically, not only with the pleasure of disillusioning his son and casting ridicule upon his wife, who was ten thousand times better in every way than he was (James thought), but also with some secret conceit at his own accuracy of judgement. What he said was true. (1.1.8)

If, in relation to this passage, one asks Auerbach's questions – 'Who is speaking ...? Who is looking ...?' (Goldman 37) – , one is likely to concur with the conclusion that he comes to in relation to his paragraph, namely that 'The writer as narrator of objective facts has almost completely vanished' (Goldman 40). Instead, we have a narrator who bends with the breezes of feeling, able to locate a temporal present, 'as now', but in such a way as to imply that that 'standing' is already seen in an emotionally charged way, presumably, by his children in whose 'breasts', we have just been told, he excited 'extremes of emotion' 'by his mere presence' (8). If that revelation depends on our trust in a reliable narrator, the rapid disappearance of such a narrator in the loaded similes is striking.

It is hard, too, to believe that the ascription of motives to Mr Ramsay is, in any sense, 'objective'. Woolf's parenthetical '(James thought)' signals as much. The supposed 'pleasure of disillusioning his son and casting ridicule upon his wife' masquerades as objective judgement; but the viewpoint is more complicated than objective judgement would allow. The phrasing could be that of an imagined surrogate guardian of the young boy, finding words for James's acute sense of grievance. The final phrases might bring to mind Mrs Ramsay expressing her reverence for a husband 'incapable of untruth'; it might, as already suggested, articulate Mr Ramsay's own idealized self-image. At any rate, the passage swiftly evokes a gravely playful swirl of Oedipal resentment, not letting Mr Ramsay off the hook, but giving us, in addition to the responses of his children, an awareness of the fact that any view of another is likely to be partial and provisional.

No wonder, then, that Clarissa Dalloway seems close to her creator, and to suggest Woolf's greatest gift to her characters and readers, when it is said of her that 'She would not say of anyone in the world now that they were this or were that.'[6] This does not mean that Woolf fights shy of judgement of or conflict between her characters. But there is in her treatment of Mr Ramsay a subdued generosity that always keeps at bay the sentimental, and never glosses over his faults. As a result, the marriage between the Ramsays seems especially if paradoxically positive when each recognizes the separateness of the other. So, in section 11 of the first part, Mr Ramsay shifts from chuckling at the thought of Hume 'stuck in a bog' to notice, as he looks at his wife's face, 'the sternness at the heart of her beauty'. In what follows Woolf allows for a more sensitive and remorseful awareness than is commonly conceded to him:

> He could do nothing to help her. He must stand by and watch her. Indeed, the infernal truth was, he made things worse for her. He was irritable – he was touchy. He had lost his temper over the Lighthouse. He looked into the hedge, into its intricacy, its darkness. (71)

Here the language slides into Mr Ramsay's mind, catching the intonations of – slightly overstated – self-reproach: 'He was irritable – he was touchy', for instance, is a sentence that could easily replace 'He' with 'I'. And yet, in the final sentence, the freedom of Woolf's method achieves another of its throat-catching successes, for in these words she stages a withdrawal from Mr Ramsay's consciousness in order to plunge into it the more fully. Yet it is a withdrawal and a plunge that work by not restricting their implications merely to one man. For what is caught, as he is imagined staring into that evidently metaphorical as well as literal 'hedge', with its 'intricacy' and 'darkness', is a brief illumination of what any of Woolf's characters, allowed enough space, will glimpse. It contrasts intriguingly with Mrs Ramsay's experience, recorded in the same section, of shrinking, in solitude, 'to being oneself, a wedge-shaped core of darkness, something invisible to others', where the appositional phrases conceal yet reveal the shift from 'oneself' to 'wedge-shaped core of darkness'. That 'darkness', at once personal and impersonal, casts its shadow over the 'sense of unlimited resources' (69) with which it is associated, and the way freedom and restriction play against one another within the minds of the characters is striking throughout the novel.

To whitewash Mr Ramsay would be as false as to simplify him into a patriarchal tyrant. In fact, Woolf's genius thrives on oversetting expectations she herself generates. After Mrs Ramsay's death, Lily takes centre-stage in Part 3, 'The Lighthouse'. In the first section, a piece of poignant, tense and, in the end, gloriously comic prose, we grow aware of her horror of Mr Ramsay's demand for sympathy: '... she pretended to drink out of her empty coffee cup so as to escape him – to escape his demand on her, to put aside a moment longer that imperious need' (160). 'Imperious' suggests his intolerably masculine assertiveness (and maybe hints at its political resonances), even as Lily's need to be 'alone somewhere' (161) ironically echoes Mr Ramsay's self-dramatizing quotation from Cowper's 'The Castaway', snatches of which Lily has just heard (160). Woolf makes us feel with Lily as she does her best to give Mr Ramsay no encouragement, lest he repeat his previous night's 'You find us much changed' (162). She captures, too, Lily's precarious self-sufficiency, her desperate need to use her art the way she uses her canvas and easel, 'as a barrier, frail, but she hoped sufficiently substantial to ward off Mr. Ramsay and his exactingness' (163). Yet, in all this, there is a human comedy, tinged with pathos, of conflicting needs, and Lily herself twists from sentence to sentence: 'Such a gift he had for gesture' passes into and is made less dismissive by the succeeding, 'He looked like a king in exile' (162).

When the denouement of this inward drama arrives, seen also from Mr Ramsay's side in section 2 of this third part ('Was she not going to say anything?' [165]), it shows

Woolf's art and emotional insight at their most unpreciously acute. This denouement takes the form of a seemingly inconsequential remark by Lily, who has just noticed Mr Ramsay's boots, and, seeing in them a synecdoche of their owner's 'pathos, surliness, ill-temper, charm', exclaims 'What beautiful boots!' (167). It is a moment that itself blends 'pathos' and 'charm', since Lily's words have the effect of lifting Mr Ramsay out of 'exactingness'. And the comic inflections to which free indirect discourse is suited since it favours a kind of mimicry are exploited to the full: 'Ah yes, he said, holding his foot up for her to look at, they were first-rate boots. There was only one man in England who could make boots like that' (167–8). Woolf's mickey-taking, caught in the gesture of the upheld foot and the repeated use of the word 'boots', is apparent. So, too, are the undercurrents of pathos that make the scene sharply symptomatic of the discontents it momentarily overcomes. Even the syntax of the first of the just-quoted sentences contributes its share to these undercurrents, since that suspended participial clause brings to mind Mrs Ramsay – 'It partook, she felt, carefully helping Mr. Bankes to a specially tender piece, of eternity' (1.18.114) – and yet, in doing so, reminds us that she is now dead (though living in that she stays in the minds of others), and of the difference between her zigzagging mind and Mr Ramsay's absorbed, even obsessive concentration on the matter in hand. This concentration in his face affects Lily in the following pages, giving it 'this unornamented beauty which so deeply impressed her' (170), one of the feelings she has about him in the wake of the 'boots' incident; others include the sense of him as 'a figure of infinite pathos. He tied knots. He bought boots' (168), and, touchingly, her twinge of 'frustration' that, just as she felt able to give him sympathy, 'he no longer needed it' (169).

What emerges from this part of the novel is Woolf's ability to trace more sensitively than just about any previous novelist a curve of complex yet recognizable feelings (without requiring lengthy Proustian excursions). Technique, in turn, bears witness to an ethical fineness in the technician, who displays, in this fiction, a remarkable understanding of human needs and fears. The boots episode, in its cathartic working-through of different feelings towards Mr Ramsay, prepares us for the finale of the novel, in which Mr Ramsay, Cam and James at last get round to visiting the Lighthouse. The children's coming to terms with the father emerges, in many ways, as the most compelling version of the novel's fascination with the process of 'liking or disliking', and the deeper recognitions underlying that process. Cam swings between opposites. On the one hand, there is the fact that 'no one attracted her more' (3.4.184) than her father, his attractions, for her, made up of 'his voice, and his words, and his haste, and his temper, and his oddity, and his passion, and his saying straight out before every one, we perish, each alone, and his remoteness' (184–5), where the endless 'ands' string together on the thread of the sentence heterogeneous beads of Mr Ramsay's character. On the other hand, there is his 'crass blindness and tyranny' (185). James also thinks of him as 'a tyrant' (3.10.206), though needing his father's approval (as Cam realizes). In his mute revolt against his father, he is both in league and at odds with his sister, who responds to her father's vulnerability in ways that make James suspect her of treachery.

Ultimately, the writing registers a recoil from merciless judgement. Lily, pursuing her reflections on Mrs Ramsay, thinks that 'One wanted fifty pairs of eyes to see with ... Fifty pairs of eyes were not enough to get round that one woman with' (3.11.214). In a comparable way, Mr Ramsay escapes condemnation: 'It was thus that he escaped, she [Cam] thought' as her father goes on 'reading quite unconsciously', unaware of their vow to 'fight tyranny to the death' (3.12.220). James's deepest feeling about his father turns out to be a sense of affinity ('They alone knew each other' (3.8.200), he thinks), and his father's praise for his steering (3.12.223) marks a moment of implicit reconciliation. Mr Ramsay, who finishes his book just as the book in which he figures is drawing to a close, cannot be read as a book; in the penultimate section, he is released, through the imaginings of his children, into the substantiated enigma of his own identity:

> He rose and stood in the bow of the boat, very straight and tall, for all the world, James thought, as if he were saying, 'There is no God,' and Cam thought, as if he were leaping into space, and they both rose to follow him as he sprang, lightly like a young man, holding his parcel, on to the rock. (3.12.224)

This sentence tallies with Lily's subsequent 'vision' (3.13.226), and encapsulates Woolf's wary trust in love, memory and imagination as modes of freedom.

II

If *Heart of Darkness* suspends final judgements, it does so less to urge upon us the value of not simplifying others than to dramatize the treacherous quicksands that beset the attempt to estimate the worth (or worthlessness) of others. Conrad's chosen form – a narrative in which an unnamed narrator reports the narrative of Marlow, who, in turn, tells us of Kurtz – puts into the foreground the question of Marlow's reliability. And yet, in some ways, the work is clear in its moral outlook. Even if its condemnation of European imperialism is conveyed as much through showing as telling, the work trenchantly condemns 'The criminality of inefficiency and pure selfishness when tackling the civilizing work in Africa', in Conrad's words (quoted in a letter, Norton Critical Edition, 201) – though the fiction is ghosted by uncertainty about whether supposedly 'civilizing work in Africa' is a legitimate ideal.

Here the complications begin. Marlow's attempt to cling to 'civilizing work' as an 'idea' trails off in memories of Kurtz's, as yet unrevealed and always dimly suggested, abuses: 'What redeems it is the idea only. An idea at the back of it, not a sentimental pretence but an idea; and an unselfish belief in the idea – something you can set up, and bow down before, and offer a sacrifice to ...' (1.10). The attempted defence of colonialism as an ideal breaks down, and provides an example of something that happens on a number of occasions: that is, Marlow's experience, under the pressure of events, of being undermined. So, the man who hates, detests, 'and can't bear a lie' because 'There is a taint of death, a flavour of mortality in lies' (1.29) concludes by falsely telling Kurtz's Intended that 'The last word he pronounced was – your name' (3.75). As Garrett Stewart argues in 'Lying as Dying in *Heart of Darkness*', 'Criticism often senses something vaguely contaminating as well as consoling about this lie', but when Stewart goes on to find Marlow discredited as 'a morally reliable narrator' (Norton Critical Edition, 369), one senses a sword being taken to a Gordian knot.

For it is the quality of Marlow's awareness that is at stake. When, at the opening of this essay, mention was made of Kurtz's 'apparent glimpse' of universal horror, 'apparent' conceded that the glimpse is known only as it is conveyed to us through Marlow's interpretation of what lies behind Kurtz's last words. Much depends on how one hears a passage such as this:

> I was within a hair's-breadth of the last opportunity for pronouncement, and I found with humiliation that probably I would have nothing to say. This is the reason why I affirm that Kurtz was a remarkable man. He had something to say. He said it. (3.69)

'Remarkable' is a term that moves between admiration and euphemistic withholding of moral approval, and Marlow's tones, here and elsewhere, are elusive; Conrad makes it difficult to distinguish between Marlow's knowing ironies (evident in the hollowness of 'pronouncement') and possible suggestions that the author is inviting us to criticize his narrator. Conrad as ironist of Marlow's glamorizing may be a tempting option. Such a view would allow us to see Marlow as distracted from the fate of those Kurtz has exploited in favour of the supposed heroism of Kurtz's nihilism. But it ignores the fact that the drive of *Heart of Darkness* is towards a vision in which ethical sentinels only pace round a whited sepulchre, at the heart of which is the corpse of European values. All that remains to record being trapped in this sepulchre is a voice, Marlow's. Though this voice's honesty cannot prevent complicity with lying, its complex rhetoric is at one with its abiding sense of irony.

III

As *Women in Love* climbs towards its icy climax in the Alps, Ursula Brangwen reviews her life and refuses to accept it as real, disowning the power of memory as 'a dirty trick played on her': 'What was this decree, that she should 'remember'! ... What had she to do with parents and antecedents? She knew herself new and unbegotten, she had no father, no mother, no anterior connections ...'.[7] Ursula experiences an emotion here to which Lawrence's use of language – at one with the absolute imperiousness of feeling – is attuned. As in Blake's Prophetic Books, we are taken into a state of mind that is somewhere between delusion and revelation. Lawrences's first duty as an artist, his language has the effect of persuading us, is not to pass an ethical judgement on the rights and wrongs of wishing to believe you have 'no anterior connections', but to evoke, through his uncanny fusion of empathy and mocking ventriloquism, what it is to 'know' that the self is 'new and unbegotten'.

The moment helps to shed light on why the presentation of Gerald Crich refuses to be adequately explained by an ethically thematic account. True, Eliseo Vivas speaks for many readers of the novel when he writes that Gerald's 'talents are the talents of destruction and evil, anti-human'.[8] There is clear textual support for this view: as the accidental (if it was accidental) killer of his brother, Gerald brings Cain to mind; his pleasure in violent control, displayed in the Arab mare scene in 'Coal Dust' (chapter 9), has about it an unpleasantly fascistic element; and in 'The Industrial Magnate' (chapter 17), Gerald is represented, with a remorseless intensity, as a creature of will, bent on subjugating the wills of others to his own instrumentalist designs. Again, just before his death, when he is on the point of strangling Gudrun, he experiences a quasi-erotic 'bliss' and 'satisfaction' as he tightens his grip on her neck, observing 'her swollen face' (30.490). At the same time, the novel brims with a dark sympathy for Gerald, so much so that it is hard not to assent to David Bradshaw's assertion that 'although Birkin was meant to have the leading role in *Women in Love* ..., it is the degenerate Gerald and Gudrun who steal the show' (xxii). Even in the passage just quoted, Lawrence, with his magnetic sensitivity to feeling, employs a version of free indirect discourse that makes us, however unwillingly, privy to Gerald's destructive impulse.

Moreover, the impulse is just that: an impulse. In a few seconds, it gives way, in very Lawrencian fashion, to a different emotion:

> A revulsion of contempt and disgust came over Gerald's soul. The disgust went to the very bottom of him, a nausea. Ah, what was he doing, to what depths was he letting himself go! As if he cared about her enough to kill her, to have his life on her hands! (490)

For all its break with tradition and Modernist rewriting of genre, the novel displays the tendency, familiar since Renaissance literature at least, for literature to bestow a kind of grace on the trapped or doomed individual. When Gerald heads off into the snows, he fears that 'Somebody was going to murder him', and Lawrence comments that the dread of being murdered 'was a dread which stood outside him, like his own ghost' (30.492). If sympathy with Gerald's condition takes the form, here, of a shift on Lawrence's part to external comment, Gerald experiences a sense of haunting himself. He has moved beyond good and evil, one might feel, and has ended up being haunted by his own feelings as though they were outside him. The glimpse of a 'half-buried Crucifix, a little Christ under a little sloping hood', along with the indirectly related final words running through his mind, 'Lord Jesus, was it then bound to be – Lord Jesus!' (492), do not show Gerald dying in a state of religious delusion. Rather, they stand in for a longing to connect suffering and salvation that is no sooner acknowledged (by both author and character) than seen to be linguistically inadequate. On the brink of extinction, Gerald, who 'wanted to go on and on, to the end' (491), comes upon a central symbol of the Christian culture whose disintegration the novel has implicitly recorded. Without seeming, exactly, to be a spiritual explorer, Gerald goes further than the other characters by embracing his tragic death.

The deepest force in the writing at this stage is the sense of an energy that has run its course, grown exhausted. Beneath it all, the desire for oblivion runs. It is easier to be detached from the pathos of this exhaustion if one reads Gerald allegorically or symptomatically, as many critics do. But there is a tension here, since if much in the novel will support a view of Gerald as embodying Lawrence's ideas about what was wrong with modern civilization, much else pulls in a different direction, inviting us to respond to Gerald as a troubled, yet in some ways potentially admirable, individual. Gudrun, ultimately his nemesis, recognizes the disjunction between essence and use in Gerald's case when, pityingly if ironically, she dismisses her Lady Macbeth-like fantasy of being the woman behind Gerald's Napoleon or Bismarck: 'You are a fine thing really – why should you be used on such a poor show!' (29.435).

This comment, an authentic tribute rather than the 'mutual hellish recognition' (250) between the two that is dramatized in 'Rabbit' (chapter 18), gets close to explaining how Gerald stays in the reader's imagination at the end of the novel. Like the other characters, he 'wander[s] in the dark woods of [his] destiny'.[9] Lawrence, only too aware of the novelist's tendency to make a character into an exemplum, allows Gerald to resist merely representative status. The remarkable ending shows that at least one of the characters, Birkin, would not be content with a dismissal of Gerald as an embodiment of the ills of industrial capitalism. That is not to say that in 'Exeunt' (chapter 31) Birkin does not mix personal distress with wider cultural reflections. His lost friend is also, it is clear, illustrative, for Birkin, of a culture that has lost his way: even had Gerald found a path over the Alps, Birkin reflects, he would only have gone down 'The Imperial road', provoking the question, 'Was it a way out?' (496). But his physical grief is powerfully dramatized, as, despite himself, 'he sat with sunken head and body convulsively shaken, making a strange, horrible sound of tears' (498). Here Birkin's grief is the more compelling for evoking revulsion in Ursula, who is reminded by his repeated 'I didn't want it to be like this' of the Kaiser's hand-wringing after the outset of the First World War (498). Female hostility to the masculine 'Brüderschaft' (20.283) hankered after by Birkin finds its nerve and voice in Ursula's response. Yet, once again, Lawrence allows a response the dignity of existence (however undignified the nature of the response), without validating it as universally right. We are reminded by Birkin's sense of loss, and need to have been loved by his dead friend, of the unsentimentally yet subtly rendered scenes of near-attraction and obscure alienation between the two men, which, in turn, have given Gerald a depth beyond that of a straightforward emblem of mechanistic instrumentalism.

Indeed, Gerald is broodingly present in the concluding dialogue between Birkin and Ursula, where Birkin's unfulfilled love for Gerald lies behind the last exchange:

'You can't have two kinds of love. Why should you!'
'It seems as if I can't,' he said. 'Yet I wanted it.'
'You can't have it, because it's wrong, impossible,' she said.
'I don't believe that,' he answered. (500)

At stake here is the possibility of a relationship between a man and woman that will survive the personal and cultural wreckage and imperfection recorded in the novel. Lawrence ends the novel on a coda of non-reconciliation; he draws the lines of conflict with flat, unsparing pessimism. It is noticeable that, whatever else is at the core of this conflict, there is a tension here between Ursula's conviction that her position is objectively valid (Birkin's desire is unattainable 'because it's wrong, impossible') and Birkin's appeal to subjective 'belief' in the final sentence of the novel. The dialogue contrasts with the moment of faltering trust established between Birkin and Gerald at the close of 'Gladiatorial', where Gerald expresses the wish to 'feel I've *lived*, somehow – and I don't care how it is – but I want to feel that – '. Birkin's gloss, 'Fulfilled', is half-accepted by Gerald, who remarks 'I don't use the same words as you', to which Birkin replies, 'It is the same' (20.286).

The lack of 'the same words' for what the characters feel impels them and Lawrence to explore provisional ways of understanding themselves and their world. The sense that understanding beckons, even if it defeats language, continually surfaces in the book, making it unsimple in its pessimism because it is always dynamic, alert and vigilant. If by the close Gerald seems reified into one version of himself, there is still hope that Ursula and Birkin will manage to find appropriate ways of moving beyond their current impasse. Yet Gerald's tragic fixity – he has 'fulfilled' one aspect of the person he might have been, where 'fulfilled' is grimy ironic – co-exists with an almost Shakespearean sense of waste. Birkin is haunted and perplexed by this Gerald who might have been ('He might have lived with his friend, a further life', 498).

It is consonant with this double perspective to observe how, even in 'The Industrial Magnate' chapter, where condemnation may seem most evident, Lawrence is able to entwine detachment with sympathy. In a sense, the novel is more interested in the workings of the psyche than the application of moral judgement. There are reasons why Gerald is as he is: they include a visceral reaction against his father's desire for 'his industry to be run on love' (17.232), a desire which Lawrence, or a narrative voice hardly distinguishable from the author's, forcibly indicates is chimerical. The chapter's rhetoric, indeed, makes it hard to know whether Gerald is always being criticized. Even when Lawrence alludes to 'the furious and destructive demon' which 'tortured' Gerald (236–7), the writing has the effect of absolving him for responsibility. At moments the writing takes on a note that is almost admiring as it describes the ruthless clarity with which Gerald 'perceived that the only way to fulfil perfectly the will of man was to establish the perfect, inhuman, machine' (236). 'Almost admiring': Lawrence does not lose a certain objectivity, employing his own kind of ruthless clarity in his analysis of what drives Gerald and the psychological cost that he pays. So, Lawrence describes how even Birkin cannot save Gerald from 'the outside real world of work and life', where 'real' mocks yet grasps Gerald's dilemma. If 'the very middle of him were a vacuum' (241), it is experienced as a vacuum by the character himself. Lawrence's artistic achievement is to depict such a sense of inner vacuum with a force that compels the reader's fascinated sympathy.

Endnotes

Introduction

1. Fredric Jameson, *The Political Unconscious: Narrative as a Socially Symbolic Act* (Ithaca NY: Cornell University Press, 1981) 9, 85.
2. Terry Eagleton, *Criticism and Ideology* (New York: New Left Books, 1976), 52, 151.
3. Introduction, *Mary Barton* (Harmondsworth: Penguin Books, 1996), xix.
4. Raymond Williams, *Marxism and Literature* (Oxford: Oxford University Press, 1997), 129, 123.
5. *The Dialogic Imagination: Four Essays by M. M. Bakhtin*, ed. Michael Holquist (Austin TX: University of Texas Press, 1981), 27.
6. See Nicola Trott, 'Loves of the Triangle: William, Mary, and Percy Bysshe', *The Wordsworth Circle*, forthcoming.
7. See Kathryn Gleadle, *The Early Feminists: Radical Unitarians and the Emergence of the Women's Rights Movement, 1831–51* (Basingstoke: Macmillan, 1995), 59–60, 116–17.
8. William Wordsworth, Preface to *Lyrical Ballads* and letter to John Wilson (1802); Joseph Conrad, Preface to *The Nigger of the 'Narcissus'* (1897).

Chapter 1

1. Ford Madox Ford, *The English Novel* (Manchester: Carcanet Press, 1997), 77–8.
2. *The History of Tom Jones*, ed. Martin C. Battestin and Fredson Bowers, 2 vols (Oxford: Clarendon Press, 1974), volume 1, page 209; book 5: chapter 1. All references are to this edition. For ease of reference to other editions, references are in the form 1: 5.1.209 (volume: book, chapter, page).
3. Horace, *Ars Poetica*, 352–3: 'which human nature has failed to avert'.

Chapter 2

1. See for example L. McCaffery, ed., *Postmodern Fiction: A Bio-Bibliographical Guide* (New York: Greenwood Press, 1986). McCaffery pronounces *Tristram Shandy* 'a thoroughly postmodern work in every respect but the period in which it is written' (xv). Numerous essays take up the question of Sterne's postmodernism in *Laurence Sterne in Modernism and Postmodernism*, ed. David Pierce and Peter de Voogd (Amsterdam and Atlanta, GA, 1996).
2. Laurence Sterne, *The Life and Opinions of Tristram Shandy* (London, 1761–67), in *The Florida Edition of the Works of Laurence Sterne*, ed. Melvin New and Joan New (Gainesville: University of Florida Press, 1978), 1.22.81. All references to *Tristram Shandy* will be to this definitive edition and will appear parenthetically in the text (book, chapter, page).
3. Summer 1759. In *Letters of Laurence Sterne*, ed. Lewis P. Curtis (Oxford: Oxford University Press, 1935), 154.
4. Unsigned review in *Critical Review* 9 (January 1760), 73; unsigned review in *Royal Female Magazine* 1 (February 1760), 56.
5. History is famously defined as 'a great chain of events' in David Hume, *Enquiry concerning Human Understanding*, in *Essays and Treatises on Several Subjects* (London, 1755), 254.
6. Jean-Jacques Mayoux, 'Variations on the Time–Sense in *Tristram Shandy*'. In *The Winged*

Skull, ed. Arthur H. Cash and John M. Stedmond (Kent, Ohio: Kent State University Press, 1971). Dorothy Van Ghent's analysis of *Tristram Shandy*'s relationship to 'time law' is classic. See *The English Novel: Form and Function* (New York: Rinehart, 1953), 88.
7. Postmodernism's characteristic gestures are catalogued in Linda Hutcheon, *A Poetics of Postmodernism: History, Theory, Fiction* (London: Routledge, 1988).
8. An especially lucid and stimulating account of Sterne's attitude toward history and the resulting problem of determining *Tristram Shandy*'s 'historical status' may be found in Carol Watts, 'The Modernity of Sterne,' in Pierce and de Voogd, 17–19.
9. Wolfgang Iser is especially illuminating on the 'frozen fantasy' of the hobby horse and its phantasmic purchase on individual subjectivity in *Tristram Shandy* (Cambridge: Cambridge University Press, 1988), 50–54.
10. Stuart Sim takes up *Tristram Shandy* with the gloves of chaos theory in 'All that exist are "islands of determinism": Shandean Sentiment and the Dilemmas of Postmodern Physics', in Pierce and de Voogd, 105–22.
11. Sterne's debt to Locke has been more than adequately explored, most thoroughly in John Traugott's classic *Tristram Shandy's World: Sterne's Philosophical Rhetoric* (Berkeley and Los Angeles: University of California Press, 1954). The 'equivocal' nature of that debt is succinctly established in W. G. Day, '*Tristram Shandy*: Locke May Not Be the Key', in *Laurence Sterne: Riddles and Mysteries*, ed. Valerie Grosvenor Myer (London: Vision, 1984), 75–83.
12. There has long been vigorous debate on whether or not Sterne finished *Tristram Shandy*, with Wayne Booth leading the affirmative charge in 'Did Sterne Complete *Tristram Shandy*?' in *Modern Philology* 47 (February 1951), 172–83. Marcia Allentuck convincingly asserts he didn't in 'In Defense of an Unfinished *Tristram Shandy*: Laurence Sterne and the *Non Finito*'. In Cash and Stedmond, 145–55.
13. William Kenrick, review of *Tristram Shandy* in *Monthly Review* 21 (July–December 1759), 565.
14. Michel Foucault, 'What is an Author?' in *Textual Strategies*, ed. Josue Harari (Ithaca, NY: Cornell University Press, 1979), 141–60.
15. Herbert Klein, 'Identity Reclaimed: The Art of Being Tristram', in Pierce and de Voogd, 124.
16. Sterne, Dedication to William Pitt, n.p., l. 9.
17. On the eighteenth-century cult of sensibility, see G. J. Barker-Benfield, *The Culture of Sensibility: Sex and Society in Eighteenth-Century Britain* (Chicago: University of Chicago Press, 1992), and John Mullan, *Sentiment and Sociability: The Language of Feeling in the Eighteenth Century* (Oxford: Oxford University Press, 1988).

Chapter 3

1. Walter Scott, *Old Mortality*, ed. Douglas S. Mack (Harmondsworth: Penguin, 1999), 173, chapter 8. All references to the text of *Old Mortality* are to this edition, which is based on the Edinburgh Edition. The Introduction to *Tales of my Landlord*, which preceded *The Black Dwarf*, can be found in the World's Classics Edition.
2. A. N. Wilson, *The Laird of Abbotsford* (Oxford: Oxford University Press, 1980), 112–13.
3. John Sutherland, *The Life of Walter Scott* (Oxford: Blackwell, 1995), 194.
4. Sutherland, 200.
5. David Hewitt, 'The Phonocentric Scott', in *Scott in Carnival*, ed. Alexander and Hewitt (Aberdeen: Association for Scottish Literary Studies, 1993), 585–6.
6. William Golding, 'Fable', *The Hot Gates* (London: Faber, 1965), 91.
7. *Old Mortality*, World's Classics Edition, ed. Peter Davidson and Jane Stevenson (Oxford:

Oxford University Press 1993), xli, xxxix, xxxi.
8. Edinburgh edition, 434; Penguin edition, 358.
9. Douglas Mack, 'Volume Divisions in *Old Mortality* and *Redgauntlet*', in *Scott in Carnival*, 186–8.
10. Kenneth M. Sroka, 'Echoes of *Old Mortality* in Dickens and Katherine Anne Porter', in *Scott and His Influence*, ed. Alexander and Hewitt (Aberdeen: Association for Scottish Literary Studies, 1983), 352.

Chapter 4

1. *The Journals of Mary Shelley, 1814–1844*, 2 vols, ed. Paula Feldman and Diana Scott-Kilvert. (Oxford: Clarendon, 1987), 1: 294. On 4 August 1819 (Percy Bysshe Shelley's 27th birthday), Mary Shelley (6 months pregnant) put the reminder to herself to 'Write' alongside the entry 'S. writes the Cenci'. Subsequent entries repeat the same instruction, 'Write'. Shelley finished a final draft of *Cenci* on 8 August 1819; Mary Shelley writes: 'he finishes his tragedy'.
2. *The Letters of Mary Wollstonecraft Shelley*, 3 vols, ed. Betty T. Bennett. (Baltimore: The Johns Hopkins University Press, 1980), 1: 215. To Maria Gisborne (18 January 1822): 'Now you are in England, we have some hope of hearing really something about his literary affairs – I hear that he is talked of. The Cenci most – I hope Charles the 1st which is now on the anvil, will raise his reputation. ... Do you remember what I wrote about Mathilda[?]' (The Gisbornes had delivered the novel to Godwin in May 1820, but he rejected their further intercession in regard to the novel.) *Maria Gisborne and Edward E. Williams, Shelley's Friends, Their Journals and Letters*, ed. Frederick Jones (Norma: University of Oklahoma Press, 1951), 76: Maria Gisborne to Mary Shelley (9 February 1822): 'With regard to Mathilda (another impediment), as your father has put a stop to all intercourse between us, I am at a lost at what step to take.'
3. *Mathilda*, ed. Elizabeth Nitchie. *Studies in Philology*, extra series no. 3 (Chapel Hill: University of North Carolina Press, 1959). The copy in the Bodleian MS Abinger Dep. d. 374 is dated 'Florence Nov. 9th 1819'. I quote from the edition of *Mathilda* in *The Mary Shelley Reader*, ed. Betty T. Bennett and Charles E. Robinson (Oxford: Oxford University Press, 1990), 173–246.
4. Nitchie, 'Mary Shelley's *Mathilda*: An Unpublished Story and its Biographical Significance', *Studies in Philology* 40 (1959), 447–62. See also: *Journals* 1: 294. Of the novel, the editors state: 'Its central theme is the relationship between the heroine and her father and strongly reflects the personal crisis between Mary and Godwin which was taking place at the time of writing.'
5. Giovanni Bocaccio, *Decameron*, trans. Frances Winward (New York: Random House, 1955), 231.
6. *Lemprière's Classical Dictionary* (1788; reprinted London: Routledge, 1879).
7. *Proserpine: A Mythological Drama in Two Acts* (1831). The reference has been noted by Alan Richardson, '*Proserpine* and *Midas*: Gender, Genre, and Mythic Revisionism in Mary Shelley's Dramas', *The Other Mary Shelley*, ed. Audrey A. Fisch, Anne K. Mellor, Esther H. Schor (Oxford: OUP, 1993), 124–39: 'Before writing *Proserpine*, Mary Shelley has already called upon the myth in her unpublished novel *Mathilda*' (128).
8. Mary Shelley, *Letters* 1: 103. To Marianne Hunt (28 August 1819): 'Shelley has written a good deal and I have done very little since I have been in Italy' – referring to Shelley's completion of *Cenci* and her own progress on *Mathilda*. *Journal* 1: 295. Her journal reveals that she was reading the plays of Beaumont and Fletcher at this same time. She finished the

184   ENDNOTES

first draft 12 Sept. 1819. John Fletcher (1579–1625) *The Captaine* (1647), in *The Works of Beaumont and Fletcher*, intr. George Darley, 2 vols (London: Routledge, 1872), 1: 617–645.
9. *The Letters of Percy Bysshe Shelley*, 2 vols, ed. Frederick Jones (Oxford: Clarendon, 1964), 2: 39–40. To Mary (22 September 1818): 'remember *Charles the 1st* & do you be prepared to bring at least *some* of Mirra translated' ... 'remember remember Charles the 1st and Myrrha – I have been already imagining how you will conduct some of the scenes.' 2: 39 note: 'In her 1839 Note on the Poems of 1822 Mary says that Shelley encouraged her to write a play on Charles I. In 1821–22 he himself took up the subject, but did not complete the drama. ... Ariosto's *Myrrha*. Nothing further is known of Mary's translation.' The reference is not to Ariosto, but to Vittorio Alfieri (1749–1803), *Myrrha*.
10. Compare Byron, *Childe Harold* Canto 3, stanza 97, 906–11: 'could I wreak / My thoughts upon expression, and thus throw/ Soul, heart, mind, passions, feelings, strong or weak, / All that I would have sought, and all I seek, / Bear, know, feel, and yet breathe—into *one* word, / And that one word were Lightning, I would speak.'
11. Mary Shelley seems to echo the incest motif of John Polidori's *The Vampyre*, the tale of Aubrey, his sister, and Lord Ruthven, written at that famous gathering during 'summer of 1816 in the environs of Geneva' when she herself began *Frankenstein*.
12. Dante, *Paradiso*, Canto 4, 142.
13. Dante, *Purgatorio*, Canto 28, 31–33.
14. Mary Shelley, *Journals* 1: 308 (11 February 1820): 'write & correct'.
15. See note 2 above; Mary Shelley, *Letters* 1: 215. To Maria Gisborne (18 January 1822). Also: *Letters* 1: 218. To Maria Gisborne (9 February 1822): 'I have sent my novel [*Valperga*] to Papa – I long to hear some news of it – as with an authors vanity I want to see it in print & hear the praises of my friends – I should like as I said when you went away – a Copy of Matilda – it might come out with the desk.' *Letters*, 1: 221. To Maria Gisborne (7 March 1822): 'could you not in any way write for Matilda? – I want it very much.' *Letters* 1: 229. To Maria Gisborne (6/10 April 1822): 'In a late letter to my father, I requested him to send you Matilda – I hope he has complied with my desire, and, in that case, you will get it copied, and send it to me by the first opportunity.' *Letters* 1: 237. To Maria Gisborne (2 June 1822): 'Did you get Matilda from Papa?' *Letters* 1: 238 (29 May 1822), note: she learned that Godwin intended to withold *Valperga* as well as *Matilda* from publication.
16. Mary Shelley, *Letters* 1, 247. To Maria Gisborne (15 August 1822); on Shelley's death; travelling with Jane Williams to Pisa.
17. *Journals* (27 October 1822), 2, 441–2.
18. Mary Shelley, *Letters* 1: 336. To Maria Gisborne (3 [6] May 1823).
19. Claire Claremont, to Byron (13 May 1819): MS in the collection of John Murray, quoted in Richard Holmes, *Shelley. The Pursuit* (New York: E. P. Dutton, 1975), 513.
20. Holmes, *Shelley*, 526.

Chapter 5

1. William Blake, *The Marriage of Heaven and Hell*, intr. Sir Geoffrey Keynes (London and New York: Oxford University Press, 1975), xx–xxi.
2. The relevance of the meaning of 'creed or system of belief' is noted in David Medalie, '"Only as the Event Decides": Contingency in *Persuasion*', *Essays in Criticism*, 49:2 (1999) 152–69, 167.
3. *Jane Austen's Letters*, ed. Deirdre Le Faye (Oxford and New York: Oxford University Press, 1995); hereafter *Letters*, 280.
4. Jane Austen, *Persuasion*, ed. Gillian Beer (Harmondsworth: Penguin, 1998), xi.

5. Beer, xi. For discussion of the 'indeterminacy' of the concept of persuasion, see Jane Austen, *Persuasion*, ed. Linda Bree (Ontario: Broadview Press, 1998), 8–10.
6. Jane Austen, *Northanger Abbey*, ed. Anne Ehrenpreis (Harmondsworth: Penguin, 1972; 1988), 115.
7. Jane Austen, *Persuasion*, ed. John Davie (Oxford and New York: Oxford University Press, 1971; repr. 1990), 100–101. All references to *Persuasion* are to this text.
8. Marilyn Butler, *Jane Austen and the War of Ideas* (Oxford: Clarendon Press, 1975; repr. 1989), 285.
9. Butler, 284. It is helpful to read Butler's argument with Malcolm Bradbury's detection of 'moral radicalism' in *Persuasion* as Anne 'originally persuaded towards rank and security, accepts the world of energetic uncertainty'. See Malcolm Bradbury, *Possibilities: Essays on the State of the Novel* (London, Oxford and New York: Oxford University Press, 1973), 76, 74.
10. 'Imposition' can also mean 'injunction' which would be in keeping with the public climate a little later in the 1790s. For the word's complex etymology (including a link with printing), see *Oxford English Dictionary*.
11. Barbara Hardy, *A Reading of Jane Austen* (London: Peter Owen, 1975), 190. Hardy's focus is on the 'distortions and illusions created by narrative imagination' (89). For Hardy Anne 'is not blinkered' (190), and she offers 'reappraisal' rather than the 'fertile narrative imagination' of other heroines (96, 86).
12. John Locke, *An Essay Concerning Human Understanding*, ed. John Yolton (London: J. M. Dent, 1993; repr. 1995), 219.
13. David Hume, *Enquiries Concerning Human Understanding and Concerning the Principles of Morals*, ed. L. A. Selby-Bigge; 3rd edn (Oxford: Clarendon Press, 1975), 294.
14. Laurence Sterne, *The Life and Opinions of Tristram Shandy*, ed. Graham Petrie (Harmondsworth: Penguin, 1967; repr. 1986), 173–4.
15. *The George Eliot Letters*, ed. Gordon S. Haight, 9 vols (New Haven and London: Yale University Press, 1954–78), 4: 472.
16. George Eliot, *Middlemarch*, ed. W. J. Harvey (Harmondsworth: Penguin, 1965; repr. 1985), 243.
17. Alain Robbe-Grillet, *La Jalousie*, ed. B. G. Garnham (London: Methuen, 1969; repr.1980), 52 (my translation).
18. Barbara Hardy observes, 'like the beginning of *Volpone* it shows a clear case of the single passion absorbing ... normal emotional energies' (42).
19. Sandra M. Gilbert and Susan Gubar, *The Madwoman in the Attic: The Woman Writer and the Nineteenth-Century Literary Imagination* (New Haven and London: Yale University Press, 1979; repr. 1984), 177.
20. Tony Tanner, *Jane Austen* (Basingstoke and London: Macmillan, 1986; repr. 1987), 220.
21. Wayne C. Booth, *The Rhetoric of Fiction*, 2nd edn (Harmondsworth: Penguin, 1987), 250.
22. W. A. Craik, *Jane Austen: The Six Novels* (London: Methuen, 1965; repr. 1968), 167.
23. Tara Ghoshal Wallace, *Jane Austen and Narrative Authority* (New York: St Martin's Press, 1995), 108. Wallace shrewdly notes that Anne 'cannot claim interpretive authority from a position of wholly disinterested observation' (105).
24. M. J. Scott, *Jane Austen: A Reassessment* (London: Vision, Barnes & Noble, 1982), 175, 189, 192.
25. Yasmine Gooneratne, *Jane Austen* (Cambridge: Cambridge University Press, 1970), 181.

Chapter 6

1. Emily Brontë, *Wuthering Heights*, ed. Ian Jack, intr. Patsy Stoneman (Oxford: Oxford University Press, 1995), Volume 1, chapter 14, 154.

186 ENDNOTES

2. Clayton Koelb, *The Incredulous Reader: Literature and the Function of Disbelief* (Ithaca, NY: Cornell University Press, 1984).
3. David Cecil, cited from Miriam Allott, ed., *Emily Brontë: Wuthering Heights* (Basingstoke: Macmillan, 1970), 137.
4. Allott, *Emily Brontë: Wuthering Heights*, 187.
5. Terry Eagleton, *Myths of Power: A Marxist Study of the Brontës* (London and Basingstoke: Macmillan, 1975), 103.
6. Arnold Kettle, *An Introduction to the English Novel*, 2nd edn (London: Hutchinson University Library, 1967), 135, 143.
7. David Wilson, 'Emily Brontë: First of the Moderns', *Modern Quarterly*, Miscellany 1, 1947.
8. Sandra M. Gilbert and Susan Gubar, *The Madwoman in the Attic: The Woman Writer and the Nineteenth-Century Imagination* (New Haven and London: Yale University Press, 1979), 282.
9. Patsy Stoneman, Introduction, *Wuthering Heights* (Oxford: Oxford University Press, 1995), xxxi–xxxii.
10. Inga Stina Ewbank, *Their Proper Sphere: A Study of the Brontë Sisters as Early Victorian Female Novelists* (Cambridge MA: Harvard University Press, 1966) cited from William J. Sale, ed., *Wuthering Heights*, Norton Critical Edition (New York: W. W. Norton, 1963), 332.
11. Heather Glen, Critical Commentary, *Wuthering Heights* (London and New York: Routledge, 1988), 379.

Chapter 7

1. *Mary Barton*, ed. MacDonald Daly (Harmondsworth: Penguin, 1996), ch. 3, 23–24.
2. Coral Lansbury, *Elizabeth Gaskell: the Novel of Social Crisis* (London: Paul Elek, 1975), 9.
3. In the introduction to the current Penguin edition, Macdonald Daly reaches the bizarre conclusion that Gaskell's mission was to 'persuade her readers to ... resign themselves to the capitalist order', xxvii. Gill allowed his readers to make up their own minds how to deal with what he saw as Gaskell's vacillation between 'what she has seen and felt to be the case, and what her middle-class upbringing has taught her is the case' (*Mary Barton*, Penguin 1970, 24). An earlier commentator, Louis Cazamian, concluded that while Gaskell had no 'economic alternative to Ricardo' her novel's 'passionate response to dismal and demanding conditions' calls tacitly for 'a new ideology' *The Social Novel in England, 1830–1850* (1903) trans. Martin Fido (London and Boston: Routledge and Kegan Paul, 1873), 214.
4. John Chapple, *Elizabeth Gaskell: the Early Years* (Manchester and New York, Manchester University Press, 1997), 248.
5. Chapple, 38, 40, 69, 277, 421.
6. See *Elizabeth Gaskell's Mary Barton and Ruth: a Challenge to Christian England*, Acta Universitatis Upsaliensis, Studia Anglistica Upsaliensia, 43 (Uppsala: University of Uppsala, 1982), passim.
7. 'Sketches Among the Poor' combines motifs from Wordsworth's 'The Reverie of Poor Susan' and 'Lucy' poems, in something of his 'Michael' or 'Ruined Cottage' style, to celebrate an Alice Barton figure, called Mary, for 'daily poesy / felt in her every action'. *Blackwood's Edinburgh Magazine*, Volume 41, January 1837, 48–50.
8. 'Libbie Marsh's Three Eras', 'The Sexton's Hero' and 'Christmas Storms and Sunshine' appeared in *Howitt's Journal* in 1847–48.
9. Wayne C. Booth, *The Rhetoric of Fiction* (Chicago and London: University of Chicago Press, 1961) 151–2.
10. *Fraser's Magazine*. Volume 39 (April 1849), 430.

11. This corrosive passage is borrowed verbatim from John Layhe's Domestic Mission report for 1842. See Fryckstedt, 90.
12. *North British Review* 14: 28 (February 1851), 417.
13. Ross D. Waller, *Letters Addressed to Mrs Gaskell by Celebrated Contemporaries*. (Manchester: Manchester University Press, 1935), 10–11.
14. *Prospective Review*, Volume 5, 1849, 53.
15. *Westminster Review*, Volume 51, April 1849, 48.
16. Jane Marcet, *Rich and Poor* (London: Longman, Brown Green and Longmans, 1851), 30–31.
17. *Illustrations of Political Economy*, 9 vols (London: Charles Fox, 1832–34), Volume 9, Part 25, *The Moral of Many Fables*, 4, 18.
18. Noel W. Thompson, *The People's Science: the Popular Political Economy of Exploitation and Crisis 1816–34* (Cambridge: Cambridge University Press, 1984), 62.
19. The theme was ubiquitous: George Eliot's *Silas Marner* was praised by Richard Holt Hutton for uniquely telling the reader what the poor say and think when *not* 'being improved'.
20. John Seed, 'Unitarianism, political economy and the antinomies of liberal culture in Manchester, 1830–50', *Social History*, 7:1 (1982) 1–27, 15–18.
21. *Report of the Proceedings of a Meeting of the British and Foreign Unitarian Association, Held in Cross Street Chapel, Manchester, and the Speeches Delivered at the Dinner, in the Town Hall, Salford* (Manchester: T. Forrest, 1830). For Fox's career see Frances E. Mineka, *The Dissidence of Dissent: the Monthly Repository, 1806–1838* (Chapel Hill NC: University of North Carolina Press, 1944).
22. *The Claims of the Poor on the Followers of Christ, a Sermon Preached at Finsbury Unitarian Chapel, November 13, by W. J. Fox; on behalf of the Unitarian Association* (London: C. Fox, [1831]), 2.
23. Monica Fryckstedt cites John Layhe's 1843 *Report of the Ministry to the Poor, in Manchester* as a particular inspiration for Mrs Gaskell: 'Now it is the duty of everyone to do what he can to remove such causes of irritation and alienation from the community. This lies within the province of every one of us. This is peculiarly the mission of Christian ladies.... To act by proxy and delegation is not sufficient; for the personal influence of every lover of mankind is imperatively required in this crisis of our country's fate.' *Report*, 1843, 53, Fryckstedt, 95.
24. *Culture and Society* (London: Chatto & Windus, 1959), 90.
25. See Thomas Cooper, *Life, written by himself*, 1872. In 1846, after his release, Cooper presented his card to Wordsworth, as author of 'The Purgatory of Suicides', and received a cordial welcome and a surprising endorsement of his principles: 'there is nothing unreasonable in your Charter; I have always said the people were right in what they asked...'. Mary Moorman, *William Wordsworth: the Later Years* (Oxford: Oxford University Press, 1965), 567.
26. Mary Eagleton and David Pierce, *Attitudes to Class in the English Novel* (London: Thames & Hudson, 1979), 35. Even John Lucas, in one of his two powerful treatments of the novel, suggests that in depicting hospitality in chapter 2 and talking of improvidence in chapter 3 'Mrs Gaskell is even prepared to go to the extent of blaming Barton for extravagance'. *The Literature of Change* (Brighton: Harvester, 1978), 43.
27. Trygve R. Tholfsen, *Working Class Radicalism in Victorian England* (London: Croom Helm, 1976), 56, citing Owen's 'Address at New Lanark'.
28. Thomas Hodgskin, *Labour defended against the Claims of Capital* (1825), 76, cited Tholfsen 56.
29. *Principles of Political Economy* (1848), 458.
30. *Illustrations of Political Economy*, Volume 3, 136.
31. Thomas Pownall, *A Memorial, most humbly addressed to the Sovereigns of Europe, on the Present State of Affairs between the Old and New World* (2nd edn, London: 1780), 87.

Chapter 8

1. Cit. George Ford, *Dickens and His Readers*, 'The Norton Library' (New York: W. W. Norton, 1965), 60. Ford also cites Wilde's original remark, giving Hesketh Pearson's biography of Wilde (1948) as his source.
2. George Gissing, *Charles Dickens* (London: Blackie and Son, 1898), 176–7.
3. Henry James, 'Preface' to *The Portrait of a Lady*, reprinted in R. P. Blackmur, *The Art of the Novel* (London: Charles Scribner, 1935), 49.
4. John Forster, *The Life of Charles Dickens* 'The Charles Dickens Edition' (London: Chapman and Hall, n.d.) 2 vols, I: 86.
5. Joan Stevens, 'Woodcuts Dropped into the Text', *Studies in Bibliography*, 20 (1967), 113–33.
6. *OCS* 413. For ease of access, page references to Dickens's novels are to the appropriate volumes of the Oxford Illustrated Dickens (Oxford: Oxford University Press), introduced by abbreviated titles. These reprint the original illustrations, although the quality of the reproductions is very variable, and there is little attempt to position them accurately.
7. Lewis Carroll, *Alice's Adventures in Wonderland* [1865] and *Through the Looking-Glass and what Alice found there* [1871], ed. Roger Lancelyn Green (London: Oxford University Press, 1971), 9. All further references to the Alice books will be to this edition.
8. Carroll drew a number of illustrations for his own manuscript, before deciding to engage Tenniel for this aspect of his work. His original illustrations are reproduced in Michael Hancher, *The Tenniel Illustrations to the 'Alice' Books* (Columbus, OH: Ohio State University Press, 1985), 27–34.
9. Rodney Engen, *Sir John Tenniel: Alice's White Knight* (Aldershot: Scolar Press, 1991), 69.
10. Donald Rackin, 'Love and Death in Carroll's *Alice*' in *Lewis Carroll: Modern Critical Views*, ed. Harold Bloom (New York: Chelsea House Publishers, 1987), 117–27.
11. James's remark comes in his review of *Our Mutual Friend*, reprinted in Leon Edel, ed., *The House of Fiction* (London: Rupert Hart-Davies, 1957, repr. 1962), 253–58.
12. Dickens, letter to Stone, 24 January 1864, cit. Michael Cotsell, *The Companion to 'Our Mutual Friend'* (London: George Allen and Unwin, 1986), 1.
13. *The Letters of Charles Dickens*, edited by his sister-in-law and his eldest daughter (London: Macmillan, 1893), 569. (To Marcus Stone, 23 February 1864.)
14. Henry James, Preface to 'The Golden Bowl', in *The Art of the Novel*, 332.

Chapter 9

1. Michael Slater, *Dickens and Women* (London: Dent, 1983), 301. Eliza Lynn, 'Rights and Wrongs of Women', *Household Words* No 210, 1 April 1854, 158–160, 160. Sarah Stickney Ellis, *The Women of England: their Social Duties and Domestic Habits*, 10th edition (London: Fisher [1839]), 155. *Bleak House*, ed. Nicola Bradbury (Harmondsworth: Penguin, 1996), 801. 'All', here includes Mr Jarndyce and Mr Woodcourt, subsumed it seems in Esther.
2. 'Declaration of Sentiments' adopted by the Seneca Falls Convention, 1848, cited from William L. O'Neill, *The Woman Movement: Feminism in the United States and England* (London: George Allen & Unwin, 1969), 109. Inter alia: 'He has never permitted to exercise her inalienable right to the elective franchise. He has compelled her to submit to laws, in the formation of which she had no voice. He has withheld from her rights which are given to most ignorant and degraded men – both natives and foreigners.... He has made her, if married, in the eye of the law, civilly dead. He has taken from her all right in property, even to the wages she earns.'
3. *Woman and her Wishes: an Essay* (Boston: 1853), 13. This essay is bound with a variety of

documents, including *Proceedings of the First National Woman's Rights Convention, held at Worcester, October 23–24, 1850*, in a collection presented to the British Library by Higginson in 1860. Harriet Martineau, in *Society in America* (New York: Saunder & Otley, 1837), initiated this critique of the gender bias of Jefferson's democracy, for excluding women from the principle of 'the consent of the governed', 1: 148.

4. Kathryn Gleadle, *The Early Feminists: Radical Unitarians and the Emergence of the Women's Rights Movement, 1831–51* (Basingstoke: Macmillan, 1995), 74.
5. Gleadle, passim.
6. Ellen Moers, exact as always, characterizes *Bleak House* as 'the single "woman question" novel in the Dickens canon' ('*Bleak House*: the Agitating Women', *The Dickensian*, 69 [1973] 13–24, 13). Suzanne Graver has diagnosed two voices in Esther, 'a dominant one that is cheerfully accepting and selflessly accommodating; and a muted one, itself double-edged, that is inquiring, critical, and discontented but also hesitant, self-disparaging and defensive' ('Writing in a Womanly Way and the Double Vision of *Bleak House*', *Dickens Quarterly* 1 [March 1987], 1–14). Pursuing this argument, Brenda Ayres asks: 'Was Dickens so insightful a writer that he was able to create a woman who might have experienced the fissure within herself that was created by domestic ideology?' (*Dissenting Women: the Subversion of Domestic Ideology*, Westport, CT: Greenwood Press, 1998, 142). Carol A. Senf has argued that the novel is set up so as to require the reader to synthesize, androgynously, perspectives that remain starkly male and female in the text ('*Bleak House*: Dickens, Esther, and the Androgynous Mind', *The Victorian Newsletter* 64 [Fall, 1983] 21–27). Virginia Blain, in 'Double Vision and the Double Standard in *Bleak House*', *Literature and History* 2 (1985) 31–46, resists these readings, finding that the death of Lady Dedlock punishes an offence against patrilinear society.
7. Coventry Patmore, Review of Maria Grey, *Thoughts on Self-Culture, Addressed to Women* (1850) and Margaret Fuller, *Woman in the Nineteenth Century* (1850), in *North British Review*, 14: 28 (February 1851) 515–31, 515–16.
8. Mrs [Sarah Stickney] Ellis, *The Daughters of England: their Position in Society, Character and Responsibilities* (London: Fisher, 1842), 15.
9. Theodore Parker, *A Sermon on the Public Function of Woman* (Boston, 1853).
10. 'The New School for Wives', *Household Words* No 107, 10 April 1852, p. 84.
11. Caroline Norton, cited by Sheila R. Herstein, in *A Mid-Victorian Feminist, Barbara Leigh Smith Bodichon* (New Haven and London: Yale University Press, 1985) from Jane G. Perkins, *Life of Mrs Norton* (New York: Henry Holt, 1909), 150.
12. Maria Grey and Emily Shirreff, *Thoughts on Self-Culture, Addressed to Women* (1850) 2nd edn (London: Hope & Co., 1854), 324.
13. 'Rights and Wrongs of Women', 160. This essay also mocked Thomas Wentworth Higginson for championing the admission of women to men's occupations: 'Imagine a follower of a certain Miss Betsy Millar, who for twelve years commanded the Dutch brig, Cloetus [...]. She might be very estimable as a human being, honourable, brave and generous, but she would not be a woman: she would not fulfil one condition of womanhood [...]. Heaven defend us from the virile energy of a race of Betsy Millars' (158).
14. Elizabeth Gaskell, for example, quailed at the idea of women doctors: women are 'at best angelic geese as to matters requiring serious and long scientific consideration' (Herstein, 81). Florence Nightingale 'would have nothing to do with the married women's property campaigns' says Herstein, and admitted to being 'brutally indifferent to the wrongs or the rights of my sex'. As for employing a female secretary she complained that 'Women cannot state a fact accurately to another, nor can that other attend to it accurately enough for it to become information' (Herstein 81–3).

15. *HW*, 210, 1 April 1854, 158–160. Eliza[beth] Lynn, then 32, was at 26 a journalist on the *Morning Chronicle* ('the first woman newspaper writer to draw a fixed salary') wrote 'some twenty-five novels and collections of stories', and contributed to 'over thirty-five periodicals'. Anne Lohrli, ed., *Household Words, a Weekly Journal, 1850–1859, conducted by Charles Dickens* (Toronto: University of Toronto Press, 1973), 343–4.
16. Olive Banks, *Faces of Feminism: A Study of Feminism as a Social Movement* (London: Basil Blackwell, 1986), 46, 88, citing Barbara M. Cross, *The Educated Woman in America* (NY: Teachers College Press, 1965), 83, 67.
17. Philippa Levine, *Victorian Feminism 1850–1900* (London: Hutchinson, 1987).
18. Mrs Ellis, *The Women of England*, 63.
19. Moers sees the treatment of Jellyby and Pardiggle as Dickens's 'immediate surface reaction'; readers who fail to progress beyond chapter 8 may see it as the whole of his reaction.
20. See John Ward, '"The Virtues of the Mothers": Powerful Women in *Bleak House*', *Dickens Studies Newsletter* 14 (1983), 37–42.
21. According to John Carey, 'Quilp's reduction of his wife to a mass of bruises gives an outlet to Dickens's punitive feelings towards women', *The Violent Effigy* (London: Faber & Faber, 1973), 25. Donald Hall argues that in *Martin Chuzzlewit* 'Merry is brutally punished for her anti-patriarchal actions and desires', while in *Great Expectations* the burning of Satis House 'serves to highlight ... the cleansing and transformation of Estella through the violence of her marriage with Drummle'. *Fixing Patriarchy: Feminism and Mid-Victorian Male Novelists* (Macmillan, 1996), 41, 194.
22. If Dickens's novels are overburdened with suffering innocents, treated at times with intolerable sentimentality, this may be because he found at a powerful tool for activating the Victorian conscience. Dickens may have been excluded as long as he was, from the academic canon, precisely because he felt (as did Marx) that the problem is not to understand the world but to change it.
23. 'They have caused themselves to be made the companions and the friends of men, as well as their sweethearts and wives; they are not to be put down, or kept in the background [...]. She will love, and she will cherish, but it is questionable how far she will obey'. Edmund Saul Dixon, 'The Rights of French Women', *Household Words* No. 113 (22 May 1852), 218–21.
24. *The Dialogic Imagination: Four Essays by M. M. Bakhtin,* ed. Michael Holquist (Austin TX: University of Texas Press, 1981), 27.
25. Carolyn G. Heilbrun, *Towards Androgyny: Aspects of Male and Female in Literature* (London: Victor Gollancz, 1973), x.
26. Barbara Charlesworth Gelpi, 'The Politics of Androgyny', *Women's Studies* 2 (1974) 151–60, 151–2.
27. Martineau's *Household Education* (London: Edward Moxon, 1849) is sometimes startlingly essentialist in its assumptions about the natural aptitudes of daughters. Her admiration for American sisters working at the mills of Lowell to send their brothers to college, in *Mind Among the Spindles* (London: Charles Knight, 1844), shares Dickens's admiration for the self-sacrificing sister, but lacks the critical edge Dickens usually adds to this topos. Writing as 'Discipulus' in the *Monthly Repository*, the twenty-year-old Martineau seems intriguingly poised between liberal feminism and domestic ideology: 'Let woman then be taught that her powers of mind were given her to be improved. Let her be taught that she is to be a rational companion to those of the other sex among whom her lot in life is cast, that her proper sphere is *home* – that there she is to provide, not only for the bodily comforts of the man, but that she is to enter also into community of mind with him.' In the same context a modestly androgynous ideal is adumbrated: though 'formed to be a domestic companion', as woman finds that 'her rank in the scale of being is elevated, she will engraft the vigorous qualities of

the mind of man on her own blooming virtues, and insinuate into his mind those softer graces and milder beauties, which will smooth the ruggedness of his character' (*Monthly Repository*, 17, October 1822).

Chapter 10

1. W. M. W. Call, 'George Eliot: Her Life and Writings', *Westminster Review* (hereafter *WR*) 116/n.s.60 (July 1881), 154–98, 180: 'a kind of village panorama, "Middlemarch" commands a wider view of the human horizon than any of her previous works'; but 'the self-unfolding unity of composition is too monotonous to be effective, the construction too colossal for satisfying survey. ... and the general inefficiency of action is so conspicuous, that we are half inclined to interpret it as an intended reflection on the futility and unprofitableness of life.' Call had close ties with his subject: he met and befriended George Eliot and George Henry Lewes in October 1857, the year of his marriage to Charles Hennell's widow (neé Brabant); was co-author, with Chapman, of 'The Religion of Positivism' (*WR*, 1858), and reviewer of the revised 1864 edition of Eliot's translation of the *Life of Jesus* by Strauss (*WR*, October 1864).
2. George Eliot, *Middlemarch*, ed. W. J. Harvey (Harmondsworth: Penguin, 1965), 890; subsequent page references are to this edition.
3. Though cf. 'A Parochial Epic, in easy verse', By Mr. J-nes, *Blackwood's Edinburgh Magazine* (hereafter *BEM*) 84 (September 1858), 327–37 (octosyllabics set in a Shropshire parish, and satirizing its turn away from comfortable old Church of England amity to enthusiastic religion and rancorous party-spirit).
4. Cf. George Eliot on George Sand: 'Fernande and Jacques are merely the masculine and the feminine nature and their early married life an everyday tragedy' (*The George Eliot Letters* [hereafter *Letters*], ed. Gordon S. Haight, 9 vols [London and New Haven: OUP, Yale U.P., 1954–78], 1: 278: to Sara Hennell, 9 February 1849).
5. Cf. Charles Kingsley's *The Heroes, or Greek Fairy Tales for My Children*, which George Eliot reviewed in the *WR* (1856), and Charlotte Yonge's *A Book of Golden Deeds* (1864), which includes the deeds of heroines.
6. George Eliot may have had the Joseph Liggins affair in mind, when her pseudonym had been taken advantage of to claim his authorship of *Scenes of Clerical Life* and *Adam Bede*.
7. The tension between the heroic and the domestic encodes a central intellectual debate of the age. As George Eliot would have been aware, Plutarch was both a model for Victorian hero-worship, and a target for its higher criticism: cf. Edward Lushington, 'Plutarch's Lives: Clough', *The National Review* (hereafter *NR*) 10 (April 1860), 259–78, 259–61: 'Since first the growing accuracy of the classical historians of the nineteenth century began to "give with Greek truth the good old Greek lie," the Lives of Plutarch may perhaps have lost something of popularity and general esteem. ... The best measure of their greatness is the power needed to destroy them. ... The individual citizen of the commonwealths of Greece or Rome may have been more like the ordinary *bourgeois* of modern Europe, or even more like the modern Greek or Roman, than our forefathers thought. ... But the fact remains, that to Plutarch's Lives we still look for the general distinguishing outline of personal story and character which has made the great men whom he deals with famous ... "One of Plutarch's heroes" is still, and will long remain, a proverbial expression in most of the languages of Europe, in one shape or other.'
8. See the entry in *George Eliot's 'Middlemarch' Notebooks. A Transcription* (hereafter *Notebooks*), ed. and introduced by John Clark Pratt and Victor A. Neufeldt (Berkeley, Los Angeles, and London: University of California Press, 1979), 57.
9. 'Particularity' because, as Will is humorously aware, the historicity of Homer was an article of faith to his idolizers, who typically venerated his work for its almost documentary realism:

see, e.g., Robert Wood's *Essay on the Original Genius of Homer* (1769); and William Ewart Gladstone, 'Homer and His Successors in Epic Poetry', *Quarterly Review* 101 (January 1857), 80–122, 80: 'Perhaps the greatest and the most pervading merit of the Iliad is its fidelity and vividness as a mirror of man and of the visible sphere in which he lived'.

10. This use of the classical 'personages' to provide character-references is widespread. They tend to pit the 'homely' against the 'heroic', often humorously (as for example Lydgate's 'you know Ladislaw's look – a sort of Daphnis in coat and waistcoat', 538); but the bourgeois is also amplified by contact with another order of magnitude: Fred is contrasted with Hercules and Theseus (723); Mrs Vincy is seen as Niobe – herself rather a homely subject (190, 293); Dorothea is both 'a sort of Christian Antigone' and a model for 'Cato's daughter' (221, 470), and Casaubon becomes a Minotaur (253); Lydgate is compared to Odysseus (by Farebrother), Rosamond to a pantomime Ariadne (333–4): previously, in Rome, Dorothea had been glimpsed by the artistic Will Ladislaw, placed in relief against, and, though 'clad in Quakerish grey', 'not shamed' by, 'the reclining Ariadne, then called the Cleopatra'– a brilliant prefiguring of the whole Rosamond-Will-Dorothea triangle (chapter 19, 219–20).

11. 'New Novels', *WR* 40 (December 1843), 446–60, 448. Cf. Margaret Oliphant, quoted, n.13, below.

12. *WR* 57/n.s.1 (April 1852), 625–62, 657: Syme is reviewing Christiana Jane Douglas's novel, *The Heir of Adrennan*, subtitled *A Story of Domestic Life in Scotland*. See also William J. Hyde, 'George Eliot and the Climate of Realism', *PMLA* 72 [i] (March 1957), 147–64; and c.f., in the first issue under Chapman's ownership, and among pages attributed to George Eliot, this view of *The Fair Carew; or, Husbands and Wives*, in *WR* 57/n.s.1 (January 1852), 'Contemporary Literature of England', 247–88, 283: 'Feminine novel writers, incognito or declared, are abundant; but few of them exhibit the subtle penetration into feeling and character, and the truthful delineation of manners, which can alone compensate for the want of philosophic breadth in their views of men and things, and for their imperfect knowledge of life outside the drawing-room.'

13. 'The Byways of Literature: Reading for the Million', *BEM* 84 (August 1858), 200–16, 206: 'the fiction feminine, which fills with mild domestic volumes the middle class of this species of literature. The lowest range, like the highest range, admits no women.'

14. *WR* LXVI (October 1856), 442–61, in *Essays of George Eliot* (hereafter *Essays*), ed. Thomas Pinney (Routledge and Kegan Paul, 1963), 300–24: George Eliot's essay takes the view that the best women's novels 'have a precious speciality, lying quite apart from masculine aptitudes and experience' which they 'can, after their kind, fully equal' (324); her title joined an existing sub-genre of criticism: cf. William Rathbone Greg, 'False Morality of Lady Novelists', *NR* 8 (January 1859), 144–67; and George Henry Lewes, 'The Lady Novelists', *WR* 58/n.s.2 (July 1852), 129–41, 131: 'the advent of female literature promises woman's view of life, woman's experience: in other words, a new element. ... And if you limit woman's sphere to the domestic circle, you must still recognise the concurrent necessity of domestic life finding its homeliest and truest expression in the woman who lives it'; 132: 'To write as men write, is the aim and besetting sin of women; to write as women, is the real office they have to perform. ... To speak in Greek, to think in Greek, was the ambition of all cultivated Romans, who could not see that it would be a grander thing to utter their pure Roman natures in sincere originality. So of women.'

15. *The Progress of Romance, through Times, Countries, and Manners; with Remarks on the good and bad effects of it, on them respectively; in a course of Evening Conversations*, by C.R., 2 vols (Colchester and London: W. Keymer and G. G. J. and J. Robinson, 1785), 1: 13.

16. Roscoe, 'Aurora Leigh', *NR* 4 (April 1857), 239–67, 240; Greg, 'Mr. Trollope's Novels', *NR* 7 (October 1858), 416–35, 416; Masson, *British Novelists and Their Styles: Being a critical*

sketch of the history of British Prose Fiction (Cambridge: Macmillan and Co., 1859), 2; hereafter Masson. At this point Professor of English at University College, London, Masson was a familiar figure to George Eliot: in July 1852 she suggested 'enlist[ing] David Masson' for *WR* (*Letters* 2: 48: to Chapman); in July 1856, she singled out his 'Life of Chatterton' from his *Essays ... on English Poets* ('Belles Lettres and Art', *WR* 66/n.s.10, 257–78, 267: 'if we have healthy sympathies, imaginary beings can never so stir our pity as the real beings of the past, as the sufferers or the heroes of whom we can say, "Such as these have lived and died."'); in October 1865, she read Masson's *Recent British Philosophy* (1865), and, partly affronted by a slighting reference to Lewes, was wary of its '"stuff"' about Comte (*Letters* 4: 206–7 and n).

17. Charles Kingsley's *Alton Locke*, 2 vols (1850), ch .9 'Poetry and Poets', 1: 139 – a novel pointed to by George Eliot for its democratic realism, 'Natural History of German Life' (*Essays*, 270). Kingsley is led by Carlyle himself: OED cites (under 'epic', '*transf.* A composition comparable to an epic poem') '1840 CARLYLE *Heroes* (1858) 267 Schlegel has a remark on his [Shakespeare's] Historical Plays, *Henry Fifth* and the others, which is worth remembering. He calls them a kind of National Epic.'

18. Masson, 2. See also William Henry Smith, 'Debit and Credit', *BEM* 83 (January 1858), 57–74, a review of *Soll und Haben* by Gustav Freytag which quotes Bunsen's Preface (on p. 57).

19. Masson, 125–6: Fielding 'distinctly refers prose fiction of every kind to the epic order of Poetry .... "The Epic," he says, "as well as the Drama, is divided into Tragedy and Comedy [Masson leaves out Fielding's reference to Aristotle, who attributes a lost satirical epic, the *Margites*, to Homer] And, further, as this Poetry may be tragic or comic, I will not scruple to say it may be likewise either in verse or in prose; for ... when any kind of writing contains all its other parts, such as Fable, Action, Characters, Sentiments, and Diction, and is deficient in Metre only, it seems, I think, reasonable to refer it to the Epic ...."'

20. Will's analogy goes back to George Eliot's 'Recollections of Ilfracombe, 1856', *The Journals of George Eliot* (hereafter *Journals*), ed. Margaret Harris and Judith Johnston (Cambridge: Cambridge University Press, 1998), 265: 'when one sees a house stuck on the side of a great hill, and still more a number of houses looking like a few barnacles clustered on the side of a great rock, we begin to think of the strong family likeness between ourselves and all other ... house-appropriating and shell secreting animals.'

21. George Eliot to Blackwood, 12 July 1857 (*Letters* 2: 362). 'Concrete' is in the positivist vocabulary: Lewes, whose essays on Comte came out in 1853, finds in Goethe the positivist hero a '*concrete* tendency determining – first, his choice of subjects; secondly, his handling of characters; and thirdly, his style' (*Life of Goethe* [1855] 2: 74). For a reading of the 'mythic' elements of *Middlemarch* as expressing George Eliot's dissatisfactions with the 'imitative realism she had practiced in her earlier fiction', see U. C. Knoepflmacher, 'Fusing fact and myth: the new reality of *Middlemarch*', in *This Particular Web: Essays on 'Middlemarch'*, ed. Ian Adam (Toronto; Buffalo: University of Toronto Press, 1975), 46–61.

22. Chapman, who had guessed the secret by November 1858, inserted a paragraph at the end of a review of *Adam Bede* (*WR* [April 1859]) insinuating that the author was a woman (Gordon S. Haight, *George Eliot: A Biography* [Oxford: Clarendon Press, 1968]), 278); by the end of June 1859, Lewes and George Eliot had decided to end the incognito.

23. Lewes, 'Dickens in Relation to Criticism', *The Fortnightly Review*, 17/n.s. 11 (February 1872), 141–54, 147, 151: 'he seized upon situations having an irresistible hold over the domestic affections and ordinary sympathies. He spoke in the mother-tongue of the heart, and was always sure of ready listeners. ... He painted nothing ideal, heroic; but all the resources of the bourgeois epic were in his grasp'; and yet the works 'are wholly without glimpses of a nobler life', since 'Not only is there a marked absence of the reflective tendency, but one sees no

indication of the past life of humanity having ever occupied him; keenly as he observes the objects before him, he never connects his observations into a general expression, never seems interested in general relations of things'.

24. *The Poems of Matthew Arnold*, ed. Kenneth Allott; 2nd edition by Miriam Allott (London and New York: Longman, 1979), 658: 'Achilles, Prometheus, Clytemnestra, Dido – what modern poem presents personages as interesting, even to us moderns, as these personages of an "exhausted past"? We have the domestic epic dealing with the details of modern life which pass daily under our eyes ... yet I fearlessly assert that *Hermann and Dorothea, Childe Harold, Jocelyn, The Excursion*, leave the reader cold in comparison with the effect produced upon him by the latter books of the *Iliad*, by the *Oresteia*, or by the episode of Dido. And why is this? Simply because in the three last-named cases the action is greater, the personages nobler, the situations more intense: and this is the true basis of the interest in a poetical work, and this alone.'
25. Goethe to Meyer, quoted, Lewes, *The Life and Works of Goethe*, 2 vols (London: David Nutt, 1855), 2: 236–7. *Hermann und Dorothea* (pub. 1796–97, read by George Eliot in Berlin in December 1854 [*Journals*, 38]) is written in Homeric hexameters, while 'The epoch is changed to that of the French Revolution'. Lewes's comments analyse the work as a 'domestic epic' of a successful sort: Goethe takes 'An ordinary story, in which the poet alone could see a poem' (2: 225); 'And in this sense *Hermann und Dorothea* may be accepted as a Hymn to the Family, a solemn vindication of the eternal claims which, as a first necessity, should occupy men' (2: 237).
26. As translated in *Middlemarch*, ed. Margaret Harris and Judith Johnston (London: J.M. Dent, 1997), 791. Literally: 'toward the highest Being constantly to strive'.
27. See 'The Antigone and its Moral', *Leader* 7 (29 March 1856), 306: *Essays*, 261–5. The terms 'collision' and 'conflict' were used by Emily Davies (founder of Girton) when reporting George Eliot's discussion of *The Mill on the Floss* in connection with 'Her own experience', 21 August 1869 (*Letters* 8: 465–6); and by George Eliot herself, when writing to John Blackwood, re. 'Janet's Repentance', 11 June 1857 (*Letters* 2: 347).
28. See especially, Book 2, 16.195; Book 5, 43.475, 45.496–8.
29. 'Alas for human fortune! When prosperous, a mere shadow can overturn it; if misfortune strikes, the dash of a wet sponge blots out the drawing' (Aeschylus, *Agamemnon*, 1329–30). My thanks to Robert Cummings for the reference.
30. In Prodicus' tale from the 5th century BC, Hercules chooses duty over pleasure; in other versions, he ends up spinning in the household of Omphale, or accidentally poisoned by his wife Deianira.
31. 'Augustus William Schlegel', *Foreign Quarterly Review* (hereafter *FQR*) 32 (October 1843), 160–81, 169.
32. 'Phantasmagoriana', *BEM* 3 (August 1818), 589–96, 590–91: 'a certain dignity of character and circumstance has always been considered as essential to the support of tragic interest, which loses its effect in proportion as it mixes itself with the every-day concerns of middling life, with customary scenes, and modern manners.'
33. Significantly, her progress in Latin coincides with her second burst of 'indignation' against her husband (317, 398; and cf. ch. 39, 425).
34. Due to the Franco-Prussian War of 1870–71: see *Journals*, 141.
35. Cf. Lewes on 'The Rise and Fall of the European Drama', *FQR* 35 (July 1845), 290–334, 311, on Aeschylus and Sophocles: 'The one paints abstractions and demigods; the other, men'; 314, on Sophocles, Shakespeare, Racine: 'They received a Cyclopean fragment, bold, but unshapely; in their hands it became a Phidian statue, the ideal of harmonious proportion. The Titan became a man. ... The Titan, no doubt, was a grand, daring being, vast in size, indomi-

table in will; but compared to man, wondrous in intelligence, inexhaustible in affection, this Titan was insignificant.'
36. See e.g. Kingsley, *Alton Locke* 1: 22: 'Those to whom the struggles of every, even the meanest, human being are scenes of an awful drama, every incident of which is to be noted with reverent interest, will not find them [Locke's boyhood scenes] void of meaning'; Percy Greg, 'Mr. Trollope's Novels', *NR* 7 (October 1858), 416–35, 417: 'the character of our novels has materially changed. There are comparatively ... few works of the heroic school, of which Scott is the unrivalled master.... Generally our contemporaries do not choose kings and statemen of high historic fame for their heroes, and brace themselves to the labour required by the dignity of an exalted subject.... the greater number of the popular fictions of the day belong to a different class. Their scenes are laid among quiet homes, and their heroes are men of peace. They are dramatic rather than narrative. Their interest is derived not from intricate situations and startling occurrences, but from the development of varieties of individual disposition and different phases of human nature.'
37. An attitude summed up in the Spanish Proverb that heads chapter 46, 'Since we cannot get what we like, let us like what we can get'; and which Cross was keen to emphasize in connection with the woman question, *George Eliot's Life as related in her letters and journals* (hereafter *Life*), arranged and edited by J. W. Cross, 3 vols (Edinburgh and London: William Blackwood and Sons, 1885), 3: 427–30: 'She was keenly anxious to redress injustices to women, and to raise their general status in the community. This, she thought, could best be effected by women improving their work – ceasing to be amateurs. But .... Nothing offended her more than the idea that because a woman had exceptional intellectual powers, therefore it was right that she should absolve herself, or be absolved, from her ordinary household duties.... She often thought it wisest not to raise too ambitious an ideal, especially for young people, but to impress on ordinary natures the immense possibilities of making a small home circle brighter and better. Few are born to do the great work of the world, but all are born to this. And to natures capable of the larger effort, the field of usefulness will constantly widen.'
38. Farebrother's depressing outlook was familiar to George Eliot herself: cf. her letter to Lady Ponsonby (*Life* 3: 245): 'With regard to the pains and limitations of one's personal lot, I suppose there is not a single man or woman who has not more or less need of that stoical resignation which is often a hidden heroism'. 'That is George Eliot all over', exclaimed the exasperated Richard Holt Hutton, in 'George Eliot', *Critical Review* 47 (March 1885), 372–91, 389: 'the low-spirited acquiescence in a depreciating estimate of human nature, and the obstinate resolve to take the more pity on it, the more dismal is its plight'. In Call's more charitable assessment, George Eliot's fiction reveals 'her cheerful acceptance of a fragmentary goodness, her wise contentment with heroes who have done some genuine work, though the rest be barren theory or blank prejudice' (166).
39. Lewes, 'Grote's History of Greece', *WR* 46 (January 1847), 381–415, 407. Cf. Lushington, 261: 'We may learn from Grote or Merivale to view the ... leading statesmen in Rome or Athens by a different light, reflected upon the single figures through a more modern and realistic conception of the multitude behind them'.
40. Lewes, 394–5: 'whether we are to suppose that before that time [of Pisistratus' arrangement of *The Iliad*] the songs had *never* been united, or that they had, subsequently to their original composition, been separated by the rhapsodists, is in truth the kernal of the whole Homeric controversy'. See Richard Jenkyns, *The Victorians and Ancient Greece* (Oxford: Basil Blackwell, 1980), 22, 207, and Hugh Lloyd-Jones, *Blood for the Ghosts: Classical Influences in the Nineteenth and Twentieth Centuries* (London: Duckworth, 1982), ch. 9.
41. Blackwood felt the effect in the transition from Books 1 to 2: 'It was a disappointment at first

not to find any of my old friends of the former part ...' (*Letters* 5: 167).
42. For George Eliot's 'growing conception of the "anti-hero"' who holds back intellectual progress, see *Notebooks*, li.
43. Cyrus' grandfather dreamed that his grandson would grow up to overthrow him, and sought (without success) to have him killed.
44. Cf. G. K. Chesterton's verdict that '*The Ring and the Book* [1868–69] is the great epic of the age', 'because it is the expression of the belief ... that no man ever lived upon this earth without possessing a point of view', a 'principle' whose 'application ... would revolutionise the old heroic epic' (*Robert Browning* [London: Macmillan, 1905], 171–2). George Eliot's narrator steps between her novel and 'the epic of free speech' (173); but, though she did not admire Browning's work (*Letters* 4: 501), the influence of its marriage-plot may be traced in her own Dorothea-Casaubon-Ladislaw triangle.
45. George Henry Lewes, 'The Novels of Jane Austen', *BEM* 86 (July 1859) (the number in which *The Lifted Veil* appeared), 99–113, 113: 'The delight derived from her pictures arises from our sympathy with ordinary characters, our relish of humour, and our intellectual pleasure in art for art's sake. But when it is admitted that she never stirs the deeper emotions, that she never fills the soul with a noble aspiration, or brightens it with a fine idea, but, at the utmost, only teaches us charity for the ordinary failings of ordinary people, and sympathy with their goodness, we have admitted an objection which lowers her claims to rank among the great benefactors of the race .... after all, miniatures are not frescoes, and her works are miniatures.'
46. Cf., in a very different vein, Frederic Myers, *Lectures on Great Men*, with a Preface by T. H. Tarlton (London: James Nisbet and Co., 1856), Preface, xi: 'We may not be Great Men, but we may render great service by fidelity to Christ, and to our brethren. The iris in the dewdrop is jsut as true and perfect an iris as the bow that measures the heavens, and betokens the safety of a world from deluge. We may not be Apostles to the Indians, but, by God's Grace, we may be Apostles of a Household – of a Profession. We may not be Reformers of Churches, but, however limited our gifts, we may remember and may imitate the deed of that poor Widow of Iona, whose cottage stood on an elevated ridge of a rugged and perilous coast, and whose heart was melted by the sight of wrecked vessels and the wail of perishing human beings. She thought, might not her lamp, if placed by her window, prove a beacon-light'.

Chapter 11

1. Charles Dickens, *The Personal History of David Copperfield* (London: Chapman & Hall, n.d.), 76.
2. Joseph Conrad, *Lord Jim*, ed. Thomas C. Moser (New York: Norton, 1996), 9.
3. The most extreme example is the testimony of the drunken chief engineer, who, in the throes of delirium, remembers the ship as being full of reptiles and toads.
4. Fredric Jameson, *The Political Unconscious: Narrative as a Socially Symbolic Act* (London: Methuen, 1981), 219.
5. 'I was becoming fanciful in the midst of my industrious scribbling; and though, when the scratching of my pen stopped for a moment, there was complete silence and stillness in the room, I suffered from that profound disturbance and confusion of thought which is caused by a violent and menacing uproar – of a heavy gale at sea, for instance' (105). According to J. Hillis Miller, this scene may be taken as 'an emblem of literature as Conrad sees it.' See *Fiction and Repetition: Seven English Novels* (Oxford: Basil Blackwell, 1982), 39.
6. One is reminded of Conrad's account of the beginning of his own literary career in *A Personal Record*. Before he began to write his first novel, he ordered his landlady's daughter to

clear away the breakfast table, 'being at the same time engaged in getting my pipe to draw' (*A Personal Record* [London: Nelson, n.d.], 154).
7. Edward W. Said, *The World, the Text, and the Critic* (London: Faber and Faber, 1984), 92.
8. J. Hillis Miller, *Fiction and Repetition: Seven English Novels* (Oxford: Basil Blackwell, 1982), 37. Subsequent references appear parenthetically.
9. Repeated several times in the course of the narrative, the word 'phantom' is one thread of a pattern of evanescence in *Lord Jim*. One meaning of the word is that of a person or thing which has the name and show of power but none of the substance. Brierly, whom many people hated because of his irresistible rise and superior attitude, is an example. He, without any warning or discernible reason, commits suicide after the inquiry. A phantom is also a weak, diminished, or faint version *of* something, as writing and speech, in the novel, are inadequate versions of experience. Finally, the word also signifies the thought or apprehension of something that haunts the imagination, such as Jim's jump from the Patna.
10. *Joseph Conrad's Letters to R. B. Cunningham-Grahame*, ed. C. T. Watts (Cambridge: Cambridge University Press, 1969), 129.
11. See Tony Tanner, *Conrad: Lord Jim* (London: Edward Arnold, 1963), 50–56.
12. Norman Sherry, ed., *Conrad: The Critical Heritage* (London: Routledge & Kegan Paul, 1973), 58.
13. Joseph Conrad, 'Author's Note' to the second edition of *Lord Jim* (London: Dent, 1917).
14. The novel's original publication in *Blackwood's Edinburgh Magazine* was extended over 14 months, ironically undermining the status of chapters 5 to 35 as a single speech act.
15. For an analysis of the theme of colonialism in the novel, see Mark Conroy, 'Colonial self-fashioning in Conrad: Writing and Remembrance in *Lord Jim*', *L'Epoque Conradienne* 19 (1993), 25–36.
16. J. H. Stape, ed., *The Cambridge Companion to Joseph Conrad* (Cambridge: Cambridge University Press, 1996), 3.
17. See Genesis 11:7, 'Go to, let us go down, and there confound their language, that they may not understand one another's speech.'
18. See, for instance, Chinua Achebe, 'An Image of Africa: Racism in Conrad's "Heart of Darkness"', *Massachusetts Review* 17:4 (1977), 782–94.
19. Jameson claims that 'Conrad's discourse – an overlay of psychoanalytically charged terms and ideological, public slogans – must be regarded as a foreign language that we have to learn in the absence of any dictionary or grammar, ourselves reconstructing its syntax and assembling hypotheses about the meaning of this or that item of vocabulary for which we ourselves have no contemporary equivalent' (245–6).

Chapter 12

1. *Heart of Darkness*, ed. Robert Kimbrough, Norton Critical Edition, 3rd edn (New York: Norton, 1988), 3: 69.
2. *Selected Critical Writings*, ed. Michael Herbert (Oxford: Oxford University Press, 1998), 183.
3. Quoted from Charles L. Ross, *Women in Love: A Novel of Mythic Realism* (Boston, MA: Twayne, 1991), 61.
4. *To the Lighthouse*, ed. Stella McNichol, intro. Hermione Lee (Harmondsworth: Penguin Books, 1992), 1.4: 28–9.
5. Quoted from *To the Lighthouse/The Waves*, ed. Jane Goldman, Icon Critical Guides (Cambridge: Icon Books, 1997), 20; hereafter Goldman.
6. *Mrs Dalloway*, 1925 (Harmondsworth: Penguin Books, 1964), 10.
7. *Women in Love*, World's Classic edition, ed. David Bradshaw (Oxford: Oxford University

Press, 1998), 29:425.
8. Quoted from *The Rainbow/Women in Love*, ed. Richard Beynon, Icon Critical Guides (Cambridge: Icon Books, 1997), 99; hereafter Beynon.
9. *Study of Thomas Hardy*; quoted from Bradshaw, World's Classics, xxxvii.

Notes on Contributors

Gerard Barrett is Lecturer in English at The College of St Mark & St John. A graduate of University College Galway, he is currently completing a doctoral thesis on the novels of John Hawkes at St Edmund's College, Cambridge. A specialist in twentieth century fiction, he has work published or forthcoming on Albert Camus, John Hawkes and Henry Green.

Frederick Burwick has taught at UCLA since completing his doctoral degree at Wisconsin (1965). Author and editor of twenty books and over a hundred articles and reviews, his research is dedicated to problems of perception, illusion, and delusion in literary representation and theatrical performance. With Grant Scott he co-edits *European Romantic Review*. His book on *Poetic Madness and the Romantic Imagination* (Penn State, 1996) won the Outstanding Book of the Year Award of the American Conference on Romanticism. He has been named Distinguished Scholar by both the British Academy (1992) and the Keats-Shelley Association (1998).

Richard Gravil is Senior Lecturer at The College of St Mark & St John, having taught at universities in Canada, Poland and New Zealand. He has edited or co-edited several collections of essays, including (with Molly Lefebure) *The Coleridge Connection: Essays for Thomas McFarland* (Macmillan, 1990), and is author of *Romantic Dialogues: Anglo-American Continuities, 1776–1862* (St Martin's, 2000).

W. B. Hutchings is Senior Lecturer in English Literature at the University of Manchester. He has published on William Cowper, Thomas Gray, Samuel Johnson and James Thomson. His most recent work has been preparing editions of Jane Austen's *Emma*, and the poetry of William Collins, Oliver Goldsmith and Thomas Gray for the British Heritage database. He is also programme editor of the Carcanet Press edition of Ford Madox Ford.

Jayne Lewis is Associate Professor of English at UCLA. Her publications, mainly in the field of Renaissance literary culture, include *The English Fable: Aesop and Literary Culture, 1651–1740* (Cambridge, 1996), *Mary Queen of Scots: Romance and Nation* (Routledge, 1998), and *The Trial of Mary Queen of Scots* (Bedford, 1998).

Michael O'Neill is Professor of English at the University of Durham. His books include *The Human Mind's Imaginings: Conflict and Achievement in Shelley's Poetry* (Oxford University Press, 1989) and *Romanticism and the Self-Conscious Poem* (Oxford University Press, 1997), and, as editor, *Literature of the Romantic Period: A Bibliographical Guide* (Oxford University Press, 1998).

Alan Shelston is Senior Lecturer in English at the University of Manchester. He specializes in the literature of the nineteenth century, English and American. He has edited works by a number of Victorian authors and, with J. A. V. Chapple, is editor of *The Further Letters of Mrs Gaskell* (Manchester University Press, 2000).

NOTES ON CONTRIBUTORS

Jane Stabler is a Lecturer in the Department of English at the University of Dundee. She is working on a study of digression and intertextuality in Byron's poetry for Cambridge University Press, and a book about text and context in the Romantic period for Macmillan. Her *Byron* Longman Critical Reader was published in 1998.

Nicola Trott is a Lecturer in the Department of English Literature at the University of Glasgow. She is editor of the Blackwell Annotated Anthology of *The Gothic Novel* and co-editor, with Seamus Perry, of *1800: The New 'Lyrical Ballads'* (Macmillan, 2000). Her interests range from Wordsworth and Coleridge to Jacobin and Victorian fiction.

Mary Wedd was head of English at St Gabriel's College, and until retirement, Principal Lecturer in English at Goldsmith's College, University of London. In addition to publishing in numerous genres she was for many years editor of the *Charles Lamb Bulletin*.

Index

Achebe, Chinua 197
Adam Bede 144
Aeschylus, *Agamemnon* 194
Aitken, Conrad 170
Alice in Wonderland see Carroll
Alfieri, Vittorio 3, 50; *Myrrha* 47, 184
Allentuck, Marcia 182
Allott, Miriam 81
allusion: in *Mathilda* 47, 49–51
Alton Locke 9, 193, 195
American slavery and the subjection of women 128
androgyny, 123, 134, 136, 190
 androgynous texts 124, 134–135
Arnold, Matthew 145, 194
 nostalgia for epic character 194
Arthur Mervyn 47, 70
Ashworth, John 89
associationism 25, 27, 32
Auerbach, Erich 171, 172
Austen, Jane 3, 55–67
 compared to Sterne, Eliot, Robbe-Grillet 60
 and stream of consciousness 62
 as Christian 55, 57
 authorial contempt 60
 characters: treatment of perception 65
 domestic dramas of persuasion 55
 Mansfield Park 56
 Northanger Abbey 56
 Persuasion 3, 3–4, 55–67
  Ann Elliot: as reliable narrator 62; fallibility of 66
  Blakean 'perswasion' 55, 58
  characters in 66
  heroine's vision 66
  and Hume's *Treatise* 58
  Johnsonian persuasion 58
  and Locke's *Essay* 58
  'moral radicalism' 185
  narrative strategy 65
  omniscient narration 60, 62
  perception as construction 62–65
  and Sterne's 'hobby-horses' 58–59
  and *Middlemarch* 59
 Pride and Prejudice 56

Sense and Sensibility 56
Austen, Cassandra 58
author 29
 and narrator 88
 author as innkeeper 14
 authorial intrusion 9
 authorial direction 59–60
 death of 30
 implied author 99
 negation of 29
 omniscient voice 60, 62
 responsibility of 15
 see also narrator
Ayres, Brenda 189

Babel 167, 197
Bakhtin, Mikhail 1, 181
 see dialogism
Banks, Olive 126
Barker-Benfield, G. J. 182
Barnes, Julian 21
Barrett, Gerard 6, 199
Beaumont and Fletcher 183
Beecher, Catherine 126, 133
Beer, Gillian 55
Bennett, Betty T. 183
Blackwood's Edinburgh Magazine 88, 191, 197
Blain, Virginia 189
Blake, William 3–4, 55, 58, 78, 134, 176; and 'perswasion' 58; *The Marriage of Heaven and Hell* 55, 78; visionary innocence 134
Bleak House see Dickens
Bocaccio, Giovanni 3; *Decameron* 47
Bodichon, Barbara 126
book illustration: illustrated fairy story 110–111; illustration of fantasy 110–111; illustrators of children's literature 121
Booth, Wayne C. 62, 88, 90, 182; implied author and undramatised narrator 90
Bradbury, Malcolm 185
Bradshaw, David 177
Bremer, Frederika: *Home; or Family Cares and Family Joys* 142

Brontë, Emily 4, 69–85
  Wuthering Heights 69–85
  and bifurcated narrative 69–72, 78–80
  and chronology 76
  and cultural time 84–85
  and evolution 84;
  and *Frankenstein* 84
  and *In Memoriam* 84
  Lockwood: as narrator 71;
    his dreams 72–73
  and multiple narration 72–78
  Nelly Dean as agent-narrator 70, 73–74
  as progress narrative 83–85
  readings of 78–83
  and revolutionary history 84
  as saga 80
  symbolic texture of 75
  subjective realities in 74–78
Brontë, Charlotte: *Shirley* 98
Brougham, Henry Lord 88
Browne, Hablot Knight 103, 104, 114
  illustrations 107, 116
Browning, Robert: *The Ring and the Book* 69, 196
Brown, Charles Brockden: *Arthur Mervyn* 47, 70
Burwick, Frederick 3, 4, 46, 199
Butler, Marilyn 57, 185
Byron, Lord 85; affair with his half-sister 53; *Childe Harold* 184

Calder, Angus 37
Call, W. M. W. 139, 191
Camus, Albert 167
canonicity: canon-formation 1–2; teaching canon 7
capital and capitalism 87, 88, 90, 93; capital accumulation 87–88; Harriet Martineau on 100; labour theory of value 97; Thomas Hodgskin on 97
Carey, John 190
Carlyle: *Sartor Resartus* 134, 135
Carpenter, Edward 127
Carroll, Lewis 109–120
  illustrations 111–113, 115, 120
  and the grotesque 112–113
  love for Alice Liddell 113
  Alice in Wonderland 109–112
  Through the Looking Glass 113–115, 119

Cartwright, John 88
Cattermole, George 103, 104
  illustrations 105–106
Cazamian, Louis 186
Cecil, David 80
Cervantes: parody of 28
chaos theory 26, 182
Chapple, John 88
characterization 7, 13, 63; consciousness 6, 24–25, 169–171; mixed characters 13; subjectivity of 63; through classical 'personages' 192
Charles II 37
Chartism 90, 91, 96, 98
Claremont, Claire 53
Clarissa 21
class murder 90; Thomas Cooper and 95
Coleridge: on androgyny 134; *The Ancient Mariner* 52, 84; *Christabel* 84
Confessions of a Justified Sinner 70
Conrad, Joseph: scepticism 6
  and modernity 163–164;
  and Romantic manifestos 7
  Heart of Darkness, 7, 175–176;
    and judgement 175–176
    Marlow in 175
  Lord Jim 6, 159–168
    ambiguity of language 160–161
    chronological displacements 160
    dramatized telling 166
    figurativeness 160–162
    generic heterogeneity 160
    and ethics 162
    and heroic literature 167
    Marlow, 165–167
    and the myth of babel 167
    as a single speech act 197
    modernity of 166
    multiple narration in 159–160
    narrative innovations 159
    writing as theme 163–168
  A Personal Record 196–197
Cooper, Thomas: 87, 95, 'The Purgatory of Suicides' 187; and Wordsworth 187
Cooper, Fenimore 3
Coutts, Angela Burdett 127
Covenanters 41
Craik, W. A. 62
Crane, Walter 121

Daly, Macdonald 1, 91, 94, 186
Dante, *Paradiso* 184; *Purgatorio* 184
Darwin, Erasmus 84
David Copperfield 5, 159
De Foe, Daniel: *Journal of the Plague Year* 3, 47
dialect: in *Old Mortality* 40–41; in *Mary Barton* 96; in *Wuthering Heights* 85
dialogic, the 99, 125, 132
Dickens, Charles 5, 89, 101–21, 123–37
   and the 'angel-in-the-house' 127
   and Angela Burdett Coutts 127
   and domestic ideology 189
   and domestic violence 131, 190
   anti-feminist 124
   and Mary Hogarth as Beatrice 110
   and his illustrators 101–109, 114–121
   and Caroline Norton 127
   and Coventry Patmore 127
   critiqued by G. H. Lewes 193–194
   and Unitarian culture 124
   Barnaby Rudge 103
   Bleak House 5, 21, 114, 123–37
     androgynous form 134–135
     and the 'angel in the house' 129–130
     the construction of Esther 127–130
     illegitimacy 123
     illustrations 114–115
     the dual narrative 134–136
     and cultural stereotypes 132–133
     synthesis of Swift and Blake 134
   Christmas Books 112
   David Copperfield 5, 159
   Dombey and Son 5
   Hard Times 100, 119, 133
   Household Words 5, 93, 126, 127, 190
   Little Dorrit: illustrations 114
   Martin Chuzzlewit 124
   Master Humphrey's Clock 102
   Our Mutual Friend 115–120, 133
     illustrations 116–118, 120
   The Old Curiosity Shop, 101–109
     treatment of the female child 103–104
     and the grotesque 104–105
     illustrations 105–107
     and Wordsworth's Lucy 109
   see also Hablot Browne, George Cattermole, Daniel Maclise, Marcus Stone, John Tenniel

Disraeli, Benjamin: *Sybil* 98
Dives and Lazarus 87
Dombey and Son 5
Don Quixote 39

Eagleton, Mary 96
Eagleton, Terry 1, 4, 80, 81, 181
écriture 160
Edgeworth, Maria: response to *Mary Barton* 92
Eliot, George 2, 5, 137, 139–57
   on feminine character 127
   democratizing impulse 150
   cites Herodotus 153
   and domestic ideology 195
   and David Masson 193
   on the domestic novel 142
   and Realism 154, 192
   on George Sand 191
   and women's writing 192
   on marriage as 'the home epic' 139
   on Fielding as the 'great historian' 143
   Works:
   Adam Bede 144
   Middlemarch 59, 139–57, 169
     allusion to *Agamemnon* 147
     Dorothea: and Milton's daughters 149
     Dorothea: emergence from egoism 156
     a revised sense of the 'epic life' 154
     on gender relations 139–140, 147
     'home epic' and mock-epic 139–142, 146, 147–148, 153
     mock-heroic register 145
     realizable heroism 151
     and the Homeric question 191, 151–52
     'epic' standard of judgement 155
     marriage as moral testing-ground 153–154, 157
     and moral guidance 59
     and moral order 157
     and persuasion 59
     and point of view 152–153
     use of classical 'personages' 192
   The Mill on the Floss 118, 136, 140
     on female subordination 140
     pictorial quality 118
   'The Natural History of German Life' 145
   Scenes of Clerical Life 150, 152
   Silas Marner 187

'Silly Novels by Lady Novelists' 142
  see also Lewes, G. H
Ellis, Havelock 127
Ellis, Sarah Stickney 123, 125, 127–28; *The Daughters of England* 133; *The Wives of England* 128
Ellis, William and Mary Turner Ellis: review of *Mary Barton* 92
Empson, William 109
Engels, Friedrich 88, 95
Ewbank, Inga-Stina 82–83

Farrell, John G. 3
feminism 124, 125, 126, 127, 133; and domestic violence 131; and domestic ideology 190, 195; essentialism 28, 127, 130–133; gender stereotypes 132; the Seneca Falls Convention 123–124, 188; slavery and the subjection of women 128
fiction: fiction feminine 192; evolution of fictional form 7; point of view 38–39, 98, 152, 170–172, 196
  see also author, fictional genres, narrative, narrators, novel
fictional genres: Condition of England novels 14, 123; generic heterogeneity in *Lord Jim* 160; historical fiction, 3; historical romances 143; hybrid genres 99; the domestic novel 142; the novel as 'prose Epic' 143; sentimental fiction 33
Fielding, Henry 2, 9–19, 23, 143
  as historian 143
  as lawyer 18
  and mock-heroic 11, 17–18
  self-conscious style 11
  Joseph Andrews 143
  Tom Jones 9–19
    and allegory 10
    on critics 12–13
    fictiveness, 14
    concern with judgement 18–19
    opening chapters as manifesto 10, 15
    mixed characters 12
    implied morality 16
    narrator: construction of 13–14, 19
    narrator: as hero 9–19
    on seriousness 10
    Squire Allworthy 10–12
    the Man of the Hill 16–17

Finnegans Wake 21
Flaubert 9
Fletcher, John 3, 184
  The Captaine 47, 49
Ford, Ford Madox 2, 9, 12, 181
  authorial intrusion 9
  literary 'impressionism' 9
Ford, George 102
Forster, John 102–103, 124
Foucault, Michel 29, 182
Fox, W. J. 89–90, 94, 124, 187
  and Saint-Simonian socialism 94
Frankenstein 3, 70, 84
Fryckstedt, Monica Correa 89, 98, 187
Fuller, Margaret 123

Gaskell, Elizabeth 87–100, 137, 189
  background 89–90
  and Christian brotherhood 95
  and feminism 189
  and Manchester Domestic Missions 89, 93–95, 98, 100
  and 'Political Economy' 89–90, 93, 97, 100
  and 'agents of virtue' 93–94
  and Unitarian culture 88–91, 89
  and William Stevenson's economics 88–89
  Mary Barton 1, 4, 87–100
    on Barton's Chartism 98
    class murder 90, 99
    cutting technique 97
    emigration as metaphor 100
    genre shift 99
    and the implied reader 96
    on 'improvidence' 96
    narrative intrusion 90
    narrative strategies 95–100
    and the Norman yoke 96
    political ambivalence in 91
    compared to propaganda fiction 92–93
    realism in 95
    reception 91–92
    republicanism 96
    working-class culture in 96
    working-class perspective of 98
  'Sketches Among the Poor' 186
Gaskell, Peter 88
Gaskell, Samuel 88
Gaskell, William 89, 94, 186

Gelpi, Barbara 136
genre *see* fiction: fictional genres
Gilbert, Sandra M. and Susan Gubar 62, 80, 186
Gisborne, Maria 53, 183, 184
Gissing, George 102
Gladstone, William Ewart 192
Gleadle, Kathryn 181
Glen, Heather 83, 84
Godwin, William 3, 47, 124, 184; trespassing the boundaries of love 54
Goethe 145, 151; *Hermann und Dorothea* 145; as domestic epic 194; *Werther* 47
Golding, William 40, 182
Gooneratne, Yasmine 63
Graver, Suzanne 189
Gravil, Richard 199
Great Expectations 131
Greg, Percy 143
Greg, W. R. 92
Grey, Maria and Emily Shirreff: *Thoughts on Self-Culture* 124, 125, 129, 130, 133, 135;
Grote, George: *History of Greece* 151
Gubar, Susan *see* Gilbert, Sandra M.

Hall, Donald 190
Hancher, Michael 188
Hard Times 100, 119, 133
Hardy, Barbara 58, 185
Hazlitt, William 88
Heart of Darkness see Conrad
Heilbrun, Carolyn 134
Henry James: on illustration 121
Herodotus 155
heroes and herosim: death of the hero 19; ideas of heroism 151, 159
Herstein, Sheila R. 126
Hewitt, David 182
Hickson, W. E. 142
Higginson, Thomas Wentworth 124, 188–189; *Woman and her Wishes: an Essay* 188–189
history 123, 143; flight from 24, 27
hobbyhorses 25, 58–59
Hoffmann, E. T. A: *Kater Murr* 70
Hogg, James: *Confessions of a Justified Sinner* 70
Holmes, Richard 53

Homer 151; historicity of 191–192; *The Iliad* 151
Horace 16
Household Words 5, 93, 126, 127, 190
Houseman, Laurence 121
Howitt, William and Mary 124
Howitt, Mary 142; translator of Bremer 142
Howitt's Journal 89, 186
Hume, David 181; *Treatise on Human Nature* 58
Hutchings, W. R. 2, 199
Hutton, Richard Holt 195

incest: literature of 47; in Romanticism 53 *see also* Alfieri, Bocaccio, Fletcher, Shelley
irony 164, 165, 167, 168
Irving, Washington 38
Isaiah 55
Iser, Wolfgang 182

Jacobite risings 40
James, Henry 5, 102, 121
Jameson, Fredric 1, 160, 181, 197
Jerrold, Douglas 124
Johnson, Samuel 9, 12, 55; and persuasion 58; *Rasselas* 15
Joseph Andrews 143
Journal of the Plague Year 3, 47
Joyce, James 21
judicial system 18

Kay-Shuttleworth, James 88
Kettle, Arnold 81
Kingsley, Charles 91
   Alton Locke 193, 195
   review of *Mary Barton* 91
Klein, Herbert 182
Knowles, Owen 167
Koelb, Clayton 69

language: in Conrad 159–168
   in Sterne 30–31, 33
   see also dialect
Lansbury, Coral 88, 90, 91
Larkin, Philip 83
Lawrence, D. H. 7, 169, 176–179
   characterization, 178
   Women and Love 169–81
   free indirect discourse 177

and ethical judgement 176–177
detachment and sympathy 177–179
and cultural wreckage 178–179
Layhe, John 187; *Report of the Ministry to the Poor* 187
Leavis, Q. D. 79, 80
Leimprière's Classical Dictionary, quoted 49
Levine, Philippa 127
Lewes, George Henry: on Aeschylus and Sophocles 194–195; on Jane Austen 196; on Comte 193; on Dickens and 'bourgeois epic' 145, 193; on the idealist reading of Greek Tragedy 148; and the 'Homeric controversy' 151, 195, 196
Lewis, Jayne 2, 199
literary 'impressionism' 9
literary text: materiality of 29
literature: ideological function 1
Little Dorrit: illustrations 114
Locke, John 27, 31, 32, 58, 182; *Essay Concerning Human Understanding* 27, 58; on language 32; on custom 58
Lockhart, J. G. 39
Lord Jim see Conrad
Lucas, John 187
Lynn, Eliza 123, 126, 130, 190; in *Household Words* 126; 'Rights and Wrongs of Women' 189

Mack, Douglas 183
Mackintosh, James 88
Maclise, Daniel 104, 108
Manchester: Domestic Missions 93–95, 98, 100
Mansfield Park 56
Marcet, Jane 87, 89, 93
Marriage of Heaven and Hell, The 4
Martin Chuzzlewit 124
Martineau, Harriet 88, 93, 125, 137; 'A Manchester Strike' 100; on capital 100; essentialism in 137; *Household Education* 190; *Illustrations of Political Economy* 93; *Society in America* 189
Martineau, James 92
Mary Barton see Gaskell
Masson, David 143, 192–193; advice to George Eliot 144
'master narratives': Fredric Jameson on, 1; and master narratives 2, 6

class conflict 81, 87–100 *passim*
class and gender 149
the condition of England 89–100, 123
emigration and empire 100
honour 6, 41–42, 159
illicit desire 47–54
liberal ideology 95–98
patriarchy 65–66, 82, 123–137 *passim*
progress 82–85
sectarianism 38–41
separate spheres ideology 5, 139–40, 145–146, 147, 149, 153–154
cultural wreckage 178–179
Mathilda see Shelley, Mary
Mayoux, Jean-Jacques 181
McCaffery, L. 181
Medalie, David 184
Mendel, Gregor 84
Middlemarch see Eliot, George
Mill, John Stuart 5, 88, 89, 124, 133; on political economy 89; *The Subjection of Women* 124
Mill, Harriet Taylor 124
Mill on the Floss 118, 136, 140
Miller, J. Hillis 164, 168, 196
mock-heroic 11, 145, 147–148
Moers, Ellen 5, 125, 189, 190
Montaigne 28
Monthly Repository, The 89, 124, 190
Mott, Lucretia 123; 'Declaration of Sentiments' 188
Mrs Dalloway 21
Mullan, John 182
Myers, Frederic: *Lectures on Great Men* 196

Napoleon 85
narratability 25
narrative: as socially symbolic act 1, 7
bifurcation 69–74
dramatized telling 166
dual narrative in *Bleak House* 134–135
narrative innovations 159–160
narrative digression 24, 26
narrative intrusion 90
narrative strategies 95–100
narrative voice 88, 90, 134
and oral narrative 39–40
point of view 19, 38–39, 76, 98, 152, 170–172

reportage 90
self-consciousness of 11, 170
see also master narratives, narrator
narrator: as agent 70
  and the author 90
  as character 38–39
  and free indirect discourse 172–174, 177
  as historiographer 24, 26
  as interpreter 16, 18
  dramatized or undramatized 14, 90, 93, 99
  reliable and unreliable 74–78, 172
  multiple narrators 38–39, 44, 72–78, 159–160
  postmodern 24
  as story-teller 39–40, 166–167
  see also author, fiction, fictional genres, novel, point of view
National Review, The 191
Nightingale, Florence 137, 189
Nitchie, Elizabeth 47
North British Review 91
Northanger Abbey 56
Northern Star, The 98
Norton, Caroline 125, 127
novel: and chronological disruption 23–24; and closure 166; between the heroic and the homely 145, 155–157; as history or anti-history 22–23, 27, 42; as escape from historical time 29; and historicity 1; and morality 16, 162; as prose epic 142–144, 153; as Natural History 144; as virtual history 14; and relativity of perception 59–60, 169; self-conscious literary status 28; two-part structure 45, 69–74; versus Romance 15
  see also author, fictional genres, narrative, narration, narrators
novelists: hostility to critics 12–13

O'Connor, Feargus 87, 98
Odyssey, The 149
Old Curiosity Shop, The see Dickens
Old Mortality see Scott
Oliphant, Margaret 142
Oliver Twist 131
omniscience 62
O'Neill, Michael 6, 199
oral tradition 40
Our Mutual Friend 5, 115, 133

Ovid: *Metamorphoses* 50
Owen, Robert 97

Paine, Tom 88
Paradise Lost 3, 9, 47
parody 28
Patmore, Coventry 125, 126, 136
Peoples's Journal, The 89
perception: imaginativeness of 66
Persuasion see Austen
persuasion: dangers of 55; Romantic meanings 4
picaresque 10
Pierce, David 181
Pirandello, Luigi 69–70
Pitt, William 34
Plutarch 47, 191; *Lives* 47
point of view and focalization 19, 38–39, 76, 98, 134, 152, 170–172; in *The Ring and the Book* 69, 196
Polidori, John: echoed by Mary Shelley 184
political correctness 40–41
political economy 89–90, 92, 93, 97
Poor Man's Guardian 87
Pope, Alexander: *The Dunciad* 13; *The Rape of the Lock* 11
post-modernism 34, 160; conventions of representation 34
Pownall, Thomas 100
Pride and Prejudice 56
Priestley, Joseph 88
Prodicus 194
Proserpine: raped by Pluto 49
Prospective Review, The 92
Proust, Marcel 160, 174
Rackham, Arthur 121
Rackin, Donald 113, 114, 188
Rambler, The 15
reading: as negotiation 66, 88–91; implied reader 96–97
realism: 2, 6, 14, 95
Reeve, Clara 143
Revolution of 1668 40
Ricardo, David 89
Richardson, Samuel 9, 21, 33
Richardson, Alan 183
Ring and the Book, The 69, 196
Robbe-Grillet, Alain: *La Jalousie* 59–60, 62
Roderick Random 2

romance 30
Roscoe, W. C. 143
Rossetti, Dante Gabriel: illustrations of 'Goblin Market' 112
Ruddick, Bill 1, 9, 46
Ruskin, John 139
Said, Edward 163, 165
Scenes of Clerical Life 150, 152
Scott, Sir Walter 2, 37–46
   and Washington Irving 38–39
   as lawyer 41
   and historicity 42;
   Old Mortality 37–46
      bigotry 38, 40
      Covenanters 37
      the fanaticism of honour 42
      and moral choice 37
      identity of narrator 38–39
      oral story-telling 39–40
      as satire 45
      two-part structure of 45
   Rob Roy 45;
   Tales of My Landlord 38;
   The Black Dwarf 38;
   Waverley 37
Scott, M. J. 62
Seed, John 93
Sense and Sensibility 56
Shelley, Percy Bysshe 46, 49, 53; *The Cenci* 46, 183; 'Epipsychidion' 82; and Mathilda's grief 49
Shelley, Mary 3, 47–54, 78;
   and Beaumont and Fletcher 183–184
   Godwin's obstruction of *Mathilda* 53
   and John Polidori 184
   death of William 53
   Frankenstein 47, 70, 84, 78
   Mathilda 47–54
      allusiveness of 49, 50, 184
      as autobiography 53
      and the literature of incest 47–50
Mathilda (character): 47–54
   as Coleridge's Ancient Mariner 52
   as Proserpine 48–49
   reading Alfieri 50
   as Shelley's 'the sensitive plant' 52
   and Fletcher's *Captaine* 49
Proserpine: A Mythological Drama 183
The Last Man 3, 47, 54

Shelston, Alan 5, 199
Shirley 98
Shirreff, Emily *see* Maria Grey
signs: arbitrariness of 31, 162
Silas Marner 187
Sim, Stuart 182
Slater, Michael 123
Smith, Adam 89
Smith, Sydney 88
Sons and Lovers 7
Sorrows of Young Werther, The 3
Sotweed Factor, The 2
Spectator, The 15
Sroka, Kenneth M. 183
Stabler, Jane 4, 200
Star Trek 95
Sterne, Laurence 2, 21–35, 60
   compared to Fielding and Richardson 23
   debt to Locke 182
   Modernist admirers 26
   and Robbe-Grillet 60
   Tristram Shandy 21–35
      as anomaly 21
      and associationism 24–25
      'biographical' veracity 34
      and chaos theory 26, 182
      chronological disruption 22, 23, 25
      digressiveness 21–22
      and fragmentation 34
      historical status 22, 182
      historicity of 23–27, 30, 34
      hobby-horses 25–26, 58–59
      incompletion 182
      physicality of language 31, 31–33
      materiality of the literary text 29
      narrative technique 21–22
      appearance of postmodernity 22, 24, 26–27, 30–35
      reception 23, 26
      as satire on Locke 27
      Shandeism 26–27, 33
      textual self-consciousness 27–30
      the *Tristrapaedia* 27, 34
Stevens, Joan 103
Stevenson, Robert Louis 160
Stevenson, William 88; as economist 89
Stewart, Garrett 175
Stone, Marcus 117–118
   illustrations of Dickens 117, 118, 120

Stoneman, Patsy 79, 82
stream of consciousness 26, 62, 170
Sutherland, John 182
Swift, Jonathan 134
Sybil 98
symbol 31, 75, 136, 160–166 passim
sympathy 7

Tanner, Tony 62
Tellers: Esther 127–130, 134–136
 Lockwood and Nelly Dean 69–74
 in *Old Mortality* 38–40
 Marlow 162–163, 165, 175
 Tristram 23–27
 in *Mary Barton* 90–96
 in *Tom Jones* 13–14, 19, 143
Tenniel, John 109; representations of Alice 110; illustrations 111–113, 115, 120
Tennyson, Alfred 131
Tholfsen, Trygve 97
Thompson, Noel 93
Thompson, William: *Appeal of One Half of the Human Race* 124
time: chronological displacements 160; cultural time 84; linear and non-linear time 22, 25, 27
To the Lighthouse see Woolf
Tom Jones see Fielding
Tristram Shandy see Sterne
Trott, Nicola 3, 5, 181, 200

Unitarianism 5, 88–90, 124

Van Ghent, Dorothy 182
Victorian fiction: illustration of 101–121
Virgil, *Aeneid* 12

Vivas, Eliseo 176

Wallace, Tara Ghoshal 62
Wars: of American Independence 85, 88; Napoleonic Wars 85; Jacobite Rising in Scott 37, 38, 40
Watts, Carol 182
Watts, Cedric 6
Webb, Beatrice 127
Wedd, Mary 3, 200
Westminster Review, The 88, 92, 124, 191
Wheeler, Anna 124
Wilde, Oscar 101, 102
Williams, Raymond 1, 95, 181
Wilson, David 8
Wilson, A. N. 38, 182
Winterson, Jeanette 21
Wollstonecraft, Mary 124
Women in Love see Lawrence
Wood, Robert 192
Woolf, Virginia 6–7, 21, 161–175
 Mrs Dalloway 21
 To the Lighthouse 169–175
  and thwarted expectations 173
  ethical fineness 174
  free indirect discourse 172–174
  and judgement 175
  rendition of consciousness 67, 169–170
  rendition of indeterminacy 170–171
  portrayal of feelings 174
Wordsworth 3, 7, 85, 109, 156, 186; echoes in Dickens 109; *The Convention of Cintra* 85; *Lyrical Ballads* 3; 'Ode to Duty' 156
Wuthering Heights see Brontë